COCKERELL

PHOTO: J. RUSSELL & SONS

SYDNEY CARLYLE COCKERELL, 1940

COCKERELL

Sydney Carlyle Cockerell,

friend of Ruskin and William Morris and

Director of the Fitzwilliam Museum, Cambridge

BY

WILFRID BLUNT

1 9 65

NEW YORK : *Alfred : A : Knopf*

L. C. catalog card number: 65–11117

THIS IS A BORZOI BOOK,
PUBLISHED BY ALFRED A. KNOPF, INC.

FIRST AMERICAN EDITION

To
Oliver and Lois

'In your account of me I wish my faults and short-comings to be emphasised and not suppressed.'

S.C.C., in a letter to the Author, 30th March 1962

'I hear there are ladies going about complaining that the Burne-Jones Memorials are not mainly about themselves! . . . Certainly the writing of a biography in such a way as not to offend half the friends of the subject of it is the most difficult of things.'

S.C.C. to Wilfrid Scawen Blunt, 23rd January 1905

FOREWORD

THIS book has not been easy to write: it would have been easier had he not insisted upon the total truth.

Sydney Cockerell's 'faults and shortcomings', which he ordered to be 'emphasised and not suppressed', are very apparent; the extraordinary empire that he exerted over his innumerable friends is more difficult to describe or to explain. There was much true kindness and goodness in his nature, though he sometimes seemed to be at pains to conceal it. He loved his wife; but his failure to understand a temperament so different from his own led finally to an indifference which wounded her more than he was able to realise. He loved his children; but he resented their inability to share his tastes and interests, and made no secret of his resentment. ('We must have been a great disappointment to him,' wrote his son. 'But are we sure that children ought to have an easy time?') His character was complex: what sometimes looked suspiciously like toadyism was, more often than not, genuine hero-worship; what could be fairly described as rudeness could often be excused for stemming from intellectual honesty combined with moral courage; when he seemed tiresomely cock-sure he was usually tiresomely right. He never spared himself; so at times he rough-handled those whose idleness or indifference or obstructionism interfered with the carrying out of what he knew to be good and necessary. It is men like Cockerell who get things done.

Arthur Benson found Cockerell 'rather *fierce* . . . not sympathetic'—that is, not *simpatico*; but he respected him and enjoyed his company. Cockerell was, as he himself told Henry Yates Thompson, 'Cockerellian—I am that, for good or ill, and cannot be otherwise, and shall remain so to the end of the chapter.' But without Cockerell's 'Cockerellianism' there would never have been the miracle of the Fitzwilliam. What his family lost, the whole world has gained in a Museum that has revolutionized the display of pictures and works of art in public collections.

'Si monumentum . . .'

W.J.W.B.

The Watts Gallery,
   Compton, Guildford.
   5th February 1964.

ACKNOWLEDGMENTS

I HAVE to acknowledge much kindness and help from Sir Sydney Cockerell's innumerable friends, and to those whose names I have inadvertently omitted I offer my apologies.

First I must thank Sir Sydney's son, Mr. Christopher Cockerell, and his two daughters, Mrs. Anthony Minns and Mrs. John Laughton. Not only did they provide me with valuable information about their father and mother, but they were also most understanding of the difficulties which confront the biographer who attempts to give an honest portrait of his subject.

I am deeply grateful to Mrs. Arthur Harrison and to Mr. Ronald Briggs for their most helpful and constructive criticism of the rough draft of this book. Mrs. Hubert Hartley, Miss Dorothy Hawksley, Mrs. F. L. Griggs, Miss Ruth Verner, Mrs. Robert Gere, Mr. F. R. Thompson and my brother Mr. Christopher Blunt also kindly read all or a part of the draft and offered useful suggestions for its improvement.

To Mr. Philip Henderson, for permission to use the sketch of Sir Sydney which he wrote for the *Journal* of the William Morris Society, and to Dr. Eric Millar for permission to reproduce part of his article on Sir Sydney as a collector, from the *Book Collector*, as also to the publishers of these periodicals, I extend my warmest thanks. I have also to thank Miss Christabel Draper for innumerable kindnesses, and for the permission of herself and Mr. Gladstone Moore to make use of published and unpublished material written by Lady Wentworth, and for a photograph of Lady Anne Blunt. Lord Lytton also made most helpful suggestions with regard to the chapters which deal with the various members of the Blunt family, and

Mrs. Gertrude Bugler added much to my knowledge of the last years of the life of Thomas Hardy.

Among the many whom I must thank for advice, for the loan of photographs or of documents, for personal recollections of Sir Sydney, or for permission to quote from letters, books or articles which they have written or of which they hold the copyright, I mention with gratitude the following:

The Abbess of Stanbrook Abbey, Lord Aldenham (for the late Lord Aldenham), Professor A. J. Berry, Mr. Howard Bliss, Brigadier Gordon Blunt, Mrs. E. Booth, Mr. John Carter, Lady Chancellor (for Henry Yates Thompson), the Marchioness of Cholmondeley, Mr. Sydney Cockerell, Dame Felicitas Corrigan, Sir Stephen Courtauld, Mr. A. Cousins, Mr. H. R. Creswick, Mr. Brian Cron, Mr. Richard de la Mare (for Walter de la Mare), Mr. J. M. de Navarro, Air Chief Marshal Sir William Elliot (for Henry Yates Thompson), Sir Claude Elliott, Mme Geoffroy-Dechaume (for Charles Geoffroy-Dechaume), Mr. Evan Gill, Mr. J. Goodison, Mr. Cosmo Gordon, Mr. A. S. F. Gow, Miss Joan Hassall, Mr. Anthony Hobson, Mr. Leonard Holder, Mr. Michael Hornby (for St John Hornby), Mr. Paul Hollister, Mr. George Hughes, Professor Muriel Hughes, the Countess of Huntingdon, the Master of St. John's College Cambridge, Dr. Kathleen Kenyon (for Sir Frederick Kenyon), the Provost of King's College Cambridge, Professor Lawrence (for T. E. Lawrence), Dr. Ethel Lindgren, Macmillan and Co. (for Mrs. Thomas Hardy), Sir Alec Martin, Dr. Jerrold Moore, Miss Mabel Moore, Sir John Murray (for the late Sir John Murray), Professor M. Postan, Mr. Peter Quennell, Mr, R. F. Rattray, Mr. John Raymond, Mrs. R. M. Robbins. Mrs. Michael Robertson, Sir John Rothenstein (for Sir William Rothenstein), Mr. Siegfried Sassoon, Mr. Stanley Scott, Lady Southwell, Miss Freya Stark, Mr. Gilbert Stead, Mrs. G. Troxell, Mrs. Vulliamy, Dr. Carl Winter and Professor Francis Wormald.

I also gratefully acknowledge to the following authors (or the holders of their copyrights) and publishers their permission to quote: Messrs. John Murray (*In a Great Tradition*, by the Benedictines of Stanbrook; *The Flame of Life* and *The*

Authentic Arabian Horse, by Baroness Wentworth); Messrs. Jonathan Cape (*Friends of a Lifetime*, edited by Viola Meynell, and *Wilfrid Scawen Blunt*, by Edith Finch); Messrs. Faber & Faber (*Siegfried's Journey*, by Siegfried Sassoon); Messrs. Rupert Hart-Davis (*The Best of Friends*, edited by Viola Meynell); and Messrs. Longmans, Green (*The Life of William Morris*, by J. W. Mackail).

The Syndics of the Fitzwilliam Museum, Cambridge and the Director of the National Portrait Gallery have kindly allowed the inclusion of certain photographs which illustrate the book. I must also thank Miss Joan Hassall, Mr. J. S. Dearden and Mr. Allan Chappelow for the loan of photographs and, last but not least, Miss Dorothy Hawksley for her fine drawing of Sir Sydney in old age.

Mrs. Terence Gates kindly read the proofs, and Miss V. Thayre once again proved herself the perfect typist.

CONTENTS

PART THREE
[1937–1961]

EPILOGUE
[1961–1962]

ILLUSTRATIONS

xvii

PROLOGUE

[1961]

PROLOGUE

'Qui non dat quod habet non accipit ille quod optat'.
(inscribed at the beginning of almost all of S.C.C.'s diaries)

ALTHOUGH I had first met Sydney Cockerell as far back as 1927, when he was still the brilliant Director of the Fitzwilliam Museum at Cambridge, the encounter was a chance one and did not immediately ripen into friendship. In 1941, however, the fortunes of war brought him into my neighbourhood and so again into my life, and thereafter I continued to see a good deal of him.

None the less I was as surprised as I was flattered when, in the spring of 1961, I received a letter from him asking me whether I would be willing to act as his principal executor and to take charge of his letters, papers and diaries.[1] For among his immense circle of friends there were many of far greater distinction in the literary world than I; and of these, not a few had known him more intimately, and for longer.

I was ill at the time; but as soon as I was well enough I went to see him at his house at Kew — the house that had once belonged to Charles Shannon and which always reminded me of a rather down-at-heels vicarage. Though he was nearing his ninety-fourth birthday, though he was very deaf and had been bed-ridden for almost ten years, he gave little outward sign of the failing powers of which he complained. His cheeks were still rosy, his beard dapper; in his neat little skull-cap he looked like the late self-portraits of Titian or G. F. Watts. And if his speech was slow and punctuated by pauses, his mind was still perfectly clear and his memory amazing.

---

[1] It was finally agreed that I should be his literary executor only.

But he would not admit to being more than half alive. 'My brain is addled,' he said. 'Sometimes—in the middle of the night—I feel as if I were already dead: so weak—that a puff of wind—would blow me out. I shan't live through next winter.' I remembered that he had said much the same thing for the last fifteen years or more,[1] and that he had been rejected for a life insurance policy in 1886. Indeed, a moment later he was talking cheerfully and rationally of the glorious days that he had spent with Ruskin at Abbeville and Beauvais in 1888, of his work with William Morris at the Kelmscott Press, of his shipwreck with Wilfrid Scawen Blunt in the Red Sea, and of his triumphs during his thirty years' Directorship of the Fitzwilliam. He said, 'I've had a very interesting life. Looking back—I am very well satisfied—with it. If I had to do it again —I don't think—it could be better done.' I thought how few of us could say the same.

While he was speaking, I looked around the familiar room. Since my last visit it had been further stripped of its treasures, and I knew that in his two studies on the first floor the walls were already half bare and the book-cases emptied of his priceless collection of medieval and other manuscripts. ('I sold my books,' he had told me, 'because I felt that, by living too long, I had kept my children out of their rightful inheritance'). But a few specially prized objects had been retained. In the bookcase that faced the bed, the little manuscripts and printed books that his wife had so exquisitely illuminated, and the volume of letters written to him by Ruskin, all beautifully 'Katied',[2] still remained. On the shelves stood photographs of some of his special friends—of Dame Laurentia of Stanbrook Abbey, Miss Freya Stark and Sir Alec Guinness; of Lady Cholmondeley, Lady Huntingdon and Lady Clarke (Mrs. Surtees) — a *Schönheitsgalerie* of the 'archangels' (as he called them) who visited him so faithfully. There was also a set of coloured postcards of his favourite *Très Riches Heures* of the duc de Berri.

[1] 'Don't be afraid of the winter. You are tough as leather, and you know it.' (Letter from T. H. White to S.C.C., 29th October 1945).

[2] i.e., bound by his friend Katie Adams, afterwards Mrs. Webb—always referred to as 'Katie', Lady Cockerell being 'Kate'.

But all this was partially eclipsed for him by the barrage of flowers which rose from a small table at the foot of his bed.

This was the first of a succession of weekly visits that I paid Cockerell during 1961 and in 1962 until within a few days of his death, for he had expressed the hope that I might collect material for a short memoir. They followed a standard pattern. I would arrive soon after three o'clock, to be greeted with, 'Well, my dear fellow, how are you?' And, peering at his diary through the magnifying-glass that was tied with a red ribbon to the leg of his bed-table he would announce, 'Do you know this is the (sixteenth) visit—of the present series.' Then we would talk until, at half-past four, a sumptuous tea was brought in by one of the little band of devoted women who ministered to him. After tea, on the excuse of fetching some letters, I would slip upstairs to smoke the long-wished-for cigarette. When I came down again, if he were not too tired we might talk a little longer.

As happens with the old, his thoughts returned most readily to early days: to Ruskin and to Morris, to his first sight of the great cathedrals of northern France, to his work with Octavia Hill in the London slums, to some peccadillo of his childhood. The mention of a half-forgotten name might rouse him and he would say, 'I think—I first got to know him— about 1891—but no doubt—you will find the exact year—in my diary.' And slowly, piece by piece, he would stitch together the story of a friendship that had very likely been terminated by death before I was born.

Meanwhile, at home, I began to tackle the thousands of letters that he had kept, most of them neatly arranged in bundles and in chronological order, and the set of diaries that contained daily entries from 1886 onwards, so that I might be able to question him on any points that seemed obscure.

Those diaries! Ultimately there were seventy-seven volumes of them, and I suppose that they ran to a couple of million words, all written in an exquisite but microscopic calligraphy that rejoiced the heart but wearied the eyes. Very probably they constitute an unbroken sequence that is without parallel. Like Queen Victoria, Cockerell dutifully recorded the weather every day. Every letter, every postcard, every parcel received, is listed. There was often a summary of the events of the year. There were addresses, telephone numbers, birthday dates, and a list of books lent. Investments and expenditure were duly entered. There were many obituaries of friends who had died And as one opened the pages, there might fall out a snapshot, a bird's feather, or a faded flower.

Admittedly a very large majority of the entries are trivial or ephemeral, for, in the main, the diaries are little more than inflated engagement books. It is no longer profitable to learn that the writer dutifully took round to the Framptons the soup tureen that had been wrongly delivered at his house, or that Dr. Scruby looked in with a bunch of sweet peas. It is tantalizing to read, 'Called on Bernard Shaw, who was out,' and merely exasperating to be told no more of a dinner party of distinguished men and women than that there was 'much interesting conversation afterwards.' For Cockerell never learnt that dull information about famous people could never be anything but dull. When, at a later date, he re-read his diaries and marked with blue chalk those passages which he considered to be of peculiar interest, he selected the great names wherever they occurred, and, curiously enough, endless references to the progress of the seasons in Kew Gardens and the birds seen on his walks. Even during the Munich crisis the fact that 'one bed of asters is fading' is singled out as being of special importance.

But of course it was *his* diary, and he was entitled to put what he liked in it. He explained his intentions and defended his policy in a letter that he wrote to the *Spectator* (16th January 1942): 'This diary has been kept for my own satisfaction, without any eye on potential great-grandchildren, or on the general public, or on anyone at all but myself.' He admitted that it might appear 'shockingly meagre' to a professional writer, but claimed justification for it on the grounds of immediate utility and of serving later as 'a sort of ladder on which recollection could climb with sure feet. In my old age I find it the most agreeable of pastimes to open one of these small volumes and to accompany my stripling self on some happy continental journey, or his mature successor on a Mediterranean cruise, or a visit to Egypt, America or Australia'.

Moreover, even if as much as ninety-eight or ninety-nine per cent is stony ground, there still remains, of so vast a field, a substantial acreage that yields a rich harvest for the reaper. In any case, few biographers can claim to know exactly what their subjects were doing every day over a period of seventy-seven years. The pity is that, by using a printed diary with a fixed space allotted to each day, he could permit himself no more than the smallest *rubato* when memorable occasions demanded expanded treatment.

If I embarked upon my task with a certain trepidation, it was because of the fact that, though I understood well enough how Cockerell had made his enemies, I could not so readily see how he had made his innumerable friends. But as I read the diaries and the letters I came to understand. Cockerell realized that friendship was a delicate plant that needed constant tending, and there was absolutely nothing that he was not prepared to do for his friends. He gave them advice and sympathy when they were in trouble; he rejoiced with them in their happiness and was never jealous of their successes. He plied them incessantly with little thoughtful gifts of books and pictures, flowers or fruit. If they were in want, he gave them money — even in times when he himself had barely enough to live on. Pressure of business never prevented him from visiting them when they were ill (nor false modesty from recording the pleasure that these visits afforded them). He remembered their birthdays and their wedding days; he would even remember the anniversary of the death of a favourite child, and write exactly the right letter on exactly the right day. He helped them with their investments, filled in their income-tax forms, read their books in manuscript, corrected ('mercilessly', as one author wrote in his preface) their galley-proofs, and encouraged them in their literary projects. When they quarrelled among themselves, he appointed himself arbiter and usually contrived to remain on the best of terms with both parties. The more I read, the more I came to admire his genius

for friendship and to forgive the abruptness that was often
indistinguishable from rudeness, the scalp-hunting, the self-
assurance, and the high-handed tactics that he employed with
potential donors to the Fitzwilliam.

Moreover, if he pursued the famous—collected them as he
had collected shells when he was a boy, and worshipped them
with the fervour the young of today reserve for pop-singers—
he also, I found, showed equal kindness to the neglected and
the unknown who won his admiration. When he read an
article or saw a stage performance that impressed him, he took
the trouble (as so few of us do) to write to the author or the
actor to tell him so; thus he came to make lifelong friends of
several famous men who were relatively unknown at the
time. A few lines of jingle, snipped from some newspaper
or other and tucked into one of his diaries, exactly describes
the attitude he approved of and himself adopted:

> If with pleasure you are viewing
> Any work a man is doing,
> If you like him, or you love him, tell him now.
> Don't withhold your approbation
> Till the parson makes oration
> As he lies with snowy lilies on his brow.
> For no matter how you shout it,
> He won't really care about it,
> He won't know how many teardrops you have shed;
> If you think some praise is due him,
> Now's the time to slip it to him,
> For he cannot read his tombstone when he's dead!

PART ONE

[1867–1908]

1

CHILDHOOD AND BOYHOOD

> She left behind her many letters and enough files of
> case histories to need a three-ton lorry to get them to
> the British Museum.
>
> (*Kingsley Martin on Dr. Marie Stopes,*
> *'Daily Telegraph', 27th May* 1962)

'MY earliest recollection,' said Cockerell,[1] 'was being
allowed to sit up late to see a comet. The cook produced some home-made ginger-beer, and the cork
shot out and marked the ceiling.' The event is recorded in a
letter that he wrote to his elder brother, Theo, in the summer
of 1874: 'We stade up very late in the eavening till ten a clock
to see the commett.' He was just seven years old, and what he
saw must have been Coggia's comet.

The Cockerells were a Suffolk family of brewers, probably of
Flemish[2] origin (Cocquerel), and Cockerell's great-great-great-
grandfather was long remembered at Framlingham for the
huge brewery (Cockerell's Folly') that he built there. The boy's

---

[1] It should be understood that, throughout this book, statements so
quoted were made to me during the conversations that I had with him
in 1961 and 1962. Since he spoke slowly, and with many pauses (which
will not in future be indicated), it was possible for me to take down his
conversation almost verbatim. I have sometimes combined conversations
which in fact occurred on different occasions.

[2] It amused Cockerell to pretend that he was descended from Galeazzo
Coquerelli, a fictitious ninth-century Sicilian bandit. William Morris and
his intimate circle used the facetious 'Coquerel' when writing of him,
and at Cambridge he was known to many as 'Cockerelli'.

father, Sydney John Cockerell, was a partner in the firm of
George Cockerell & Co., Coal Merchants — a man of the highest
integrity, well-read, and associated with Octavia Hill in her
social work in Southwark. His mother was Alice, daughter of
Sir John Bennett; and one of his uncles by marriage, Sir
Richard Douglas Powell, Bt., became President of the Royal
College of Physicians. It has been suggested, but without any
evidence, that there might be some Jewish blood on one side or
the other of his family.[1]

Sydney Carlyle Cockerell was born at Brighton on 16th July
1867. He was a chubby baby — 'so fat,' wrote his father three
months later, 'that we sometimes call him "the Butcher".'
The boy owed his second name to his father's admiration of the
author of *The French Revolution*, and, to avoid confusion with
his father, was known as 'Carlie'. Within the space of nine
years, Alice Cockerell presented her husband with six children:
Theo, a year older than Carlie; Olive, a year younger; then
Douglas, Leslie and Una.

When Carlie was five, the family moved from Sydenham to
nearby Beckenham, still within striking distance of the delect-
able joys of the Crystal Palace, which had been transferred from
Hyde Park to Sydenham less than twenty years earlier. 'It was
a splendid place for children,' said Cockerell, 'and we were
often taken there. I remember the pool, and the expert
swimmers and divers. There was incessant music — classical
music, great choruses. There was a theatre, and Nonconfor-
mists who wouldn't go to London theatres went to it. In the
gardens was a famous collection of casts of prehistoric animals
— round the corner you might suddenly come upon a hippo-
gryph or something.'

The two elder boys were often taken by their father for
Sunday walks, during which he read Walter Scott aloud to
them. (On one of these walks Carlie noticed a fossil starfish in a
pile of stones by the side of the road — 'rather a *clever* find, I
think'). 'I can remember my father very clearly,' he said. 'He
once said to me, "When you grow up, I expect you to be a

[1] When asked if this was so, Cockerell was delighted. 'That's where I
get my *taste* from,' he said. But he neither denied nor confirmed it.

better man than I am". Though I was only ten when he died, I was old enough to realize the impossibility of this. He was very keen on intellectual things, and I recollect how pleased he was when I brought home a prize for Greek. I started learning Greek when I was nine—but later I forgot it all, like nearly everything else I learned at school. Spelling Bees were very popular at that time, and my father told me that on one occasion he beat Mrs. Craik—she wrote *John Halifax, Gentleman*, and was a great friend of ours—by a single word. I asked him what the word was, and he said, "mulligatawny".'

'My mother was a remarkable woman. She was very witty and very pretty. William Morris was quite bowled over the first time he met her. But she was always something of an invalid—just before her wedding she fell off her horse, and had to be married lying down.' And in a letter to a friend he wrote, 'She was left a widow at 32, with six children and very little money. When she was dying she asked me to write down [i.e. attest] her declaration that she had brought us up very well and that no one could have done it better.'

Soon after the family had moved to Beckenham, a Miss Sarah Marshall was engaged to give Theo and Carlie lessons in natural history. A faded photograph shows this remarkable woman staring into space with the monumental placidity of an Assyrian bull. The boys owed much to her stimulating teaching. Theo became in due course a professional naturalist of some distinction; and Carlie's boyhood passion for collecting shells and fossils taught him, not merely how great was the pleasure of being a collector, but also the value of close observation and the systematic keeping of records. Natural history was, incidentally, to provide Carlie with an introduction to Ruskin —the most important event in his early life.

'I was a passionate collector from the cradle,' he said. 'I collected mosses, butterflies and moths, all sorts of insects, shells, fossils, stamps—everything. I was very ardent, and very quick in determining what they were. The differences are often very small and it was a most useful training. We used to keep privet hawk caterpillars in the playroom at the top of our house at Beckenham. There was one with lots of long hair

which we christened "the King of the caterpillars." I trod on
it by mistake. It was the greatest grief I ever felt in my life —
dreadful *dreadful* anguish!'—And he shuddered at the mere
recollection of what he had unwittingly done, nearly ninety
years before. It was even worse than the misery of his discovery that Father Christmas was nothing more nor less than
'Uncle Jack dressed up.'

In 1875, after two or three years at a Kindergarten, Carlie
entered the Abbey School, Beckenham, as a day-boy. A letter
to his mother, who was away from home that autumn, has
been preserved; it is interesting to note that in it he draws
attention to a spelling mistake made by his mother, although
his own spelling leaves much to be desired:

> My dear Mama as I promiced to rite to you when I had
> one I must do so I got on butifly with my lessons yesterday
> and i think it was very very kind of you to rite so sone I
> hope your headace is better . . . Dougee has been a very
> good and if you please in dougees letter you spellt
> Cockerell Cockrell did you get to Margate . . . Douglas
> sends his love and a Thousand kisses he is at the present
> time takeing that shell of the brechfastroom mantle
> piece and putting up a lot of boots and calling the sheell
> the boot that the queen rides in and the boots the men of
> wars Una is quite well good by yours most affectionate son
> Carlie Cockerell.

On the whole Carlie was happy at school (though 'I get
knocked about a little by my schoolfellows I'm afraid,' he told
his mother). He was happy, too, at home, in a family that was
closely united; he worshipped his father.

Mr. Cockerell was very upright, very earnest, very sure of
himself. He knew what was right, and could not imagine it
possible that any honest man could entertain other opinions.
So, at least, it would seem from a handful of letters that he
addressed to his youngest sister, Adah. When he was twenty-
six and she twenty, he told her that he was 'sorry and vexed'
that she should spend her time 'reading nothing, knowing

nothing, content to live in a purposeless, frivolous, inane fashion, just like the women the *Saturday Review* is always holding up to ridicule and contempt. Some people can't help it, but you can. I imagine that you don't care to have any opinions of your own, either on religion, or social affairs, or politics. . . . What do you know of the current history of France, Germany, America or Italy?' He tells her to avoid slang words such as 'awfully' and 'scrumptious', not to write on 'grocers' paper', and never to date her letters '/67' instead of '1867'. He longs to see her 'beautiful eyes full of a light of seriousness and cultivated intelligence' — a light that could easily be kindled, he assured her, by reading the *Pall Mall* instead of 'fifteenth-rate novels;' he 'trembles' for her and urges her to wrestle with her soul for strength. And so on — page after page.

We have no knowledge whether Adah deserved such strictures, but there remains the impression that Mr. Cockerell, for all his virtue, may have been something of a prig. And it is interesting to speculate whether, had he lived his allotted span of three score years and ten, Carlie would have avoided quarrelling with him. But in 1877, when he was only thirty-five, Mr. Cockerell died suddenly, leaving his young wife and six children ill-provided for.

Cockerell & Co. agreed, it is true, to make the widow an allowance of £500 a year for ten years, but this was little enough upon which to bring up a large family of young children. She therefore moved to a smaller house and the brisker air of Margate, and Carlie became a boarder at the Abbey School. Here every economy had to be practised. 'I might have done quite well at cricket,' Cockerell said, 'but I had to make do with a very old bat. And it was the same with jumping: I was rather a good jumper, but I always lost because my shoes were so bad.' But, though he found it hard at the time, later he was often to say how thankful he was that he had been brought up without luxuries.

For a student of natural history Margate had endless possibilities that were lacking at Beckenham, and during his holidays Carlie eagerly collected shells on the beach and fossils near the fort. Sometimes, too, he went to stay with his maternal grandfather at Chislehurst, whose caves were an inexhaustible source of excitement, or with his father's family at the Banks, Mountfield, Sussex—'a very good place for butterfles.' That Carlie rapidly became something of an expert naturalist is revealed in his correspondence with Dr. Arthur Rowe, a leading authority on chalk fossils. Rowe writes to the fourteen-year-old boy: 'I have no scruple in accepting the M(icraster) Gibbus: many thanks. Sorry you smashed the Spondylus latus, but let me tell you, it was all your own fault. Unless you soak them in water, you will never get a good result. . . . You are a lucky youth to find that Apocrinus Ellipticus. It is nearly as good as mine, and think how long I had to look before I found it! That cockle is a Lima, I guess. . . . The shell you got at Pegwell I should imagine is either Cerithrum trimonile, or C. Bowerbankii. . . .'

When Rowe died in 1926, Cockerell wrote: 'I made his acquaintance when I was a boy at Margate by showing him at a soirée a tiny fossil echinus from the cliff at Margate called the Fort, which he had not seen before. I subsequently (more than twenty years later) learnt that it was new to science and that it had been called after Rowe, to whom I gave the specimen.'

From his Margate days Cockerell recalled two links with the past. The first concerned Dickens's mistress, Ellen Ternan, who had by that time married the Rev. G. Wharton Robinson, a Margate schoolmaster. 'Mrs. Robinson,' said Cockerell, 'was a great friend of my mother's. She used to recite *The Christmas Carol* at Christmas parties given by my mother, both at Margate and in London—and very well she did it.' He wrote that by that time Mrs. Robinson's attractions had become 'mental rather than physical.'

At Margate there also lived two of Tennyson's sisters, 'Mrs. Jesse and—I forget the name of the other,' he said. 'Jesse was a sea captain and both sisters were very trying. They kept a lot of dogs, and each dog had its own dish. Old Captain Jesse used to say, "Marriage should be for 5, 10 or 30 years, not a permanent arrangement".'

*   *   *

In 1880, Carlie sat for a scholarship at Winchester. At that time the examination lasted for five days, the number of candidates being reduced at the end of each day. Carlie was among the last batch to be sent home. But though he failed, his visit to Winchester was not wholly fruitless; for it gave him the chance of seeing his first cathedral, and he was overwhelmed by the majesty of it.

After a year's private coaching at Margate, he won a scholarship at St. Paul's; he entered the school in May, 1882, as a day-boy, travelling to London each morning from Chislehurst. 'St. Paul's School was then under the shadow of the Cathedral,' he said; 'but my last term was spent in the then brand-new magnificence of Hammersmith. At the opening of the new buildings, Benjamin Jowett handed me a prize. I made many friends at school, but Laurence Binyon was the only one I kept up with.' There was, however, another boy — Algernon Brown — with whom he remained in touch for a number of years. Brown, who was Captain of the School when he left in 1884, was extremely able; but for all his good degrees at Cambridge he never rose to greater heights than a country vicarage.

During the summer holidays of 1883 Carlie and Olive were taken by their mother on a week's excursion to Bruges, Ghent and Antwerp. This was the boy's first visit to the Continent, and as memorable as his first sight of an English cathedral. While he was still a schoolboy he also made his début in print: a list of shells found in the neighbourhood of Margate, published in *Hardwicke's Science Gossip*. In August 1884 he walked with Theo from Winchester to Torquay, shell-collecting; and that same summer he won the Smee Prize at St. Paul's with an erudite thesis on 'The British Representatives of the Genus Limnæa,' illustrated by a case of shells that he had collected. There was also about this time an expedition with a friend in search of buildings and places mentioned in the works of Dickens.

Carlie left St. Paul's at the end of the Christmas term of 1884, significantly exchanging his school books for a copy of Ruskin's *Lectures on Art*, and at the age of seventeen and a half joined, as a clerk, the family firm of George Cockerell & Co., then under the direction of his grandfather and two of his uncles. At the same time his mother and her family moved from Margate to Bedford Park, Chiswick, so that it again became possible for him to live at home.

Mr. Walner, his form master at St. Paul's, wrote to Mrs. Cockerell: 'I believe that on the whole what has happened is the best for your son. He is a boy of great ability and fine feeling. If as he grows a man he adds strength of will and perseverance, he will be heard of.' To Carlie he wrote: 'I am glad you see your way to a decision. Work hard and make yourself useful. A life of business is in my judgment the happiest and your scholarship will make it happier.'

But from the very start the boy was unhappy. The pay — ten shillings a week — was meagre, the hours fairly long, the work dreary. He visited potential clients, pursued those who were slow with their payments, reasoned with the dissatisfied, and sat up half the night over the accounts. But, boring and unimaginative though it all was, he persisted; he could not, however, have survived the seven years he spent in coal had he not been able, out of business hours, to keep his soul alive. He made marvellous use of his leisure, stretching it to its utmost limits. He went to lectures and the theatre, visited art exhibitions of all kinds. He explored the City churches and spent his brief holidays among the French cathedrals. Again and again, by curtailing his lunch, he returned to Westminster Abbey and the National Gallery, till he knew every monument, every picture, by heart. He read Shakespeare, Keats, Browning and Carlyle and filled the spare corners of his diary with extracts from their works. He bought his first picture — an etching by W. L. Wyllie. He went for long walks, played tennis and chess.

When he was nineteen he was ill for three months — sufficiently ill for him to make a will and to be refused a life insurance.[1]

[1] He suffered from albuminuria. *Black's Medical Dictionary* states, 'Most good [Life Assurance] companies will not issue a life policy to anyone with permanent albuminuria lest this be due to Bright's disease.' This was the disease that had caused his father's death.

It was perhaps at this time that he experimented with vegetarianism, but was soon disillusioned by a monotonous diet of 'stodgy greens.' ('It was all very well for Shaw,' he said. 'Shaw, after his marriage, could afford a good cook, and vegetarianism saved his life.')

Carlie 'sampled' the most prominent preachers, Haweis and Stopford Brooke in particular, and entered into correspondence with Alfred Watson whom he begged 'to denounce the craving for riches' in his next sermon and to explain the resurrection of the body and other stumbling-blocks to faith. Watson replied kindly and at length, but was forced to the conclusion that he could be of no help: 'For me to attempt to argue with you in your present state of mind,' he wrote, 'would only be madness . . . I sympathize with you in your difficulties; I feel my helplessness . . . I have no nostrum to propound to you. I trust and pray that God will guide you in your search for truth.' But Carlie could not accept God—neither then nor later, when half a century of prayers at Stanbrook Abbey proved insufficient to deliver him from agnosticism.

By far the most important thing that happened to him at this time was, however, his incomparable good fortune (or good management) in making the acquaintance and soon winning the friendship of three of the most outstanding men and women of the day—Octavia Hill, John Ruskin and William Morris. Miss Hill's influence was only temporary; but Ruskin and Morris were to change the whole course of his life.

2

COAL AND PHILANTHROPY

THE entry in Cockerell's diary for 12th March 1887 records a typical Saturday: 'Went collecting [i.e., collecting money owed by customers] and saw the depths of British degradation in Upper Whitecross Street. Squalid sickly women bargaining for putrid meat. To South Kensington Museum in afternoon. In evening to brilliant and intensely interesting lecture by Alfred Ainger on Jonathan Swift. Then to Whittington Club where I met John Lea and found them swearing in members over a sword and a "Complete Peerage, Baronetage, etc." which did duty for a Testament!'

For some time past he had been having 'searchings of heart about always condemning the defects and inequalities of our social structure and doing nothing to reduce them.' A talk with his father's old friend, Edward Bond,[1] one of the Charity Commissioners, took him no further, because Bond rejected Socialism as a solution but had no alternative to offer. That the problem continued to worry Cockerell is shown by two letters he received in 1889 from his Pauline friend Algernon Brown. In the first, Brown writes:

I allude now to the closing paragraph of your letter: 'London, like Sodom and ancient Carthage, must be *blotted out*.[2] The disease has gone so far that there is no hope save in the knife . . .' (Lordly sentence: ought to be printed in the *Star*, if indeed it is not borrowed therefrom) . . . 'But who shall be the operator?' (I never can

---

[1] Bond was at one time engaged to Octavia Hill.   [2] See p. 34.

guess conundrums, but fortunately you append the answer to this one — 'Your's always, Sydney C. Cockerell). You have a grand work before you. Please let me know when the sabre, sword or cigar-cutter is about to be unsheathed, and I will not select that morning for a visit to the metropolis. . . .

Three months later, Brown writes again:

On re-reading your letter I find one query. You consider that London ought to be 'blotted out' on account of the uneven distribution of happiness, cleanliness and wealth. If you mean that the *evil* in London is to be blotted out, then sensible people must be with you. But surely what ought to be done is to investigate what are the ultimate causes of hunger and squalor, and to attempt to stop the evil at its source. . . .

That was precisely what was being done, in Southwark and elsewhere, by a very remarkable woman — Octavia Hill. Miss Hill had long been a friend of the family; Cockerell's father had often helped her with money and advice, and his sister Olive was her godchild. At the age of five, dressed in a little holland frock, he had taken part with her in a play at Barrett's Court — the tenement building that had been bought for her by Lady Ducie, and which she rebuilt and renamed St. Christopher's Buildings.[1] In the spring of 1887, Cockerell became Secretary to the Red Cross Hall, Miss Hill's latest venture to bring light to darkest Southwark, and organizer of the various activities that took place there.

The name of Florence Nightingale must be known to almost every man, woman and child in England; that of Octavia Hill, whose work was in its way as astonishing, and in its effect as far-reaching, is known to but few. Few people realize that it was she who was chiefly responsible for creating a state of

---

[1] Now St. Christopher's Place, Wigmore St.

public opinion which forced Parliament and Local Authorities to improve the housing conditions of the London poor; and probably only a mere handful of the hundreds of thousands who each year enjoy the magnificent houses and fine scenery preserved for the nation by the National Trust, know that Octavia Hill, with the help of Canon Rawnsley and Sir Robert Hunter, founded the Trust in 1895.

It was in 1864, when she was twenty-six, that Miss Hill had made her first experiment in housing reform. In that year Ruskin bought and placed at her disposal three slum houses in what was most inappropriately named Paradise Place. 'The unprecedented feat of buying three slum houses, with the slummiest of tenants, and by sheer business ability and great-ness of heart turning them, without any monetary loss, into decent dwellings, and their pig-like occupants into decent folk, refuted for ever the lie of the slum-landlord, heard even today, that it is useless to give better homes to the poorest because were they palaces their inhabitants would turn them into pig-sties.'[1] Her work has been called 'as brave a battle against in-difference and opposition as has ever been fought by man or woman in the interests of intelligence against stupidity, and therefore good against evil.'

Miss Hill's system was to substitute a good for a bad landlord by purchasing the latter's property and putting it in order, and to exert a civilizing influence on the tenants by the use of trained women rent-collectors of an educated class. From small beginnings she gradually expanded her activities: when she died in 1912, she had over 1,800 houses and flats under her control.

When 'off duty', Octavia Hill seemed unassuming enough. Mr. Cockerell senior, writing to his sister in 1871, described her as 'an unobtrusive, plainly dressed little lady, everlastingly knitting an extraordinary fine piece of work, whose face attracts you at first, and charms you as you become acquainted with the power of the mind, and sweetness of character to which it gives expression, a lady of great force and energy,

[1] Sir Reginald Rowe, in his Foreword to *Octavia Hill* by E. Moberly Bell, Constable, 1942.

with a wide, open, and well stored brain, but withal as gentle and womanly as a woman can be, and possessed of a wonderful tact, which makes her the most instructive, and the pleasantest companion in the establishment.' But when she took the chair at a Meeting she appeared, wrote H. W. Nevinson, like 'Queen Elizabeth among her admirals and pirate explorers. For the solid, little figure with powerful head, masses of loose grey hair, large, benign, but watchful brown eyes, and mouth closing tight like a trap when she was displeased, displayed all the great Queen's indomitable resolution, power of command, personal affection or dislike, and scrupulous regard for every halfpenny spent or received.'

In 1885 Miss Hill acquired from the Ecclesiastical Commissioners a derelict site in Southwark, and when young Cockerell agreed to give her his services she was about to collect money to buy 'an old dilapidated skin factory' that adjoined it. The former was to be turned into a garden and playground, and on the latter she proposed building a Hall and a few cottages. Writing sixty years later to *The Times* Cockerell described the making of the garden, whose progress he watched with keen interest:

> Six weeks of bonfires night and day disposed of accumulations of rubbish, and it was laid out partly as a covered playground for children and partly as a garden in which there were flower beds and flowering trees and shrubs, as well as two plane trees with circular seats round them — not to mention a bandstand, a bridge, and a little pond with goldfish in it. It was a gay oasis amidst all that dreariness, an open-air sitting room for the tired inhabitants of the adjoining tenements.[1]

[1] He was writing to tell of the sad fate that had befallen it in the interval, at the hands of hooligans. 'I revisited it the other day . . . and was dismayed to find not a flower, not a shrub, not a tree surviving, no covered playground, no pond, no bridge, no bandstand—merely a desolate flat space, part of it newly asphalted and the rest in course of reclamation by the employees of the Southwark Borough Council. The clock had been turned back to 1887, when the area was first taken in hand.'

The money for the Hall was quickly collected, and within a few months of the launching of her appeal Miss Hill could write: 'The walls of my hall begin to rise, and three of my cottages are getting their roofs on.' For the Hall, Walter Crane painted a series of decorative panels illustrating heroic themes; the garden wall was inscribed, in enormous red letters on a white ground festooned with flowers, 'THE WILDERNESS SHALL BLOSSOM AS THE ROSE'; and on a radiant June day in 1888 the Archbishop of Canterbury, in the presence of 'a concourse of grandees and Southwarkians,' declared the Hall and gardens open.

The Hall, which was put in Cockerell's charge, immediately became the centre of innumerable festivities of every kind. There might be 'a delightful and boisterous dance,' a performance of *Rumpelstiltzkin* by the children of St. Christopher's Court, a party of blackface minstrels, a gymnastic display by members of the Working Men's Club, or an evening with 'musical chairs and Sir Roger lively enough, but the other dances funereal.' At first Cockerell found the work interesting and rewarding; but as the months pass, the diary entries become less and less enthusiastic. In March 1891 he writes, 'Indescribably dull waxworks etc. The last Thursday entertainment of the season, heaven be praised!' What he was later to call his 'philanthropic wild oats' had been sown, and though he continued to help and advise Miss Hill until her death in 1912, the days of his active association with the Red Cross Hall now drew to an end. 'I do not know how far this [withdrawal] was due to selfishness and hatred of fatigue,' he wrote. 'Still I felt that what little I did was done half-heartedly, and that I was really helping no one.'

But seen in perspective, what he had achieved appeared to him to have been of some value after all. 'Looking back,' he said, 'I feel rather proud of what I did for the Hall after a hard day's work.'

That Cockerell, while he was working for Miss Hill, took a personal interest in some of the poor of Southwark, is shown in a handful of letters written to him by a man named Richard Greenwood, who in his spare time helped him with the library at the Red Cross Hall.

In his diary (14th August 1887) Cockerell writes: 'Greenwood came to lunch, and stayed till 9.45. Had long conversation and respect him more than ever. Only had 3 months schooling in his life and has fainted for want of food. Very shrewd and refined.' Ten days later, Greenwood expresses his gratitude for 'one of the most pleasurable days I have ever had . . . I think I learnt more in that one day, of the beauties of nature, than I had done before in the whole course of my life.' Though he was always excusing himself for his illiteracy, in fact Greenwood wrote admirable letters with very few mistakes in them beyond an occasional misspelling. Sometimes he can hardly find words to express his indebtedness to his benefactor; and when Cockerell urges him to abandon the formal 'Dear Sir' in favour of 'Dear Mr. Cockerell', he feels that condescension is being carried indecently far. So he writes:

> I cannot for the life of me see why you (in spite of your advanced socialism) should object to the word 'Sir'. Surely it is the proper term from one in my position to one in yours, and I must impress on you however much you may differ that there is a certain line beyond which I ought not to go. The refined and cultivated life which you have led lifts you into a sphere totally different from mine. . . . I have seen that your thoughts and aspirations are much nobler and purer than mine, and this is no flattery when I tell you that I have been a better man since I knew you than I ever was before. . . . Of course I know you will say that we are all equal and so on, but in my humble opinion that will never be and I feel I am doing wrong in addressing you so freely; but as we all defer to those whom we like and respect, so will I defer to you.

Cockerell also helped Greenwood with small loans of money and gifts of old clothes. Then, just before Christmas 1889, and apparently through no fault of his own, Greenwood lost his job. He wrote pathetically to his benefactor. He could not face, once again, the long and hopeless search for work, the pitiful cries of his starving children. He felt this must be a judgment on him for having wasted his opportunities, for youthful peccadillos that really were only the result of high spirits. He wrote page after page. Fate was always against him. A 'glint of silver' (i.e. Cockerell's kindness) had lined for a moment his black cloud; but now the cloud had grown blacker than ever. He wanted to die. 'I wish you,' he abruptly concluded, 'a very merry Xmas and a bright and prosperous New Year.'

No doubt Cockerell came to the rescue, for in February we find Greenwood working as a commercial traveller in the north of England. The letters now become yet longer, yet more remarkable. In them he tells of the people whom he meets ('I don't care for the commercials much') and the books ('Carlisle [sic] Heroes and, don't laugh, Browning') that he is reading. He relates in detail the triumphant occasion when he 'banged Carlisle' at a party of commercials who were discussing Mahomet and was left 'master of the field.' He describes the crumbling beauty of York, the unforgettable splendour of a sunset over the Humber, his loneliness in Leeds, his 'moment of temptation' and subsequent remorse in Bradford, and the state of his jacket—'awfully shabby, torn in two places, and it looks so bad when I take the [i.e. Cockerell's] overcoat off. Have you an old one . . . ?'

Three years now elapse in silence, and the last letter, written from Southwark and edged with black, is dated 6th January 1893. Greenwood's little girl has been run over and killed on her way home from school. It seems that this was the *coup de grâce*; Greenwood gave up the hopeless struggle and embarked upon a life of crime.

'Yes, alas it ended in disaster!' said Cockerell. 'He became a thief again. He had good intentions, but everything was against him. I could do no more.'

Meanwhile the Cockerell family was becoming scattered. In 1885, Douglas, then a boy of fifteen, was sent out steerage to Canada, 'in the company of terrible riff-raffs—a dreadful

experience,' to work on a farm.[1] Two years later both Theo
and Leslie[2] developed consumption and were obliged to go and
live abroad. Theo went to Colorado with a former school friend
named Payn, who was also tubercular. 'Payn was well-to-do,'
said Cockerell, 'and paid Theo's passage. But he was rather a
wild young man. Theo was just the opposite, and they soon
parted company.'

Theo was indeed portentously earnest for his age, as is
shown in the letters that he wrote to Sydney. They were not
so much letters as lectures — lectures on themes such as friendship, love (sub-headed 'theoretical', 'aesthetic', 'Christian',
'historical' and 'practical'), tolerance and immortality. They
contained much, also, about Annie Fenn, the girl he had left
behind him, and even more about slugs and insects. Theo's
exquisite and microscopic calligraphy at that time is hardly dis-
tinguishable from Sydney's, and his letters have the added
charm of illustration. His industry, in spite of ill-health, was
very considerable; in the year 1887, for example, he published
no less than eighty-three papers and notes on natural history
subjects in various journals.[3]

There were other family sorrows and troubles besides the
expatriation of half the children. In 1887 Grandpapa Cockerell
died. He was 'a stiff old boy' but 'very kind to me always. He
had a sound judgment and was strictly and unswervingly
honest in his business dealings.' It is doubtful whether the
same could have been said of Sir John Bennett, Sydney's

---

[1] Later he got a job in the Imperial Bank at Toronto, where he saved
enough money to return to England. William Morris, on being shown a
book that he had bound in his spare time, gave him employment, and in
due course he became one of the leading book-binders in England and the
author of the principal manual on the subject. He died in 1945.

[2] After various vicissitudes in America, Leslie settled in London as a
mining engineer. He became something of a 'man about town', dressed
smartly, enjoyed sport, and was entirely different in character from his
three brothers. He died in 1943.

[3] After holding various posts in natural history in museums and
colleges in the New World, Theo was appointed Professor of Biology at
the University of Colorado, at Boulder. He first married Anne Fenn, who
died in childbirth, then his pupil Wilmatte Porter. He died in 1948.

maternal grandfather. Theo called him 'abominable', and even seventy years later Cockerell could still speak of him as 'something of a monster.' Sir John, who had a famous clock shop in Cheapside and was (like Grandpapa Cockerell) a Sheriff of the City of London, had been knighted in the mass investiture which celebrated the Prince of Wales's recovery from typhoid fever in 1872. Lady Bennett was deeply religious, and her letters to her grandchildren (especially those to Leslie, whom she constantly urges to smoke less and pray more) are full of pious exhortation; it is not, therefore, difficult to imagine her shame and misery when, in the summer of 1889, her husband was declared a bankrupt.

Almost at the same moment it was discovered that she herself was suffering from an inoperable form of cancer. 'I dare say you have heard,' Sydney wrote to Leslie, 'of the distressing aggravation of our anxiety, owing to the importunity of Grandpapa's creditors. . . . The next few days will decide whether or no Grannie's last few days are to be embittered and shortened by the shame she would feel if she knew what was taking place beneath her. There is happily some hope that she will be allowed to remain in ignorance, and that she will look out from her bed on to the oak trees and see the grass dappled with their shadow until she dies.' It was, however, decided that it would be better to move Lady Bennett to her daughter's house before the bailiffs arrived.

She died there in October. 'Olive was with her at the time and the end was tranquil,' Cockerell wrote in his diary. 'She was a pure and single-hearted woman, and tried to obey the precepts of Christ, in whom, and the resurrection, she had an unshaken trust. The wind moaned and the heavens sobbed as she passed away. Grandpapa arrived from Paris at midnight, heard the news and went away until the morning.'

Sir John died in 1897, leaving what little he possessed to Aimée Guilbert of Huon, Tasmania.

On the death of old Mr. Cockerell, Sydney had received the sum of £2,000. In January 1889, when he was twenty-two, he

was invited by the partners to invest the sum in George
Cockerell & Co. and become a partner.

He himself was half inclined to abandon coal in favour of
Cambridge. He did not like his present work; he did not like
his two uncles who were partners, nor did they like him. But
those whose advice he sought were against his going up to the
University. One of these was an old family friend, Henry
Attlee, a City solicitor and father of the future Lord Attlee.
Another was Octavia Hill, who wrote:

> I shall think very much of you on Monday. I cannot but
> feel how very hard the sacrifice is to you just now, but do
> you know I really *do* believe that the partnership will be
> the best. I remember so well a somewhat similar trial in
> my own early life and how I seemed to have to turn away
> from my ideal, and—by unexpected ways I found years
> afterwards that just the sacrifice I had to make brought
> me by ways I did not know to that ideal.

On 8th May Cockerell signed the partnership deed. He
wrote, 'I have done this out of deference to my grandfather's
and mother's wishes, and to the advice of all my friends—but
very much against my own judgment and inclination.'

3

THE GOD REVEALS HIMSELF

OVER Octavia Hill—over, indeed, almost every social worker, painter or poet of the day—towered the gigantic figure of John Ruskin. The friendship that young Cockerell struck up with the old and disillusioned seer of Brantwood was the most precious thing that ever happened to him in the course of his long life.

It was an enlightened schoolmaster at St. Paul's—Dr. King, afterwards Head Master of Clifton—who, by the reading aloud of a striking passage from *Modern Painters*, first stirred the boy's interest in Ruskin; 'the magic of the words took hold of me,' Cockerell wrote later, 'and gave me a thirst for more.' By good fortune the cashier at the head office of George Cockerell & Co. in Cornhill was a Ruskinian, from whom Cockerell was able to borrow several volumes of *Fors Clavigera*; these entranced him, 'both the political and the artistic teaching being wholly to my taste,' and by the time he had finished the sixth volume he was 'a convert to Ruskinian socialism and convinced of the dishonesty of usury.'

But how was he to establish contact with his god? It was now that his patient study of conchology reaped its reward; a gift of shells ('I had nothing else to lay at his feet') elicited a polite acknowledgment from the Master, and a year later a further instalment, accompanied by a letter pointing out a small conchological error in *Fors*, received a friendly answer. Meanwhile, on 23rd May 1885, Cockerell had succeeded in setting eyes on his hero, who had come to Chiswick to address the members of a children's society, the Friends of Living Creatures. He could not gain admission to the lecture, but after it was over he saw Ruskin 'led to his carriage by a pretty child, Katie Macdonald. He clapped his hands as he drove away.'

The exchange of letters[1] continued throughout 1886, and in March Cockerell disclosed the awful secret that he was not 'a venerable conchologist, bald, bearded and spectacled as I have since become,' but a mere stripling of nineteen. He slipped little questions into the letters to draw Ruskin out—such as, was usury always dishonest? The Master dutifully replied—but sometimes rather tardily, so that Cockerell, like any impatient lover, was driven to write again to ask whether he had given offence. 'How could you possibly think I was "angry"!!!' came the swift answer from Brantwood. 'I never received letters from anyone for which I was more grateful; but I can't answer the tenth of what I receive . . .'; and he asks Cockerell to try to find out 'why the sand-jumper jumps, and when.'

Only one of Cockerell's letters to Ruskin appears to have survived:[2]

5, Priory Rd.
Bedford Park
Chiswick W

Nov 22nd 1886

My dear Mr. Ruskin,

I have this morning despatched the long-promised collection of British shells, to be, so please you, a gift from *yourself* to the Barnsley Museum. It contains almost all the commoner species and some of the rarer ones as well, so it should serve its purpose of reference. I have made a catalogue with every other leaf blank for notes of such as wish to make them; and I have a copy of this myself. For guidance in sending other things at a future time, *Please* let me know that you are not dissatisfied.

In one of your letters you say that you 'may take advantage of my kindness' more than I shall be glad of.

[1] Ruskin's letters to Cockerell, and a fuller account of their friendship, will be found in *Friends of a Lifetime* (pp. 20–61), from which certain passages in this chapter are taken.

[2] In the possession of Mr. Evan Gill.

Let me tell you that you *cannot* do that. Few things would give me greater pleasure than to know that I was giving *you* pleasure. Any work you give me to do I will do it to the best of my ability; and if you bid me prepare further collections for other Museums in which you are interested, I will set to work at once.

Please tell me whether you will accept for St. George my own collection of British shells. It shall be worthy of him, and if you will undertake to find room for it I will spend the winter in remounting the specimens. There are about a dozen cases, 15 inches square. I do not think there are half a dozen better collections in the kingdom, if so many.

I am delighted to read of the bold step taken by Mr. Geo Thomson, and I hope that with this example of your teaching in practice others will be stimulated to follow suit. People are more and more turning to you for advice as to the only preacher of Christianity, the only great teacher insisting on the necessity of Society being based on things just, honest, true, pure, lovable, and of good report. Mill and his school are every day losing influence and prestige — and well they may. The divine law of Supply and Demand is dealing out less than 1d. per hour, and less than 1/– per day to the toiling Sempstresses in the East End of London, while death releases them from slavery at an age which is to others the prime of life. Is there any solution of the question other than Revolution of some kind? Will people ever learn that they are murdering their fellows when they live in idleness and luxury on *their* toil? or that Dishonesty is *not* the best Policy?

I took an American artist-friend to Watts' studio[1] the other day, thinking to show him something great, but he found great fault with the drawing and the colouring, and wouldn't hear of its being good and noble work. *Do* tell me that he knows nothing about it, it would be such a

[1] Where they no doubt saw his 'Song of the Shirt'—showing a 'toiling sempstress'.

relief to me. I am convinced that we have no other Artist except Burne Jones who can compare with Watts, since his pictures all set one thinking and tell a mighty truth in mighty poetry—but by last night's post I received five sheets from Boston hurling at my head the technique of the Old Masters etc till I am quite bewildered.

I wonder whether I shall ever speak to you face to face. I sometimes think I shall, but perhaps the wish is father to the thought. Though I have never spoken to you I love you very dearly and think of you always with greatest reverence. *Do* set me another task to do.

Ever yours most respectfully
S. Carlyle Cockerell

By the beginning of 1887, and by what to Cockerell had seemed 'needlessly protracted steps,' his salary had been advanced from ten to thirty shillings a week, and he now found himself in a position to afford an Easter excursion to Coniston to see (if he would show himself) the man he 'worshipped'. Ruskin replied amiably to his anxious enquiry: he would be visible, for an hour or so, at half past three on Easter Eve. He concluded, 'How very odd it should make you so happy to come and see an old Cynic.'

Cockerell left London jubilantly by the midnight train on the Wednesday before Easter. At Carnforth, where he had two hours to wait for a connection, he collected seventeen species of land shells on the limestone hillside, and by midday he was at Coniston. Such was now his state of elation that he immediately set off to climb the Old Man, 'a somewhat arduous matter, but eventually I managed to stroke his hoary locks.' It was not merely the first mountain that he had ever climbed, it was the first that he had ever seen; from the cairn at the top he looked delightedly at the wide landscape and upon Windermere below him, then he began the hard descent. 'That night I went to bed at 7.30 and slept like a stone.'

But there were still thirty-six hours to fill in before the god was due to reveal himself. Cockerell spent the time exploring the country, collecting more shells and observing the wild

flowers. Then, 'palpitating with anticipation,' he walked up
the drive of Brantwood.

'Saw Him and talked to Him for an hour,' runs the diary.
The Master greeted him cordially and immediately put him at
his ease:

> He was fairly tall but his height was already diminished by
> a little hunch in the shoulders. His hair was dark, long and
> thick, his beard iron-grey. His head was of the long type.
> His forehead sloped, and on each side, between his temples
> and his ears, there was a noticeable depression. He had
> heavy eyebrows and the bluest of blue eyes. Their colour
> was repeated with a difference in his large blue neckties.
> . . . His hands were small and delicate (I have one of his
> little gloves). He wore very old-fashioned clothes —
> trousers and double-breasted waistcoat of home-spun and
> a long dark coat. Round his neck was a gold chain attached
> to his watch. His smile was kindness itself, his voice some-
> times almost caressing. He could not quite pronounce his
> r's.[1]

Cockerell relates in his diary the conversation that ensued.[2]
Ruskin, delighted at Cockerell's youth and eagerness, was

> awfully kind and showed everything — books, pictures,
> minerals, garden — and lent me his boat to row over the
> lake in. Morris is 'beaten gold', 'a great rock, with a little
> moss on it perhaps.' His 'love of Turner, primroses and
> little girls' had prevented his ever becoming Morris's fast
> friend, but he has great reverence for him and for his
> views. Surprised that I don't know Burne Jones, who is
> 'the central figure in England.' Doesn't believe Carlyle
> ever loved his wife, or had any power of comprehending
> beauty. He saw, however, that 'out of evil nothing but
> evil can come.' London and Paris must be obliterated.

[1] *Friends of a Lifetime*, p. 30.
[2] A more polished version of it appears in *Friends of a Lifetime*,
pp. 30–3.

Sorry to be so nearly done for. Christian in ethics, like all true men, but cannot but believe that death is the end of all things. Wants to visit onceloved spots. Never saw Walden. Doesn't read the Americans much. French novels and plays. In his drawing room were pictures by Turner, W. Hunt, Holman Hunt, Burne Jones, Francesca etc., Punch from beginning, Encyclopedia Britannica, Dickens 1st ed., Pope, Grote's History, Pinkerton's Voyages, Couch's British Fishes, books by G. Macdonald, Froude, Patmore, Hood etc. Chess board set out. Musical instruments.

After an hour or so, Cockerell was led into the garden to play shuttlecock with Ruskin's Saturday afternoon class of village girls, and invited to return to lunch the following day.

Easter morning was warm and sunny. Towards one o'clock Cockerell, who had been rowing lazily on the lake in Ruskin's blue-painted boat, saw the Master approaching the water's edge. He pulled to the shore and joined him.

As we strolled back to Brantwood, he called my attention to the unpaintable bloom on the hills, and pointed out an upright tilt in the strata by the roadside. Then he spoke of the feeling of solitude that comes over one as one sits in a boat far out in the lake. A tortoiseshell butterfly settled in our path, but he refused to notice it. 'I cannot admire anything lower in the scale than a fish,' he said jestingly. 'I have the best disposition towards slugs and flies and gnats, but why they exist I don't understand.' But he stooped to caress some wild flowers on a bank.

During lunch Cockerell mentioned to Ruskin that he had read that many scientific men were joining the Church of Rome. This Ruskin denied, pointing out the danger of generalizing from particular instances. Of his books, Ruskin said that he set most store by *Unto this Last*, and that he dreaded the sad things — 'his father's death and so on' — that lay ahead of him in the third volume of his autobiography, *Praeterita*. On the walls of the dining-room hung Northcote's portraits of his parents and of himself as a child, Titian's *Doge*, a portrait of Turner and a study of a girl by Gainsborough.

After lunch there were the Turners in his bedroom to be seen, and in his study Turner's view of Rouen from St. Catherine's Hill — a view that Cockerell knew and that Ruskin proclaimed 'the finest thing there is to see in all this damned world.'

In his books and lectures [wrote Cockerell] Ruskin was apt to lay down the law with an air of papal infallibility and to trample without mercy on those who differed from him. In his conversation he was singularly unassuming. He seemed anxious to learn, even from babes and suck-lings. He had in a remarkable degree the power of making any person to whom he was attracted at the moment feel like a special favourite and confidant. When later we were at Beauvais he treated me as though I had known him always, and as if out of my little knowledge and experi-ence I could give him precious help and counsel. It was more than a year later and I had advanced somewhat in understanding. But I was still a bumptious fledgeling just under twenty-one, and, as far as I can judge, had no qualities of a solid kind except loyalty, enthusiasm, and unworldly aspirations, to counter-balance gaucherie, ignorance, and a double allowance of juvenile assurance. Readers of these notes and letters must not suppose that my existence was of more than passing importance to him. He was all the world to me, or nearly all, and I chanced to come in and out of his life when he was weary and perplexed and ready to lean on any young man or woman who seemed worthy of his affection. . . .[1]

[1] *Friends of a Lifetime*, p. 33. In 1939, in a letter to Mrs. Dallyn, Cockerell wrote: 'I find it hard to agree with your partial condemnation of the Ruskin letters. I think them wonderful as letters from a famous man (no one now is nearly so famous, no writer I mean, as he was then) to an insignificant suburban youth. The "self-consciousness and conceit" that you find in them was not an indication of old age—it is present just as much in the letters of twenty years earlier and in *Fors Clavigera*, his most characteristic work. . . . I have pointed out that in conversation I found him humble to a degree.'

As the afternoon wore on, Cockerell found himself sufficiently at ease with his host to broach a matter which had long been a source of sorrow to him: Ruskin's lamentable quarrel with Octavia Hill. For many years the two had been close friends, and Ruskin had helped to finance her projects; then some busybody had made trouble: Ruskin was told that she had been saying that his teaching was not to be taken too literally. He seized his pen and wrote to her in biting terms, adding insult to injury by publishing in due course their correspondence in *Fors Clavigera*. All this had happened ten years before. Ruskin, at the time, had been on the verge of his first mental breakdown, though Miss Hill had not been aware of it; she herself, miserable at this quarrel for which she could not feel responsible, became ill for many months.

'Will you not now forgive Miss Hill,' Cockerell begged, though he felt that it was she who had as much, or more, to forgive.

'I never forgive,' said Ruskin firmly. 'It was too great an injury.'

Cockerell saw that for the present there was nothing more he could do.

4

RUSKIN

BUT the visit had been a success—so great a success that Ruskin invited the boy to bring his sister Olive to spend their summer holiday with him. Cockerell, in ecstasy, wrote to tell her the great news:

Easter Sunday 1887   Coniston
                                            Lancashire

My Dear Olive,
    MR. RUSKIN HAS INVITED *YOU* AND *ME* TO COME AND SPEND OUR SUMMER HOLIDAY WITH HIM AT BRANTWOOD ! ! ! hip! hip! hourra.a.ay! . . . You must draw a daffodil or something —with a fairy—*as well as ever you can*—if the first isn't satisfactory you must do another—and write and say how delighted you are to know of his kindness, and that you were never so glad in your life! Sign 'Olive' not 'O' as he likes the name—John Ruskin LLD etc., Brantwood, Coniston, Lancashire. He likes daffodils—and they are all now about in his grounds. . . .

In May, however, came news from Mrs. Arthur Severn, who kept house for Ruskin and whom Cockerell had not yet met, that Ruskin was ill. 'Grievous things have been happening to me at Brantwood,' Ruskin wrote to Cockerell in June, and when the time came for the eagerly-awaited visit the Master was no better. Mrs. Severn kindly suggested that Cockerell and his sister should stay as Ruskin's guests in rooms in the neighbourhood, but they felt that they ought to be independent. They came to Coniston, however, where they made the acquaintance of Mrs. Severn, and also of Ruskin's secretary, Sara Anderson, who flattered the young man by proposing that he should take over the secretaryship. She did not conceal the difficulties of the job; but Cockerell, tempted though he was to accept, felt that he could not abandon the family business so soon after his grandfather's death.

But in spite of their disappointment in not being able to see Ruskin, the fortnight's holiday was enjoyable. Whole days were spent on the lake in Ruskin's boat, reading Shakespeare aloud, and one morning they set out before dawn to see the sunrise from the top of the Old Man.

In the New Year Ruskin wrote from Sandgate, where he was recuperating, sending his 'pensive and tremulously patient love' and inviting Cockerell and his sister to spend any Saturday to Monday there as his guests. They set out at once, Cockerell armed with two large cases of his best shells, reaching Sandgate in time for tea. Ruskin welcomed them warmly, kissing Olive, whom he had not met before, and led them to rooms which he had taken for them in the neighbourhood and hung with watercolours by Turner, and by T. M. Rooke.[1]

In *Friends of a Lifetime* Cockerell has recorded the conversations of that memorable week-end. 'With his exquisite old-world courtesy [Ruskin] drew us out, made as though our little suburban opinions interested him, and seemed as ready to listen as to talk.' He spoke much of art and of artists — with enthusiasm of Rossetti and Millais, and with regret that he had not recognized Fred Walker's worth in his lifetime; of the splendid technique of the Old Masters 'and the evident determination of each of them to do his very best.' When Cockerell mentioned that Walter Crane's early development

---

[1] 'Afterwards my very dear friend', wrote Cockerell, who later helped him to get Rooke commissions to paint the French cathedrals. Rooke died in 1942 in his hundredth year, his wife ('the brick of a wife to a saint of a man') in 1929. Two hundred and thirty letters from Rooke are among Cockerell's papers.

had been hindered by poverty, Ruskin replied that *his* had been hindered by luxury; had he lived in a garret on short rations he could have advocated such a life to the highest in the land. 'The way to abolish the East End,' he said, 'is to abolish the West End first.'

When Cockerell found himself alone with Ruskin, he consulted him about his own course of life. Should he abandon business and go up to the University? Ruskin was of the opinion that it was his duty to follow his grandfather's wishes; he himself, he said, had gained little from Oxford. The second evening closed with Ruskin reading a new chapter of *Praeterita*. 'I have since had the good fortune to hear many distinguished authors read from their works,' wrote Cockerell; 'Ruskin surpassed them all in the charm of his manner and in the humorous relish with which he drove home every point, responding with glance and voice to each tiny demonstration of his spell-bound listeners, as though they were an instrument on which he was playing and for them alone his theme had been composed.'

It was on the last morning that Cockerell bravely returned to the subject of Ruskin's quarrel with Octavia Hill and succeeded in persuading him to 'forgive' her:

> First gently, and then vehemently, I took him to task. . . .
> At first he appeared obdurate, but Olive, who was
> Octavia Hill's godchild, seconded me bravely, and we
> continued the attack until finally he could but surrender
> to our alternate demands and entreaties. . . . Then he
> kissed us both, joined our hands, gave us an affectionate
> blessing, and bade us farewell, we being touched to the
> heart and in tears.
>
> Such things can happen sometimes between young and
> old, while the flaming wings of Love are beating about
> them and the air is full of heavenly music. Back at home,
> when the wings were furled and the music had ceased,
> we were amazed at our temerity and began to fear that
> by recurring to this painful episode we might contribute
> to another breakdown. . . .

In April Cockerell attended the Private View of the Old
Water-colour Society at which, to his surprise and joy, he
came upon Ruskin:

> As we were talking I was suddenly conscious that Brown-
> ing was beside us waiting for an audience. Ruskin had
> not seen him for some time and failed to recognize him,
> so it fell to me to introduce them. 'Here is Mr. Browning,'
> I said and moved to a little distance. Then I was to witness
> a pretty spectacle. Ruskin instantly removed his hat and
> held it in his hand — Browning as quickly did the same,
> and they stood together with heads uncovered.[1]

Ruskin's books, especially the *Seven Lamps*, had fired Cockerell
with a longing to see more French gothic architecture; in June
therefore, when his fortnight's holiday became due, he set out
with Detmar Blow, a young architect of his own age, and a
copy of *The Bible of Amiens*, for northern France. Ruskin had
written to Cockerell in May that he had no intention of going
abroad; great therefore was the astonishment of the two young
men when, at the Tête de Boeuf in Abbeville, they saw
Ruskin and Arthur Severn enter the breakfast-room. It was of
course for Ruskin to make the first move. This he did: introductions were effected, and for the rest of Cockerell's holiday
(which he managed to get extended by a week) they were a
party of four.

Those nineteen days were probably the most memorable in
the whole of Cockerell's long life. With Ruskin at his side he
saw Abbeville and Beauvais. He watched the Master as he
drew — and of course succeeded in becoming possessed of the
drawings. ('Get me a sketchbook and you shall have whatever I put in it.') They lunched and dined together, and when
they drove together round the countryside Cockerell was even
allowed to take his turn at holding the precious rosewood box
that contained, between two sheets of gold, one of Rose La

[1] *Friends of a Lifetime*, p. 48. But in Cockerell's diary there is no
mention of his effecting this introduction.

Touche's letters.[1] In the evenings they played reversi; and sometimes Ruskin would read aloud — Legouvé's *La Fleur de Tlemcen* or *La Cigale chez les Fourmis* — translating as he read. The climax was reached when Ruskin, 'a little flushed and excited', read another chapter from the third volume of *Praeterita.*

On the whole they were unlucky with the weather, but nothing could damp Cockerell's ardour. Ruskin, too, was full of eagerness to show the young men everything. Cockerell wrote:

> July 6th. Went out at 8 a.m. with Mr. R and explored the town [Beauvais] and Cathedral. Climbed to the topmost parapet of the latter and looked down upon the sublime poising of the flying buttresses. Amazed with the majesty of the apse. Looked at the old houses round about. Drove to the hill, saw vines growing, lay for long in a hayfield and had altogether the delightfullest day since we started. R in splendid spirits and full of vigour. . . .

The diary makes no mention of a small contretemps at Beauvais. Cockerell said: 'There were bugs in the hotel and I suggested to Ruskin that we should move elsewhere. Ruskin replied, "Damn the bugs! If they'd been scorpions you'd have had a right to complain." So Detmar and I found another hotel.' It seems very strange that Cockerell should have considered the absence of bugs as of greater importance than the presence of Ruskin. But all turned out well: Cockerell added, 'Ruskin and Severn followed us.'

It is curious, too, that on the day (9th July) when, according to Cockerell's account in *Friends of a Lifetime*, Ruskin talked

[1] There is an interesting entry in Cockerell's diary for 27th June 1914: 'After dinner had a talk with Mrs. Severn [at Brantwood] about Rose Latouche (sic) and heard much that astonished me greatly about her wayward and eccentric nature. Mrs. Severn was engaged to her brother for a year. Mrs. Severn said that J.R. did not really want to marry Rosie, though she fascinated and tormented him, and that he was not greatly upset when she died.'

dismally of illnesses and approaching death, the diary merely records, 'R. declared himself to be in better health than he had been for a long time.'

Cockerell had lost no time in telling his mother of his glorious and unexpected encounter. His wild enthusiasm must have alarmed her, for she replied at once: 'I am *so afraid* of Mr. R's getting tired of you, and I think it is almost better for you to leave him *before* that happens; but you will be the best judge of that.' Cockerell was: his mother's letter had been written barely a week after he had come upon Ruskin; yet when, at the end of three weeks, Cockerell was obliged to return to England, the Master showed nothing but regret at his departure.

'Carlyle carries my umbrella for me as if he were attending the Emperor of Japan,' Ruskin had written to Mrs. Severn, and 'Detmar is as good as gold.' Shortly afterwards he told H. W. Nevinson, whom he met at Sallenche, that Cockerell was 'a very remarkable young man, so sweet and thoughtful, and of high scientific power too. If he had been here, he would have filled the whole place with shells by now.'[1]

Cockerell was obliged to leave for England at a very early hour, but Ruskin had begged him to come to his bedroom to say goodbye to him. 'This I did at a quarter to five. He was awake and expecting me. As I tried to express my gratitude to him and kissed his hand in a final good-bye I was pierced by the thought that I might never see him again.'

Detmar Blow remained with Ruskin and Severn on their leisurely journey through France, Italy and Switzerland. Ruskin was now on the verge of another breakdown, and in December he had to be brought back to England. Though he rallied for a time, the 'sorrowful mood' soon took full possession of him once more. After 1890 he never left Brantwood.

Cockerell did, however, see him again — and on more than one occasion. In 1892, while staying with W. G. Collingwood

[1] H. W. Nevinson, *Changes and Chances*, 1923.

at Lanehead, Coniston, to help him with his biography of Ruskin,[1] he paid two visits to Brantwood:

> April 17th (Easter Day). . . . After supper and a little quiet talk the Professor came in at 9.15, looking much like his old self (older, more feeble, more bent — his beard longer and a little whiter, his hair still dark steel grey and very abundant, his smile subdued, his eye less bright, as I expected to find him, though less altered than I anticipated) altogether a most impressive figure. He took my hand, referred to our last meeting at Beauvais. *The Nature of Gothic* with the inscription 'John Ruskin from William Morris with affectionate regards, April 11th, 1892,' was on the table and I took it up. He was pleased with it and interested in my telling him about the new black letter fount. He said that Morris was the ablest man of his time. I was stirred and embarrassed at the sight of the dear old man, and too full of reflections to say much — he also being inclined to silence, and speaking in a very low tone. A chessboard was soon produced by Mrs. Severn, and we had a game, he and I. It was a long one, J.R.'s moves being rapid and well thought out — but eventually by some mischance I won. Then Mrs. Severn sang a song or two, and he retired. I left soon after, walking back along the dark road under the stars to Lanehead, full of thought and emotion, very thankful to have been permitted to speak again with the man to whom I owe so much more than I can ever realise.

A second visit followed on the Monday, when Joan Severn sang the little Agincourt chant composed in 1415:

> I kept my eyes on J.R. as she sang it, and I shall never hear it now without seeing him. . . . It was strange and pathetic to look at that bent figure and noble head, and to

---

[1] Cockerell had compiled a skeleton biography of Ruskin which proved of considerable use to Collingwood, who had at first suggested collaboration in the writing of the Life.

Sydney Carlyle Cockerell,
c. 1869

Cockrellius
eving a poore traveller
manuscript, 1934
TO: STEARN

St Cockerellius RELIEVING a
poore traveller of a manuscript

Octavia Hill, 1899
PHOTO: NATIONAL PORTRAIT GALLERY

William Morris, 1886

Ruskin in his study

PHOTO: DEARDEN

The Morris and Burne-Jones families at The Grange, Fulham, c. 1875

BACK ROW, FROM LEFT TO RIGHT: Philip Burne-Jones, Edward Richard Jones,
Edward Burne-Jones, William Morris and Mary (May) Morris
FRONT ROW, FROM LEFT TO RIGHT: Mrs (later Lady) Georgiana Burne-Jones,
Jane Alice (Jenny) Morris, Margaret Burne-Jones, Mrs. Jane Morris

Sydney Carlyle Cockerell,
from a photograph by
Bernard Shaw, 1905

Shaw at the
Fitzwilliam,
1933

The Fitzwilliam Museum in 1887, showing Gallery III approximately as Cockerell found it when he became director in 1908. M. R. James is in the centre of the

The Fitzwilliam Museum in 1963, showing the same corner of Gallery III
approximately as Cockerell left it when he retired in 1937
PHOTO: STEARN

Kate Cockerell and her children, 1920

think of the part it had played in the 19th century drama, and to touch the very hand that had written so much, from *Modern Painters* onwards. The world seemed so empty when at 10.30 he moved slowly from the room . . .

Next day, 'carrying the warped and mildewed fragments of the two shell cases . . . which I had left at Sandgate in 1888,' Cockerell returned to London, wondering once again 'whether I should ever meet him more.' But he did, though seven years were to pass before he took his final farewell of the man who had been 'by far the most powerful influence' on his early life:

7th November 1899. . . . Got to Brantwood about 11. . . . Was taken up to see J.R., who was sitting in his chair with a little book before him and his hands encased in fur mittens. I do not think he recognized me, though when I said I had been to Beauvais 9 times since were we there together he answered, 'and I have not been there once!' Did he remember Detmar Blow? 'No'. Did he remember Rooke? 'No'. To other questions yes or no, never a longer sentence, except the one already quoted. He looked tranquil, rather wistful, but very little changed in face since I saw him last in 1892. . . . It was like interviewing a ghost, but very wonderful — and as I was prepared to find him looking much more pinched I was not cast down. I stayed only a few minutes with him and spent the rest of the time till 4 at his table in his study looking at his manuscripts, and especially at the wonderful 'St. Louis' Psalter'.[1]

Ten weeks later, on 20th January 1900, Ruskin died. 'I was walking from Richmond to Hammersmith . . . when I saw the announcement. Much moved, I turned aside to share the tidings with dear old Arthur Hughes,[2] then living on Kew Green. He felt as I did, that a mighty spirit had gone out.'

[1] This Psalter, of which Cockerell was later to write a description, was acquired for the Fitzwilliam Museum in 1919.
[2] Arthur Hughes (1832–1915), artist, friend of William Morris. Painted 'April Love', etc.

5

WILLIAM MORRIS

O N 15th November 1885 Theo and Sydney went to
their first Socialist[1] meeting at Kelmscott House,
Hammersmith. William Morris was announced to
read a paper on Socialism, but it was read in his absence by his
younger daughter, May. Theo at once declared his adherence,
and a fortnight later was elected to the Hammersmith Branch
of the Socialist League.

A year elapsed before Cockerell met the man who was to
become the second of his great heroes.[2] Morris, who was to
speak in Chiswick, came with Emery Walker to a meal with
Mrs. Cockerell beforehand. Theo and Sydney attended the
meeting, at which Morris's paper on *The Dawn of a New Epoch*
was ill received by an audience 'discourteous and wanting in
intelligence', and walked the two miles to Hammersmith
with him afterwards, questioning him all the way.

After Theo had left for America, Sydney, who had at first
played with Morris the minor rôle of 'Theo's brother', became
by degrees his intimate friend and most ardent disciple. He
went to concerts at Kelmscott House, where May Morris would
play the guitar and sing and her father read passages from his
own works. He saw Morris's socialistic play *The Tables Turned,
or Nupkins Awakened*, in which the author was 'rather funny
as the Archbishop of Canterbury, but otherwise dreadfully

[1] 'I had *leanings* towards Socialism,' said Cockerell, 'but nothing more
than that. I was brought up a Liberal—pro-Gladstone, anti-Beacons-
field. . . .'
[2] His worship of Morris was never to waver; but many years later he
said of Ruskin, 'I now see his limitations.'

dull,' and *The Duchess of Bayswater and Co.*, also with Morris taking part. But it was not until he was elected, in March 1890, to the Committee of the Society for the Protection of Ancient Buildings that Sydney was able to establish close and regular contact with Morris.

The S.P.A.B., familiarly known as 'Anti-Scrape', had been brought into being by Morris in the seventies to combat what he termed those 'acts of barbarism which the modern architect, parson, and squire call "restoration"'. The Committee met every Thursday at 5 p.m. in Buckingham Street to plan how to prevent the latest sacrilege threatened by the great Sir Gilbert Scott or some lesser vandal. Often it was disheartening work, for there was both apathy to be combated and powerful opposition to be overcome. But however wearisome or frustrating the meeting, for Cockerell there was great reward when, at the stroke of 7 o'clock, he adjourned with Morris, Philip Webb, Emery Walker and W. R. Lethaby to high tea at Gatti's.[1]

The meal was simple enough—for Cockerell a roll and butter, a couple of poached eggs on toast, and a pot of tea, unless some special triumph called for celebration with a bottle of cheap claret. It was the talk that mattered, and the amiable Italian waiter who always served them never tried to hustle them away afterwards. They relaxed completely: jottings such as, 'Morris very jovial,' 'much merriment,' 'abundant laughter,' and 'the usual chaff' occur frequently in the diary, and diners at neighbouring tables were sometimes puzzled, and even a little shocked, by their hilarity. But there was serious talk also. Morris might produce for inspection, from the satchel slung over his shoulder, a newly-acquired medieval manuscript or (after the Kelmscott Press had been started) a specimen of his own printing. There might be photographs of French or Italian cathedrals, the trophies of a recent continental

---

[1] Philip Webb (1831–1915), architect; Sir Emery Walker (1857–1933), process-engraver and typographical expert; W. R. Lethaby (1857–1931), author and architect. These three men, all of whom had been closely associated with William Morris and his various activities for many years, became and remained Cockerell's most intimate friends.

tour by one of the party. And sometimes the conversation would turn upon general problems of ethics or aesthetics. Though gout or lecturing occasionally kept Morris away, Cockerell's diary shows that he shared his company at Gatti's on no less than one hundred and twenty-five evenings, some of which were prolonged until nearly midnight in the library at Kelmscott House.

In March 1890 Morris took Cockerell with him to Merton Abbey, near Epsom, where the dyeing, fabric-printing, weaving and other activities of Morris & Co. were carried on. The banks of the river Wandle, which flowed through the grounds, were bright with daffodils and looking a 'dream of beauty.' Morris explained the various technical processes, and Cockerell, ever a collector of souvenirs, dipped his handkerchief in the indigo vat before leaving. The following year he had his first sight of the Kelmscott Press, which Morris had recently set up in a cottage on the Upper Mall at Hammersmith, a few yards from Kelmscott House. Sheets of *The Story of the Glittering Plain*, Morris's first essay in printing from type designed by himself, were being pulled from a little old-fashioned press.

Ruskin had told Cockerell that Morris was 'beaten gold,' and he could not doubt it. Sixty years later, in his admirable Introduction to a new edition of J. W. Mackail's *The Life of William Morris*,[1] Cockerell wrote:

> He was, indeed, utterly unlike anyone I have since encountered. . . . He was sound and sweet and genuine through and through, wholly without pose, fustian, or pretence. There was nothing petty in his nature. He was self-sufficing, but was never self-centred, though he became utterly absorbed in any work on which he was engaged. So little vain was he of his striking appearance that he had no looking-glass in his bedroom. . . . His industry was amazing—his output was that of twenty men. And yet he never seemed too busy to see a friend.

[1] World's Classics edition, 1950.

. . . We thought him flawless and it would never have occurred to any of us to criticize him.

It is not difficult to imagine how unsettling, to a rather disillusioned young coal-merchant, were the glimpses of a fuller and richer life that his contact with Ruskin and the Morris circle had opened up for him. Not only was Cockerell bored with his work, but the profits were meagre and the future of the firm very uncertain. He was now twenty-four; if he was to break away and make a new start, there was no time to lose. But what odds there were against him! He wrote to seek the advice of Albert Fleming, a man twenty years older than himself who was a close friend of Ruskin.[1] Fleming's reply (19th November 1891) was as frank as it was discouraging:

Dear Man,
Be as sulky as you like but don't be rash and wild. If coals give you the merest bread and cheese, stick to them until something better turns up. Even an £80 berth in the B.M. isn't to be had for the asking, and even then to potter over that heart-breaking Catalogue, or to sit all day with a rod in your hand amongst Greek pots or stuffed birds, isn't exhilarating work. Do you know how desperately hard it is to get work nowadays? A man called here one evening (his brother is a great pal of mine) literally *starving*, had been driving a cab, tried the stage, had no vice nor disqualifications, but there he was on my hearthrug with no shirt to his back and no food in his belly.
Then again, brutal as it may sound, you're no very great catch, are you now? You'd make a splendid secretary, but you know you hate dull hard drudgery, and you're happy if you are dabbling about in literature and architecture, and scraping up dates for somebody else to use; but you're not a great scholar or linguist, nor do you

---

[1] Fleming revived the industry of hand-spinning in the Lake District. Cockerell admitted to having destroyed almost the whole of his large collection of letters from him. Possibly he considered Fleming too candid; but their loss would seem to be a great misfortune.

know much about general literature and you know
nothing at all about art. You won't write for the Press,
and I don't suppose you'd lecture; and though you are
always ready and capable of helping others, you're not
especially capable of helping yourself. Moreover there is
a quixotic vein in you which is adorable, but in one sense
a drawback.

Pray stick to the coals till you can drop them for an
actual opening. You're not strong, and the world is most
damnably cruel, and I am ever your sincere friend

A.F.

Cockerell consulted Philip Webb, who was 'unspeakably
kind and nice and full of wise counsel;' he also talked with his
uncle, Douglas Powell, but he does not mention what they
advised. 'Much worried what to do,' he wrote in his diary
(16th December 1891). 'Stiff competitive examination to be
passed before one can get into South Kensington Museum.
Must therefore think of something else.' The decision was
taken on New Year's Eve: 'Arranged to sell my share in the
business to Mr. T. G. Nevill for £1000.' With great generosity
he divided this money equally between himself and his five
brothers and sisters; then, finding that one of the clerks had
never received a sum of £100 promised him at the time of old
Mr. Cockerell's death, he paid this out of his own share. Of the
£2000 that, some six years before, he had invested in the
family business, only about £66 remained to him.

Doubtless it seemed to Cockerell at the time that he had
squandered six precious years of his youth. But the years had
not, in fact, be wholly wasted. Just as his conchological studies
had quickened his powers of observation, so the discipline of
the City had taught him business-like habits. 'I learned,' he
said, 'to be orderly and methodical, and to answer every letter
by return of post; and I learned that if two jobs have to be
done, the duller one must be done first.' These virtues, not
too commonly found in the world of art, were to prove

invaluable to him when he became Director of the Fitzwilliam Museum.

On the last day of May 1892 Cockerell walked out of the doors of George Cockerell & Co. 'feeling as though I were leaving school. Some of the clerks really sorry for my departure, and I heavy-hearted when the time for the last handshaking came. It was nice to feel that there was no one in the office against whom I bore the slightest grudge . . .'

Five days later he was in Abbeville.

Foreign travel was to become one of Cockerell's greatest pleasures. Already he had slipped across the Channel on a number of occasions to spend a few days among the cathedrals of northern France; in September 1891, shortly before he made his fateful decision to abandon coal for ever, he had gone with a party on his first visit to Italy.

The trip had been organized for the Art Workers' Guild by a remarkable man named Thomas Okey, the son of a Bethnal Green basket-maker, who ultimately became the first Professor of Italian at Cambridge. Of the twenty-seven men whom Okey conducted to Venice, Emery Walker and Bernard Shaw were the two best known to Cockerell. The inclusive cost of the twelve-day holiday was £13 10s. a head.

In a long and scintillating letter[1] to Morris, Shaw described his companions and the impact of Italy upon him. 'I write,' he said, 'because I must work off my growing irritation and escape for a moment from the fearful solitude created by these twenty-seven men, about twenty of whom seem to be capable of admiring everything except beauty.' Italy frankly disappointed him. There was 'the very expensive wedding-cake' at Milan that posed as a cathedral, and the exterior of St. Mark's, Venice, which would have been 'ideal for a railway station.' Even the gondoliers disillusioned him by declining to chant the verses of Tasso. 'You should see Walker and Cockerell,' Shaw continued. 'Their faces and necks are pure mosquito pastures — all red spots . . .' He himself kept the

[1] See *A Basketful of Memories* by Thomas Okey, 1930.

mosquitoes at bay by means of pastilles that burned with 'a
fume so noxious that I have all but succumbed to it myself;'
nor was he troubled, as were the others, by fleas: 'The fact is
I perspire freely . . . I am convinced that the damp gives the
fleas rheumatism, which must be a hideously unpleasant complaint for an insect which has to jump for its life every few
seconds.'

'Walker and I took Shaw's extravagances as part of the
game,' said Cockerell. None the less, Shaw's gay account is
brisker reading than Cockerell's earnest appraisal of churches,
palaces and pictures, made the more unappetizing by the
reduction in size of his script to near-invisibility. He was never
to acquire the light touch. There is little mention of Shaw,
whose frivolity probably irritated him and whose subsequent
fame he did not then foresee. A second expedition by the Art
Workers' Guild, with much the same team but this time with
Florence as its goal, was to be made in 1894.

With the single exception of a visit to friends in France to
recuperate after an illness in 1886, all Cockerell's previous
excursions abroad had been tantalizingly brief; when he
stepped out of the Coal Office into the boat train to Newhaven
he was embarking upon the longest continental holiday he had
yet had. During the next seven weeks he visited most of the
great cathedrals of northern France, sometimes in the company of friends, sometimes alone, but always with Beowulf and
the Odyssey (in Greek) under his arm for relaxation. Chartres,
which he had not seen before, filled him with such delight that
he 'shouted for joy;' its Cathedral was, in fact, to become for
him something so precious that he could not tolerate the
slightest criticism of it. When he was there on one occasion
with John Tweed, the sculptor, he was 'troubled by his critical
attitude to the statues . . . which made me glad of his departure. His remarks, based on technical experience, would have
interested me more at a later period, when my own eyes and
judgment had become better trained. I reported my annoy-
ance to William Morris, who said, "I don't want to meet the

man who would criticize Chartres Cathedral. It is like finding fault with a geological epoch.'"[1]

Filled with the joy of Chartres and in his newly-won freedom, Cockerell took no thought for the morrow when his small savings would have been swallowed up. But once back in London, facts had to be faced. He had already applied for the Curatorship of the Sheffield Museum, only to discover that the post was not after all vacant. He visited the Public Library and pored over the 'Appointments Vacant' columns in the newspapers, but in vain. Meanwhile he was doing a little work for Octavia Hill, verifying footpaths and rights-of-way which had been closed by unscrupulous farmers and land-owners, but receiving no more for his labours than his expenses. In his diary he frankly admitted to being 'worried' about the future.

Perhaps at the back of his mind Cockerell felt that, somehow or other, Morris would come to his rescue. He had been assiduously, and almost brazenly, cultivating his new hero. After attending a lecture at the Art Workers Guild ('I squeezed in, although not an art worker'), at which Morris had taken the chair, he wrote (4th March 1892): 'Came home with Morris—thoroughly ashamed of my impudence in taking such constant advantages of my opportunities for associating with him. I never felt his greatness more completely.' In August Morris invited him to spend a week at Kelmscott Manor, his country retreat on the upper Thames near Lechlade.

'Except Hever and Ightham I don't think I have ever seen any house so beautiful,' Cockerell wrote. 'It looks as if it had risen from the ground with the old fruit trees about it—its grey stones, like them, tinted yellow with lichen.' There were mullioned windows and panelled walls, and a room hung with tapestries; in the garden, which stretched down to the banks of the Thames, old clipped yew hedges rose darkly against the

---

[1] This was written in 1933, at the time of Tweed's death. Cockerell's visit to Chartres with Tweed was made in August 1902, six years after Morris's death; Morris's comment must therefore have been made in some other connection.

pale walls and gabled roofs. It was — as it still is — a house of enormous charm.

Morris was at the door to greet him. 'Burly and thick-set, but not tall,' he was wearing, as he always did, 'a dark blue serge suit — a little untidy . . . a linen shirt dyed indigo in his own vats,' and no tie. Mrs. Morris (the lovely Jane Burden) and their younger daughter, May, awaited him indoors; poor Jenny, their epileptic elder daughter, was not at home.

For Cockerell 'it seemed almost like being in heaven' to find himself for a whole week in Morris's company. For a while he was shy — so shy, indeed, that on the first evening, having failed to get to his bedroom, which could only be reached by passing through Morris's, before his host had gone to bed, he spent the night on a sofa in the tapestry room rather than disturb him. But Jane and May took compassion on him, and he soon felt at his ease.

Cockerell had no creative talent. 'I look despairingly at my useless hands that have not been taught to fashion the smallest thing,' he once wrote; and again, 'I haven't a spark of imagination, and am only good for dry-as-dust cataloguing.'[1] But he soon began to make himself useful to Morris in various ways. At least he could hold a brush steadily enough to paint in the flat background of a wallpaper design; and he was a born reader of proofs, never missing the minutest error. He could also effortlessly provide the worship that, coming from the lips of the young, must fall sweetly on the ears of even the most modest of middle-aged artists. Together the two men visited Great Coxwell barn and some of the local churches, or fished for perch and gudgeon in the infant Thames that flowed past the house; and in the evening there was whist or 'twenty questions' or talk about printing. Cockerell proved the perfect protégé; the visit was repeated in October, and before it was over he found himself invited to catalogue Morris's library at Kelmscott House, Hammersmith. This was not — or at all events it did not then appear to be — a permanent solution to his problem, but for the moment it provided him with a perfect

[1] To W. S. Blunt, to whom he also wrote, 'Modesty—one of the virtues with which I am seldom credited.'

job—the most congenial work in the world, to be performed at the very feet of the Master. He was to receive two guineas a week and a copy of *The Golden Legend*.

Albert Fleming heard the news and, fearing that before long Cockerell would find himself in need of a new job, sent him a mock-testimonial in his usual racy style:

I have known this most promising candidate for years. He devoted many years of his youth to collecting shells, and having acquired some really valuable information on the subject, as well as 'one of the best collections of native shells in the kingdom' (J.R.), he declined either to use the information or to sell the collection (though worth some hundreds). I cannot precisely recall *what* he did with the shells, but one may be sure that it was something unwise, unpractical and unselfish. He then became partner in one of the leading coal merchants' firms. Although not privileged to be a member of the ever-honoured 'Guyld' he has adopted the craziest portion of their creed, and he therefore spent some hours every day debating whether selling coals was in harmony with the ethics of Ruskin, Morris, Miss Octavia Hill and Ibsen. He addressed voluminous memoranda to his partners on this point. The rest of the day he spent in following the carts, and detected the men on several occasions in supplying quite 3 ozs short measure. At last a virtuous lady from Wimbledon wrote saying she had ordered *coals*, and not being an ironclad she objected to be bombarded by projectiles from the grate. . . .

This proving the trade to be of a pestilent and immoral nature, S.C.C. compelled his partners to buy him out, and he turned his back for ever on the coal trade. Going home he flung down the notes in the drawing-room and told the family to help themselves, he himself presenting £100 to a faithful family retainer. Being then penniless he started off for a prolonged tour of the Continent.

He is a prominent (and very aggravating) member of the Anti-Scrape Society, and no owner of an old house

within 50 miles of Bedford Park ventures to mend a
broken window-pane or put on a new tile without sub-
mitting the matter to S.C.C. He is also a member of a
Secret Society of socialists — anarchists, poets, painters and
suchlike dangerous persons — who meet in Barnards Inn,
and he may often be seen, after dark, gliding thither in
a villainous-looking brigand's hat. . . . He goaded W.M.
into reprinting, in fantastic form, an isolated fragment
of the master of the aforesaid ever-remarkable Guyld,
and doing it up in sham parchment and ribbon and
generally frivolling round and pandering to luxury. He
is now hopelessly and remorselessly Gothic. He has
quarrelled with his sisters because they declined to be
Early English, and he has hired a Breton peasant as cook,
that he may practise Norman French with her. He is at
present cataloguing W.M.'s collection of Early Printed
Books. He says practically there have been no real books
produced since 1450.

Time fails me to tell of the vast national work he did on
quite four Kentish foot-paths, and how he induced
several 'oldest inhabitants' to commit flagrant perjury.

Cockerell also felt that he ought not to count upon permanent employment with Morris, delightful though this would be.
In December the Curatorship of the Soane Museum fell
vacant, and he immediately asked Ruskin and Morris to provide him with testimonials. Ruskin, too ill to write himself,
dictated a letter to Mrs. Severn in which he described his
protégé as

in every way a most desirable, and suitable, person for
the curatorship. He has a special gift for research, and
classification . . ,. and is an earnest reader with considerable knowledge of art — wonderfully neat and careful in
his work and in collecting and arranging things admirable — and with a love, a power, of keeping things in
beautiful order — always genial and pleasant, whether as
a guest in this house or in doing services for his friends . . .

Morris wrote:

> Mr. Sydney Cockerell has been working for me, on the
> cataloguing of a library of ancient books, and in addition
> I have known him for some years. He is a man of great
> intelligence, and very careful and exact in his work, in
> which he takes much interest: he has a very good general
> knowledge of Archaeology, and I should think him on all
> grounds a very suitable person for the Curatorship of the
> Soane Museum.

Cockerell also asked the advice of Philip Webb, who
approved the project if it did not entail the sacrifice of too
much time and energy in the service of an institution. Webb
added:

> I believe it would be an advantage to the institution your
> not being an architect. For architecture, embracing — as
> it does — all the other arts should be looked upon with a
> much wider estimate of its highest value, than a practice
> of it usually allows — I am sorry to say! Your business
> aptitude and experience would serve you well, and your
> power of writing pointedly and clearly on various sub-
> jects would be a great help to the institution.

It was not until many wheels had been set in motion that
Cockerell discovered that the statutes provided that the
Curator must be a trained architect. He could not, therefore,
apply, and the post was in due course filled by a distinguished
but rather reluctant septuagenarian architect and antiquary
named Wyatt Angelicus van Sandau Papworth, who died the
following year. Papworth's successor was mild and ineffective,
and there can be little doubt that Cockerell, could he have
been appointed, would have done very valuable work; he
would, however, have thereby missed one of the most important experiences of his life — the further years that he spent
with Morris and as Secretary to the Kelmscott Press.

6

THE KELMSCOTT PRESS

MEANWHILE Cockerell was prodigiously enjoying himself at Kelmscott House:

'Tuesday 1st November [1892]. Spent the morning and afternoon at Kelmscott House and started the catalogue of W.M.'s books. W.M. designed two borders for Crane's Glittering Plain designs while I was there, and had some stanzas of Venus and Adonis set up . . .' A fortnight later he wrote, 'I was never so happy in my work before.' Yet the work was laborious, 'entailing an exhaustive scrutiny of each volume, the counting of the leaves and illustrations, the discovery of defects, and frequent researches in the British Museum to verify details. It took me three whole weeks to count and tabulate for the first time the 1,809 woodcut illustrations in the *Nuremberg Chronicle* of 1493, of which as many as 1,164 are repeats.'

At first Cockerell sat at a small and inconvenient table in Morris's study, but later he moved into a room connected with the study by a little staircase. Day after day he watched the designs take shape, the proofs arrive from the press, and finally the emergence of the bound volumes. He ran errands between Morris and Burne-Jones ('the Bart', as they all called him after he received his baronetcy in 1894), and thus had many opportunities of seeing the latter at work also. Almost imperceptibly he found himself promoted to being Morris's private secretary, and in 1894 he was officially appointed Secretary to the Kelmscott Press. 'He was,' said May Morris, 'my father's right hand.' He was constantly with Morris in working hours, and often his guest at lunch or dinner. One evening 'when I went up into the drawing-room to say good-night,' wrote Cockerell, 'Morris and his wife were playing at draughts, with large ivory pieces, red and white. Mrs. Morris was dressed in a glorious blue gown, and as she sat on the sofa, she looked like an animated Rossetti picture or page from some old MS of a king and queen.' There were visits together to the National Gallery, to the sale rooms, and to Messrs. Quaritch from whom Morris rarely returned without a manuscript or two. And there was the daily privilege of his conversation, for Morris liked to be talked to while he was drawing. Cockerell jotted down scraps in his diary at the end of the day; these will be found in May Morris's life of her father.[1]

At Hammersmith Morris sought little relaxation beyond a change of occupation—from designing to writing, or vice versa. But at Kelmscott Manor, where Cockerell was now a frequent guest, there were walks and drives, fishing, reading — and sometimes sheer idleness: ' 1st September [1895]. In afternoon lolled about and picked nuts and plums, and lay on the grass chatting. In evening W.M. read some of his favourite bits out of *Handley Cross*. A very happy day.'

Two expeditions which Cockerell made with Morris were memorable. In April 1895 they went with Philip Webb, Emery Walker and F. S. Ellis to Epping Forest to take note of excessive tree-felling that had been reported in the newspapers. The second was a week's visit to northern France with Walker and another friend, organized by Cockerell in order that he might have the 'felicity' of seeing Beauvais with Morris. 'On the first morning after we reached Beauvais, Morris rapped on my door soon after 7 o'clock and summoned me to "come out and buy a manuscript". . . . By an extraordinary stroke of luck we found a thirteenth-century Justinian going for a song at an old curiosity shop and carried it back in triumph.' Cockerell said: 'I went to Beauvais sixteen times in all. The last was in 1939. The Cathedral was like an old hen with her chicks round her. Then came the War: it's no use going there now . . .'

[1] *William Morris, Artist, Writer, Socialist*, pp. 84–93.

The genius of Morris, and the magnitude of his achievements in very varied fields, have never been in dispute, though the fluctuations of taste have left their mark on his popularity at certain moments. Morris 'made no fewer than 644 designs for woodcut initials, borders and ornaments for the Press,' wrote Cockerell:

> It had an existence of only seven years. Fifty-two works in sixty-six volumes, including the folio Chaucer, were produced on hand-presses in that short period. I saw this going on. For much of the time I was in the thick of it. And yet it would puzzle me to say how such a miracle was accomplished. Printing was the last of Morris's artistic activities. He had previously been at one time or another a painter, an embroiderer, a weaver, a dyer, a modeller, a carver in wood, a calligrapher and illuminator, a wood-engraver, and a cook. Well might he claim for himself the modest title of master-artisan.[1]

Cockerell's loyalty to Morris kept him for many years silent on the subject of his 'flawless' hero's Achilles heel: his temper. But on the publication, in 1950, of *The Letters of William Morris* (with an introduction by Philip Henderson), he joined in a correspondence in the *Observer* provoked by Mr. B. Ifor Evans's review of the book: 'As to Morris's famous rages, they antedated his married life and were due, I imagine, to some taint in the blood. I witnessed about half a dozen of them. They were startling at the moment, but they were over in a very few minutes, and when he became calm he was like a penitent child.' And he said, 'I once saw him tear his waistcoat into shreds.'

Mackail had, in fact, touched lightly upon Morris's temper in his biography; but his hands had been to some extent tied by Mrs. Morris, who would not even allow him to refer to her own humble origin. Mackail wrote to Cockerell (22nd September 1898):

[1] From S.C.C.'s Introduction to Mackail's *Life of William Morris* (1950).

What I feel is that it does grave injustice to Morris himself to slur over the fact that he married 'beneath him' and did so with perfect simplicity and as a thing which he had no reason whatever to feel ashamed of in any way. I have been obliged to some degree to slur it over, and the loss will be the book's, and Mrs. Morris's own I think, if she knew it. As to the picture [of the Burdens' house], it would hardly have relevance in the book unless it were explained what it represented. If Mrs. Morris feels ashamed of having lived in a little house among surroundings of extreme beauty before she was married, all I can say is that such a feeling is to me unintelligible.

The Victorians, by the blindness of their worship and their refusal to allow unpalatable facts (even such as did not affect the living) to see the light of day, defeated their own ends and invited the iconoclasm that followed. There is evidence elsewhere in Cockerell's letters that steps were sometimes taken to destroy or conceal evidence that tarnished the glitter of the legend, and he himself admitted to having burnt a page of one of Ruskin's letters to him (though Ruskin stated more than once that any letter of his might be read by all the world). Fairfax Murray, writing to Cockerell in 1915, said that no full life of Swinburne could then be written: 'It will be very difficult ever to be fair to the really fine qualities of his nature once the truth is told . . . and a certain whitewashing would be necessary for outsiders.' Of Lady Burne-Jones's *Memorials* of her husband, Murray wrote that the picture it gave was incomplete 'from much being omitted, purposely of course.' 'All Kipling's "saucy" letters to Burne-Jones,' said Cockerell, 'were destroyed.'

But truth will out. Posterity has taken its revenge, and one cannot but agree with Mr. Ifor Evans that 'it is a part of the penalty of the artist that the public wants the material of his life as common property.'

In 1896 Morris, who was now sixty-three, fell seriously ill. 'Four mouldy Sundays in a mouldy row, the Press shut and

Chaucer at a standstill,' he wrote sadly of the Easter holidays. Alone his determination to see the completion of the great Chaucer, and his unabated enthusiasm for the purchase of manuscripts, gave him the will to fight on. Cockerell was sent to Stuttgart, with full powers, to negotiate for a superb twelfth-century English Bestiary, which he purchased for £900 and carried back exultantly to Kelmscott Manor. On June 2nd the first two copies of the Chaucer came from the binder; it was the triumphant conclusion of a project conceived five years earlier.

In July, after a fruitless visit to Folkestone, Morris went on a cruise to Norway in the hope that the keener northern air might help; he returned no better, and the doctors diagnosed his illness as tubercular and incurable. Cockerell, diary in hand, was constantly at his bedside, noting each day the fluctuations in his health, rejoicing in the little improvements and sadly recording the more frequent relapses. Friends rallied round: 'The illness of our *captain* glooms us terribly,' wrote Lethaby. 'I don't care for anything.' On 27th August Morris dictated to Cockerell the end of *The Sundering Flood* — four and a half pages of foolscap; 'this was a great relief to him, I think.' A final twelve lines were added a fortnight later.

August 30th. W.M. asked me whether I should be prepared to carry on the Press after his death, with Walker, and I said that I was in favour of its ceasing — as otherwise it would fizzle out by degrees, and the books already issued would suffer by inferior ones following them. He said he thought I was perhaps right.

September 10th. W.M. was disturbed with fancies in the night — e.g. that he was writing Farrar's *Life of Christ* . . .

September 29th. W.M. said that he felt much better. It was a bright morning, and we took him out in the bath-chair. . . . We went into Ravenscourt Park and round by the Library, the longest turn we have yet had — and W.M. was in good spirits and declared that he was not a bit tired, and that he felt able to do some walking. . . . At 4.45 I went to the post and on returning found W.M. upstairs with blood streaming from his mouth. F. S. Ellis was with him. We helped him downstairs and put him to bed. Dr. Hogg came soon after.

'Mr. Cockerell was ceaseless in his zeal and care,' wrote Mackail, 'and Mr. Emery Walker nursed him with the patience and tenderness of a woman.' Morris died four days later: '3rd October. W.M. died peacefully at 11.15,' Cockerell noted in his diary. 'Lady Burne-Jones, Mrs. Morris, May, Detmar Blow and Miss De Morgan were in the room. Miss De Morgan and Walker started off to Kelmscott to tell Jenny. Carruthers, Crom Price, Philip Webb and Murray called. Murray made two drawings[1], one of which he gave to me. I had never seen a dead man before, and was startled to see how little it resembled the living Morris. The face was singularly beautiful, but the repose of it made it the more unlike what I had known.'

On 3rd October 1940 Cockerell wrote in his diary:

It is the 44th anniversary of William Morris's death. I was in his study across the passage from his bedroom on the ground floor of Kelmscott House, but I did not actually see him die. . . . As his most active executor I had to make all arrangements for his funeral at Kelmscott, to interview journalists, etc., etc. Burne-Jones was among the visitors. He asked me to lead him by the hand into the death chamber and then to leave him alone there. When he came out he said, 'There is nothing I would not do for you for your devotion to dear Morris.' When I had been previously left alone there myself I burst into an uncontrollable paroxysm of tears and was led back into the study by Catterson Smith, where for some time I went on sobbing. When it abated I set to work on all there was to be done.

[1] I have not been able to trace these.

And there was a great deal, for no executor could have been more conscientious. All Morris's friends were given little things which he had handled, even to a tube of Chinese white that he had squeezed and a brush whose end he had chewed. For himself, Cockerell had systematically been retrieving discarded proof sheets of every kind; these fruits of his 'pious regard for history in the making' and 'instinct for the preservation of the significant and the beautiful', together with presentation copies of Kelmscott books from Morris, and other Morrisiana, fetched a very large sum when they came to be sold at Sotheby's in December 1956.

Morris was dead. Millais had died two months before, and Burne-Jones was to die two years later. Ruskin was suffering, with increasing frequency, from fits of insanity. It was, for Cockerell, the *Götterdämmerung*.

But as one of Morris's executors and trustees, Cockerell's connection with the family was by no means at an end. There was also the winding up of the Press, a task that took him eighteen months to complete and which involved the supervision, with Emery Walker's help, of the production of several books which were already on the stocks. Among these was *A Note by William Morris on his Aims in Founding the Kelmscott Press*, to which Cockerell contributed 'a short description of the Press'. This little essay shows already the rare qualities of precision that were to characterize all that he later wrote.

Cockerell's vast correspondence with Mrs. Morris and May testifies to the extreme conscientiousness with which he carried out his duties as a trustee. Nothing was too much trouble to him. After Mrs. Morris's death in 1914 he helped May with the great Memorial Edition of her father's works, advised her over the endless problems connected with Jenny's illness, watched over her investments and safeguarded her interests.

He was present, of course, at Mrs. Morris's funeral at Kelmscott: '29th January. To my surprise Jenny came to the funeral, a pathetic figure, muttering sentences that had a meaning but were very difficult to follow. She took my arm, May took Walker's.'

On Jenny's death in 1935, he wrote in his diary:

When I was in and out of the house at Hammersmith and Kelmscott, she, being an invalid suffering from epilepsy from about her sixteenth year and seeing very few men, became much attached to me. She was of a very guileless, downright and affectionate disposition, the only person with whom her father was habitually demonstrative. For many years she has lived a secluded life with a nurse in the country and her mind has latterly been clouded with bromide. It is quite eight years since I saw her.[1]

Meanwhile, May Morris had become the personal property, as it were, of the extraordinary Miss Lobb—

a strange great masculine creature [wrote Cockerell] who always dressed in man's clothes—rather violent in some of her behaviour and perhaps a little mad—much resented by most of May's other friends, but no doubt useful to May and on the whole devoted to her. She came to Kelmscott from Cornwall as a land girl during the [First World] War.

When May Morris died in 1938, Cockerell wrote:

I first saw her, a beautiful girl of 23, in 1885. We soon afterwards became good friends. After her father's death, as his trustee I managed her finances and those of her mother and sister. We were on mildly affectionate terms. With many excellent qualities she combined a dissatisfied attitude on life which interfered greatly with her happiness and with that of others. Probably this was due to some taint in the blood which in her sister's case

[1] Brilliant brief obituaries of his friends were a regular feature of Cockerell's diaries between 1925 and 1940.

caused epilepsy. She inherited Kelmscott Manor after her mother's death.

A fortnight later, on re-reading her letters to him, he added, 'They recall much that I had forgotten and show a deep love of her stricken sister Jenny. If only she had married the right man what a different, more effective, and far happier woman she would have been! Full of so many fine qualities, she suffered from a gnawing discontent all her life, as it seems to me.'

He said, 'I saw her into her coffin. She always wanted something out of her reach: if she got the moon, she wanted the sun. She married a rather second-rate Socialist named Sparling. She was in love with Bernard Shaw before he was famous, and he with her. Shaw said that "a Mystical Betrothal was written in heaven," but that on earth his poverty prevented their marriage. Stanley Baldwin fell in love with her too, and so did Burne-Jones.' It is just possible that he was at one time rather in love with her himself.

Thus came to a close, after fifty years, Cockerell's close association with William Morris and his family. Though with the passing of the years the limitations of Ruskin became increasingly apparent to him, Cockerell's burning reverence for Morris — a man so different from himself in temperament and attainments — remained unquenched to the end of his life. He was the greatest hero of them all.

7

WILFRID SCAWEN BLUNT

'NOVEMBER 4th 1892. All day at Kelmscott House. Met Wilfrid Blunt there . . .' This was Cockerell's first meeting with Wilfrid Scawen Blunt (1840–1922)—poet, orientalist, traveller, anti-imperialist, amorist, sportsman and breeder of Arab horses—with whom he was to form a friendship that lasted until Blunt's death.[1]

Though they continued to meet from time to time at Kelmscott House, it was not until five years later that Cockerell came to know him. Blunt now invited him to stay at Newbuildings, one of his two country-houses in Sussex. Philip Webb, conscious that Cockerell was about to find himself in a wholly unfamiliar *milieu*,[2] urged him at least to learn the points of the horse before going: 'It would be bad,' he wrote, 'if the talk was of hocks, and you were thinking of Rhine wines.' Cockerell no doubt concealed the fact that he thought Arab horses 'queer little creatures,' for he made so favourable an impression that he was invited by Blunt to undertake research, at the British Museum and elsewhere, into 'the origins of the horse and especially of the Arab stock from which it is derived.'

---

[1] For Wilfrid Blunt, see: *My Diaries*, by Wilfrid Blunt, 2 vols., 1919, 1920; *Wilfrid Scawen Blunt*, by Edith Finch, Cape, 1938; and *Wilfrid Scawen Blunt, a Memoir by his grandson*, by The Earl of Lytton, Macdonald, 1961. In order to understand the tangled story of Wilfrid Blunt and his family, the reader must consult Miss Finch's and Lord Lytton's books.

[2] In a letter to Blunt's daughter, Cockerell described himself as a 'cockney sparrow'.

Blunt immediately won Cockerell's allegiance by his praise
of Morris ('certainly the greatest man I ever met'), by his
well-stored mind, his irresistible charm and his excellence as
a host. 'He introduced me into a new world,' said Cockerell —
'the world of the British aristocracy. This led to very agreeable week-ends at fine houses, and to my getting to know
many interesting and delightful people.' As for Blunt, he soon
saw that he had found something both unique and vitally
necessary to him: the perfect, the faithful and utterly reliable
factotum.[1]

Blunt was dangerously ill throughout much of the year
1898, and Cockerell paid constant visits to Newbuildings
where he made himself useful in a hundred ways; he was,
wrote Blunt, 'a treasure'. In a household where there was
often considerable tension, Cockerell contrived to win the
friendship and confidence, not only of his host, but also of
Lady Anne Blunt (Byron's grand-daughter) and of their only
surviving child, Judith.[2] In October, Judith became engaged
to Neville Lytton;[3] and soon after this Cockerell agreed to give
the half of his time to Blunt (who was to pay him £200 a year),
the remainder being subsequently devoted to Yates Thompson's manuscripts.[4] A subsequent offer to become Blunt's agent
at Newbuildings he declined.

Life at Newbuildings was never dull, though it was some
times difficult and even embarrassing. Cockerell grew accustomed, though he never became reconciled, to family tension.
He soon became used to being woken by what he called the
'braying' of the peacocks on the terrace, and to the strange

[1] In the sense of 'one who is called upon or employed to do all kinds of
work for another' (*Century Dictionary*), not 'servant managing his
master's affairs' (*Concise Oxford Dictionary*).

[2] She wrote, 'I was a seven-month, seventh and only surviving child of
eight'. Burke's *Landed Gentry* mentions only four children.

[3] Subsequently third Earl of Lytton, d. 1951. Judith, who obtained a
divorce in 1923, succeeded her mother as Baroness Wentworth in 1917.
There were three children of the marriage—Anthony (fourth and present
Earl of Lytton), Anne, and Winifrid (Lady Winifrid Tryon). Lady
Wentworth died in 1957 at the age of eighty-four.

[4] See p. 76.

ways of a house where dinner might be at any hour and host and hostess in Arab dress. He enjoyed the brilliant conversation of Blunt and his guests; and he loved the surrounding country, whose primroses and wild roses were hardly to be rivalled anywhere in England. He helped Blunt in many ways — he assisted with the publication of his poems and the preparation of his Diaries, interviewed publishers, corrected proofs, searched museum files and village registers, took speeches to be typed, booked boat and train reservations, entertained his guests, and by lending a sympathetic ear to the story of his many troubles became his close confidant. And if Blunt did not quite become for him a second Ruskin or Morris, he did at least come to rank, along with Webb, Lethaby and Walker, among his lesser deities, as one to be worshipped as well as loved.

One of Cockerell's useful services to Blunt was the restraining influence that he exerted, though not always successfully, when Blunt contemplated some particularly rash letter or futile piece of litigation. It must not, however, for a moment be imagined that he in any way influenced Blunt in his political opinions, with which he was often quite out of sympathy. He was always a loyal Briton whose esteem for Blunt was personal and literary, but who had a Socialist's dislike of inheritances, was keen on death duties (as he told the present Lord Lytton), thought horses rather absurd and hunting worse than absurd, and did not begin to understand the tradition of country landowners. It was merely that on many occasions he was able to prevent Blunt from rushing wildly into ill-considered print. On 30th November 1901 he wrote to Blunt:

> I still cannot help regretting that you are going to spend time and strength on attacking Rennell Rodd, who has now been safely removed from Egypt, and about whose action in the fox-hunting matter[1] few people outside the

[1] Some English officers, out fox-hunting, had broken into Blunt's property and had arrested the Arab servants who attempted to eject them. See W. S. Blunt, *My Diaries*, ii, pp. 9, 13, 15.

circle of your friends would care to know more than they can gather for themselves from the blue book.

And again, six years later:

My own attitude is that of a person averse both to quarrels and to the throwing away of money — and I don't think it is worth £20, much less £100 or more, together with a vast expenditure of energy, to make a newspaper manager, who is nobody in the eyes of the public, feel uncomfortable, or to prove to B—, what everyone else knows, that his reputation for honesty cannot be injured as it does not exist. However I will of course do all I can to help you in the matter.

In 1900, Blunt invited Cockerell to spend a few weeks as his guest at Sheykh Obeyd, his country house and small stud farm near Cairo. Cockerell left London early in February and passing by way of Paris to Marseilles, boarded the *Sénégal* for Alexandria. Within a week he had exchanged the fogs and chill of London for the palm groves and apricot orchards of Sheykh Obeyd, his graceless London clothes for the white draperies of Arabia, and his suburban train for the trotting donkey.

Life at Sheykh Obeyd was a perpetual joy to him. Visitors would turn up from England, and conversation at table was lively. 'We always had breakfast on the roof at six o'clock,' said Cockerell. 'The kites used to swoop down with a shriek and carry away half a pigeon from our plates. The birds at Sheykh Obeyd are wonderful;' among them, he observed with special pleasure, were several different species of his favourite bird, the kingfisher.

'Cockerell arrived last night from London very keen for sightseeing,' Blunt wrote in his diary. He was indeed! After a day's rest he began at once to explore the bazaars and the mosques, the libraries and the museums, of Cairo. With unflagging enthusiasm he visited every accessible pyramid. He made an expedition to Luxor and Thebes. And, straddling the little grey African donkey which always makes a man look slightly ridiculous,[1] he accompanied Blunt and Lady Anne when they rode majestically on their Arabs into the desert. With Blunt he visited the Grand Mufti and Lord Cromer, and camped for an uncomfortable but unforgettable night in the desert. But the principal attraction that had been arranged for him was a visit to Mount Sinai.

> I am to dress like a Bedouin [Cockerell wrote to Olive], and I believe carry a gun — so you will be able to imagine the picturesque figure that I shall look. There is not the least danger from beast or man — but this is the correct garb of travellers who do not wish to be a blot on the landscape.

On 7th March Blunt, Cockerell, Miss Lawrence (Blunt's devoted nurse) and two native servants sailed from Suez in the *Chibine*, a small steamship of the Khedivial Line.

The *Chibine* was a poor ship with an incompetent captain, an inadequate crew and a regrettable shortage of life-belts; and she was badly overloaded with several hundred pilgrims bound for Mecca and Medina. At three o'clock on the first morning at sea, the ship struck a coral reef off the Sherratib peninsula. Four anxious days and nights followed, during which it seemed increasingly probable that the heavy seas might break her in two. A life-boat which attempted to make a landing capsized, and one of its occupants was drowned. Two pilgrims died on board. But the passengers behaved admirably, and Blunt noted that there was 'none of the affectation of merriment one would see under like circumstances on board a P. and O.' The pilgrims prayed to Allah; Blunt prayed for the dead and to St. Winefride — 'a superstition which quiets the mind.' He also read Tolstoy's *Resurrection* ('a most depressing book') and the Gospels, while Cockerell made friends with everyone who

[1] Or it may have been the large white Egyptian donkey, which is more dignified.

could speak a word of English; 'It greatly eased the contemplation of death,' he wrote later, 'to know that my little affairs were in perfect order.'[1] As for Miss Lawrence, she calmly pursued her gentle and efficient ministrations. 'I cannot think we shall be drowned,' she said; 'God would not allow all these good people who call on him to perish.'

When the cabins became flooded, Blunt and his party camped under an awning on deck, where by making common cause with the pilgrims against the Captain, and by a lavish distribution of oranges, they soon overcame some initial unpopularity. The principal anxiety, other than the possibility of the ship breaking up, was now the shortage of drinking water. Two of the three remaining life-boats had been swept away by the high seas, but Suleyman, one of Blunt's servants, finally succeeded in effecting a landing in the only surviving one; his orders were to run the forty miles to Tor to summon help.

Suleyman's cable from Tor having confirmed the anxiety that had been growing at Suez, Lord Cromer immediately ordered the gunboat *Hebe* to the rescue. Blunt and his companions were taken on board, and the pilgrims were picked up by other vessels that appeared on the scene and carried to Jeddah. But Blunt had 'a superstition against continuing a journey in face of a strong warning,' and the *Hebe* returned to Suez.

At Blunt's instigation a naval court of inquiry was appointed, at which he and Cockerell gave evidence. The Court found against the Khedivial Company, and the witnesses were publicly thanked for 'public-spirited action' that eventually led to better conditions in the pilgrim ships.

The shipwreck was the only occasion in Cockerell's life when he was dramatically exposed to danger. Though he always maintained that he was incapable of all courage other than moral courage, he kept his head through four difficult days and nights. He also kept, for the rest of his long life

[1] To May Morris, July 2, 1915, when vainly attempting, for about the hundredth time, to get her to make her will.

and in spite of Jenny Morris's protestations, his newly-grown beard: 'I had not shaved since Thursday,' he wrote, 'and I resolved to dedicate my razors to the nymphs of Sherratib.'

In April, Cockerell sailed with Blunt and Miss Lawrence for Brindisi, where they took the train for Florence. Here they spent ten days, paying visits to friends and seeing the galleries (though Blunt proved 'a not very eager sight-seer'). At Poggio Gherardo, the villa where Boccaccio had set his *Decamerone*, Cockerell met Janet Ross, and her niece 'Miss Duff Gordon the beautiful' (Mrs. Waterfield) with whom he fell in love at sight. 'I was deeply attached to Lina Duff Gordon,' he said; 'but I was not in a position to marry.'

At Lucca, Blunt and Cockerell called upon Ouida, with whom Blunt, who shared her extreme political views, had been in correspondence. Once rich and famous, the hostess of wildly extravagant parties in London and Paris and Rome, the author of novels that had won hundreds of thousands of readers, Ouida now languished in penury in a fisherman's cottage on the Tuscan coast. They found her, wrote Cockerell, 'surrounded with dogs — an old lady of sixty or more, with rather a long, impressive face, large forehead, large ears, fine slate-blue eyes, and a bright complexion — a slight body arrayed in light grey satin — very gentle in her manner and wise in her speech which was mostly about European politics. We were both agreeably surprised to find her thus and not vulgar, masculine or loud.' 'She rose,' wrote Blunt, 'to meet us and reprove her dogs, still yelping at us in chorus. A mild reproof it was, nor did it save us from their caresses. The largest poodle placed himself upon my knees, and another took my hat in his mouth. "They do not often bite," she explained, "except beggars".' Blunt found it difficult to believe her capable of the malevolence shown in her novel, *Friendship*. 'With Cockerell she was immensely taken, and was curious to know who he could be, for I had not introduced him, and persisted in thinking him a personage in disguise.' Cockerell, though he never saw her again, corresponded with her regularly until her death eight years later, and some of her lively and vitriolic

letters to him, written in her enormous sprawling hand,[1] may
be read in *Friends of a Lifetime.*[2]

It had been agreed that Cockerell should work for Blunt for
two years, and this time had now elapsed. Blunt was anxious
for the arrangement to continue; but Cockerell felt obliged to
refuse. He said, 'It was a most agreeable existence, but I was
not doing anything that was really worth while. I said to
Blunt, "I'm frightfully happy looking at your woods and your
flowers, but I don't feel that it's right for me to spend all my
time in my own enjoyment".' But though he now found
full-time employment elsewhere, he was always ready to come
at a moment's notice to Newbuildings. The debt that Blunt
and entourage owed him in the years that followed, and which
will be told later, cannot be exaggerated. Nor was Blunt unaware of Cockerell's worth: in 1898 he addressed to him the
following acrostic sonnet:

TO A DISCIPLE OF WILLIAM MORRIS

Stand fast by the ideal. Hero be,
You in your youth, as he from youth to age.
Dare to be last, in all good modesty,
Nor fret thy soul for speedier heritage.
Even as he lived, live thou, laborious, sage,
Yielding thy flower, leaf, fruitage seasonably,

[1] In an average letter, Cockerell wrote eighteen words in the space
occupied by *one* of Ouida's!

[2] pp. 144–52. Extracts of these and other letters to Cockerell may be
found in Elizabeth Lee's *Ouida: a Memoir*, 1914. An unpublished letter
to Cockerell, written on learning of the death of Queen Victoria, is typical:
'She made herself ridiculous (if not worse) with her gillie J. Brown. She
loved Disraeli because he flattered her. She hated Gladstone because he
did not flatter her. She did nothing for India at any time; only vulgarised
it and herself by a tawdry and absurd title. For forty years she never ful-
filled her duties in public functions; nor passed a season in London as she
was bound to do. She was a professing Christian and she was at war
throughout her reign. She prated of peace, and incessantly shed blood.
She had the temper of the Tudors, but none of the charm of the Stuarts.
She was German—a German hausfrau—down to her fingertips. Worst of
all, when her dogs were ill, or old, she sent them away, and took new
ones! . . .'

Content if but some beauty in Time's page
Out of thy pains shall spring and live through thee.
Churl Fame shall grudge (ah, let it grudge!) the glory.
Knaves have earned that. Behold, the blossoming thorn
Emblazoneth the hedge where fools made foray,
Redeemeth their sad flouts and jibes forlorn.
Ere thou shalt know, the nightingale her story
Learning shall sing of thee and shame men's scorn.

8

WALKER & COCKERELL
PROCESS ENGRAVERS

IT was in the company of William Morris that Cockerell
had first looked seriously at medieval manuscripts. He
then began to reap the benefits of his study of natural
history, which had prepared his eye to detect minute differences of style and of detail. A distinguished authority on manuscripts was later to say of him, 'He had an unfailing eye. He
could always be relied upon to bring something new to any
manuscript he was shown.' In 1898, soon after he had agreed
to devote the half of his time to Blunt, Cockerell was invited by
Henry Yates Thompson to give the remainder to assisting him
with his collection of manuscripts.

Cockerell had first met Yates Thompson, a wealthy collector,
when the latter came to Kelmscott House after Morris's death
to look at the library. Yates Thompson had recently enriched
his own collection by the purchase *en bloc* of a section of Lord
Ashburnham's famous library. It was his policy to limit the
number of his manuscripts to one hundred, gradually discard-
ing what was inferior; Cockerell's first task was to help him to
decide which of the Ashburnham MSS. he should retain, and
which volumes in his own collection should make way for them.
Cockerell also helped Dr. M. R. James[1] and others in the compiling of the four-volume catalogue of Yates Thompson's
collection (1898–1912), and described the fourteenth-century

---

[1] Cockerell's predecessor as Director of the Fitzwilliam Museum,
Cambridge. Provost of King's College, Cambridge, 1905; Provost of Eton
College, 1918. Died 1936.

Book of Hours of Yolande of Flanders, and the thirteenth-century Psalter and Book of Hours of Isabelle of France, in two volumes published by the Chiswick Press in 1905.

The Yates Thompsons did Cockerell many kindnesses, and he was often their guest at Oving. They were the first to offer him financial help when he was badly let down by a fraudulent collector for whom he had been purchasing manuscripts on commission.[1] But Cockerell also knew that his knowledge and 'flair' had been of the greatest value to Yates Thompson who, though he had inherited a few manuscripts from his grand-father, had not himself entered the saleroom until 1895. Moreover there was something about Yates Thompson's manner of giving that he did not like. 'I think his generosity is overpraised,' he wrote to J. W. Robertson Scott, who had submitted an account of Yates Thompson to Cockerell for his opinion. 'His wife was as rich as himself, and he gave from his superfluity — not always without a little touch of vanity.'

It is hardly surprising that, as will be told later, this friend-ship ended in tears.

In the autumn of 1899 Cockerell took the decision to look for a single steady job in place of his work for Blunt and Yates Thompson. First he considered entering into partnership with his brother Douglas, now a successful bookbinder. Then John Murray invited him to prepare a new edition of his *Handbook to France*; but he did not want merely temporary employ-ment and therefore declined the offer. Next he consulted Quaritch about the prospects of bookselling, for which both Blunt and Mrs. Morris generously offered to advance the necessary capital. In October he told Noël Rooke, son of his friend T. M. Rooke, 'I am going to turn bookseller in the New Year — second-hand, of course, and "enormously dear".' But on 25th November he wrote in his diary, 'Came to the con-clusion that I would rather not turn bookseller, if I have not

---

[1] Blunt also offered to help him. The sum involved was about a thousand pounds, and Cockerell's courage in rejecting assistance in what must have been a most serious crisis for him is very remarkable.

already gone too far to retreat.' Finally he turned to Emery
Walker, the distinguished process-engraver, who invited him
to take the place of his partner, Boutall, when he left the
following summer. Walker offered to divide the profits
equally, but Cockerell—and it was very characteristic of him—
refused to accept more than a quarter share.

Emery Walker—'my greatest friend after Philip Webb's
death for forty years, although Lethaby was very near to him
in my affections'—was born in 1851 and was the son of a
coach-builder. When he was twenty-one he met by chance a
man of remarkable inventive gifts, Alfred Dawson, who was at
that time occupied in perfecting a form of process-engraving.
Walker joined him, and later founded, with William Boutall,
the well-known firm in Clifford's Inn, Walker & Boutall,
which subsequently became Walker & Cockerell and finally
Emery Walker, Limited.

In 1883 Walker had met Morris, his near neighbour in
Hammersmith. They soon became fast friends, and Morris
used to say that he did not think a day complete without a
sight of him.

> Among the subjects in which they were both deeply
> interested [wrote Cockerell], but of which the younger
> man possessed all the technical knowledge, was the art of
> typography, then at a low ebb. Out of their eager talks
> and some preliminary experiments arose the Kelmscott
> Press . . . Walker had declined to be a partner in this
> costly undertaking, as he had no capital to risk. Neverthe-
> less he was all the while a virtual partner, and no impor-
> tant step was taken without his advice and approval.[1]

Walker was one of the founders of the Arts and Crafts
Exhibition Society (1888) and a member of the Committee
of Anti-Scrape. He was also a keen supporter of the then
young and unpopular Socialist movement and Secretary to its

[1] *Friends of a Lifetime*, p. 220.

Hammersmith branch; he organized Sunday evening lectures in the little hall adjoining Morris's house, and among the lecturers were Morris himself, Ramsay MacDonald, Bernard Shaw, Lord Haldane, and other men subsequently famous.

It was at one of these lectures, in 1885, that Cockerell first met Walker. The following year Walker supped with the Cockerells in Bedford Park, and a warm friendship soon grew up between the eighteen-year-old boy and himself. They were in Italy together with the Art Workers' Guild. 'When I became Morris's secretary in 1892,' wrote Cockerell, 'Walker and I saw still more of each other and when Morris died in 1896 it was to each other that we turned for consolation.'

Cockerell has described what his work with Emery Walker entailed. 'I wrote most of the letters,' he said; 'and I had been taught by my severe discipline in youth to answer every letter by return of post. I interviewed people, and introduced new business—the Burlington Fine Arts Club, for instance. I never went to the works and I knew absolutely nothing about how to make a photogravure.'

No one could have been a more sympathetic partner than Walker, but Cockerell soon began to tire again of city life. After six months he wrote: 'This work has proved on the whole congenial and I do not think that Walker has regretted taking me—but I feel more and more the oppressiveness of London, and I wish I could get my living without having to spend all my days in it. When I think over possibilities my eyes turn wistfully towards Florence, where it seems to me that a very human sort of life might be led.' Florence was also, of course, the city of Miss Duff Gordon the beautiful.

Moreover, as he wrote in a letter to Lethaby, 'It was very nice being at Clifford's Inn, and seeing Walker every day and other good friends—but I found that at the end of the year I had done almost nothing except gossip and keep easy accounts, and that I simply must get back to my work.' He had entered into a three-years' agreement with Walker; after remaining a fourth year with him he decided that the firm was in so flourishing a state that he could leave it without damage to his partner. 'It remains to be seen,' he wrote, 'whether I can

earn enough money by describing MSS. and occasionally buying them on commission to keep me going—but I feel pretty
confident about it, as my needs and expenses are moderate.'

In 1900 Walker had joined forces with T. J. Cobden-Sanderson
in founding the Doves Press (1900–1911). With the Kelmscott
Press, and the Ashendene Press (1894–1933, founded by St.
John Hornby), this was to form what has been called the
Great Trinity of early Private Presses, and Cockerell was
fortunate in being closely associated with all three of them.

Cobden-Sanderson, son-in-law of Richard Cobden, the poli-
tician, whose name he had added to his own on his marriage,
had been called to the bar but had broken down under the
strain of a life that proved both hard and uncongenial. Friendship with the Morrises and Burne-Joneses had turned his
thoughts in the direction of 'arts and crafts' (a term of his own
coining); at the suggestion of Mrs. Morris he took up book-
binding, and in 1893 founded the Doves Bindery. His most
famous pupil was Cockerell's brother, Douglas. Cobden-
Sanderson was sixty when his next venture, the Doves Press,
opened its doors.

The type of the Kelmscott Press had been criticized for
being heavy-faced; Walker therefore, when designing the
Doves Press type, took as his principal model the light fount
used by Jensen in his Pliny of 1476. Walker also aimed to
show that beauty could be achieved without ornament; the
finest production of the Press, the famous five-volume Bible
(1902–5), can hold its own in any company and is far less
'dated' in appearance than its rival the Kelmscott Chaucer.

Doubtless Cockerell was in close touch with the Press, whose
principal productions he possessed in copies inscribed to him by
Walker or Cobden-Sanderson. But the most important assistance he gave to it was when he constituted himself arbiter in
the dispute which arose between the two partners over the
final destination of the Press's type—a quarrel which came to
a head in 1909.[1]

[1] See *Friends of a Lifetime*, pp. 223–43

This is no place to discuss the rights and wrongs of Walker's claim, after his resignation from the Press, to continue to make independent use of the type; what concerns us is the part Cockerell played in effecting at least a temporary reconciliation between the disputants. 'You must please forgive me for speaking thus frankly,' he wrote to Cobden-Sanderson. 'I honestly believe that I take an impartial view of the matter. . . .' His opinion was that, though Walker may have played only a small part in the actual conduct of the Press, Cobden-Sanderson ought to appreciate the benefit to him of his association with 'the most distinguished master of the craft of printing, and the man of the most consummate taste in such matters, living when the Press was started.' So Cockerell proposed a compromise to Cobden-Sanderson:

A modus vivendi has now occurred to me as possible — which is that you should have the sole use of the type for your lifetime, and that if you survive Walker it should remain your property, and that if he survives you it should become his. You are an older man than he is, but I should think your life is still as good as his[1]. . . . If Walker survives you there could be no better or more appropriate hands for the type to pass into — for whatever your mutual exasperation may make you think of each other, each of you perfectly well knows in his heart of hearts that the other is the best of men and a valiant fighter in the cause of artistic and political progress.

So please let your reasonable self get the better of your unreasonable self, and think this over calmly as a way out of the impasse. Say yes to it and I will do my utmost to bring Walker to the same way of thinking. . . .

Walker, after consulting his solicitor, agreed. 'You are certainly the best of friends a man in a difficulty ever had,' he told Cockerell. Cobden-Sanderson agreed also. He wrote to Cockerell:

[1] Cobden-Sanderson was eleven years older than Walker; each lived to the age of eighty-two.

I am sending for your acceptance *Hamlet*, the last book
printed at the old address and the first published (today)
at the new, and offer it in token of my gratitude for your
kindly and felicitous intervention, without which there
would surely have been strife to the bitter end . . .

Cobden-Sanderson carried on the Press alone until 1916;
then, in contravention of his agreement, he went — 'night
after night' — to Hammersmith Bridge and threw the punches,
matrices and type into the Thames.[1] Walker's solicitor sent to
the *Times Literary Supplement* two letters on the subject from
Cobden-Sanderson, in which the latter baldly admitted that he
had 'irresistibly returned to his original intention' to prevent
the Doves Press type from being used elsewhere.

The agreement had been 'shamefully broken.' Cockerell
wrote indignantly to Cobden-Sanderson, who replied that
while he could not explain he could yet uphold his act.
Cobden-Sanderson was nearly thirty years Cockerell's senior;
but Cockerell, in a final letter, bravely summed up the situation as he saw it, making no secret of whom he considered to
be, and who undoubtedly was, the villain of the piece:

10th September 1917   3, Shaftesbury Road,
                                          Cambridge.

Dear Mr. Cobden-Sanderson,

It has always seemed to me that you combined in one
person one of the most rational and one of the most
irrational of beings. Your letter, like the action to which
it refers, appears to have been dictated by the second of
these two. But I cannot hope now to persuade you of this,
any more than you can persuade me that it was the
rational and admired and level-headed C.S. who was
guilty of breaking a solemn compact in what most people
would regard as a very mean way — with the stars for his
only witness. They have been the only witnesses of many

[1] The first consignment fell onto an inaccessible ledge of one of the
piers; another narrowly missed a barge that was passing under the bridge.
'My idea was magnificent,' Cobden-Sanderson wrote; 'the act ridiculous.'
See Cobden-Sanderson's neurotic *Journals* (vol. II, pp. 296–307).

a stealthy misdeed which the doers have afterwards regretted — and I believe that you will come to see that your sacrifice to the River Thames was neither a worthy nor an honourable one, and will cry peccavi and desire to make reparation. So much faith have I in the rational C.S. to whom (and not to his irrational counterpart) I am still affectionately

Sydney C. Cockerell.

More than twenty years later, after Cockerell had published his full and factual account of the affair, Douglas Cockerell (who had been Cobden-Sanderson's pupil) wrote to his brother:

The unhappy Walker Cobden-Sanderson controversy you have dealt with so impartially that although your opinion is obvious most people's sympathy will be with Cobden-Sanderson, regardless of the legal rights or wrongs . . .

Cobden-Sanderson's egotism was almost pathological. He lacked the power of co-operation almost entirely and was almost insanely jealous of any reputation, even Morris's, that might rival his own. He lived in a world of his own creation, swayed by emotional storms of great intensity, and I doubt if he was capable of true friendship. He was, however, capable of very generous actions, and without doubt had a remarkable brain. . . .

The Ashendene Press, destined to be the longest-lived of the pioneer Private Presses in England, had been founded by St. John Hornby in 1894. Five years later he transferred it from his father's country-house, Ashendene, in Hertfordshire to Shelley House, Chelsea, where the great *Dante* (1909) and other splendid books were printed.

Cockerell first met Hornby, his exact contemporary, in March 1895 at Kelmscott House. Hornby, writing to Cockerell many years later, recalls the memorable visit:

How well I remember that afternoon. . . . It was shortly after I started the Ashendene Press, and I was brimful of enthusiasm for Morris and all his works. I remember my talk with him in his book-lined room, and going with you to see the sheets of the Chaucer on the Press, and having tea on the scrubbed oak table with the beautiful Mrs. Morris sitting at one end — all as if it were yesterday, and it is forty-five years ago. Incredible!

It was through Cockerell that Hornby came in due course to know Emery Walker. From Cockerell and Walker, wrote Hornby in 1935:

> I received inspiration and encouragement in my venture, and unstinted help and advice . . . Cockerell was an unsparing and outspoken but withal kindly critic, and Walker a mine from which to draw a wealth of counsel ever at the free disposal of any struggling beginner. I owe them both a great debt which can never be repaid; and I am only one of the many whom that kindly enthusiasm has fired and guided towards what is best in craftsmanship, and indeed in life itself.[1]

Cockerell's first, and greatest, contribution to the Press was made when, in 1900, he suggested to Hornby that he should have a type of his own. Like Morris, Hornby had always wished for this; but he had been under the impression that the cost would be far beyond his means, and had used types from the Oxford University Press. Cockerell hazarded that for about a hundred pounds this 'luxury' could be his. In a little over a year the Subiaco type, based on that of Sweynheym and Pannartz (Subiaco, 1465), had been prepared by Walker and Cockerell, and the cost was exactly a hundred pounds. Another proprietary type, the Ptolemy, was added in 1927. Among the volumes issued by the Ashendene Press was *The Song of Solomon* (1902); forty copies were printed, all on vellum, and these were exquisitely illuminated by Kate Kingsford, whom Cockerell was later to marry.

[1] Foreword to the *Ashendene Press Bibliography* by C. H. St. John Hornby.

9

ARCHITECTS AND SCRIBES

COCKERELL often said, and more than once wrote, that his closest friends were — and in this order, for he loved to list, grade and tabulate — Philip Webb, Emery Walker, W. R. Lethaby and St. John Hornby. (He was thinking, of course, of mortals; gods such as Ruskin and Morris, and demi-gods such as Blunt, came in a different category). It cannot be denied that this little group became something of a mutual admiration society, there being a strong tendency among its members to describe one another as 'flawless' or 'beaten gold'.

Of Webb, Cockerell wrote, 'We all feel a boundless love and veneration for him. He is the noblest man I ever knew, the most resolute, the most steadfast, the most guileless and the most saintlike in every way.'

Webb was three years senior to William Morris, with whom he had been closely associated since they had found themselves side by side in Street's office in Oxford in 1856. It was Morris who had given Webb his first architectural commission when the latter set up on his own — that for the historic Red House, for which Webb also designed most of the furniture and fittings; and when Morris & Co. was founded in 1861 it was Webb who, after Morris himself, was for long its most active member.

Cockerell first met Webb ('Signor Filippo' or 'Webbone' to his friends) in 1890 at the weekly Committee Meetings of Anti-Scrape. By August of that year Cockerell had begun to appreciate the worth of a man who was 'absolutely modest,

like all really great persons; learned withal, well read, witty,
generous, and unselfish—in fine a Christian gentleman,
although neither a Christian nor a gentleman, I suppose, in
the ordinary acceptation of these terms.' So began another
friendship in which the disparity of age—for the one was in
his sixtieth year and the other in his early twenties—created
no barrier.

There is a great deal of information about Webb to be found
scattered through Cockerell's correspondence, and in the
Victoria and Albert Museum are three 'Katied' volumes of
letters exchanged between the two men. Webb's contributions
are interesting but his style is laboured and there is a tendency
to facetiousness. To Cockerell, about to leave for Italy with the
Art Workers' Guild in 1894, he could write:

> Ye maun sleep before you gae awa to the Italian land,
> therefore this may catch you—if not napping—still, only
> half awake whilst sucking the mental lollipops of coming
> holiday. . . .

In a letter written to Cockerell shortly after Webb's death,
Lethaby discusses Webb's taste in reading and gives his impression of the range of his achievement. In a postscript he
adds:

> I have found in myself sometimes the thought that Webb
> was a funny old buffer who *somehow* had a way of doing
> things in building. But his power of getting *at greatness*
> was his central self. This is what he had for books and his
> power of reading them must have been intensive to get
> that range of tags. It was he I'm sure [who] got settled the
> *early* Morris method in stained glass, and later it got
> heavy and overdone. He too must have been the first
> *reformed* drawer of Heraldry. His cast iron was wonder-
> ful, his *lettering* beautiful. I have never known anybody
> with the same intimate love of the books he did know.
> We all treat them disdainfully as water laid on to shelves;
> to him they were persons.

Cockerell replied that he rather doubted whether Webb was as widely read as Lethaby imagined: 'I should say his range was small compared with that of Burne-Jones. . . .' But

Of course we agree about nearly everything – only it wouldn't do not to be perverse! I have been thinking of those men in terms of Cathedrals – and Morris was Lincoln and Webb Durham and Burne-Jones Wells and [Madox] Brown Peterborough. Rossetti will not fit into this scheme. He was of the passionate south. Is Monreale the nearest we can get to him? Burne-Jones was not of the south, much as he tried to be. They were all mighty men in their different ways.

But though there might be dispute as to whether or not Webb should be considered a widely-read man, and though Webb's buildings may today seem ponderous and dated, there was no doubt as to the importance of his position in the development of English domestic architecture. Mackail, in his *Life of William Morris*, wrote, 'It is hardly too much to say that the work of these three men [Webb, Morris and Norman Shaw] has, in the course of a generation, revolutionized domestic architecture throughout England.'

As the century drew to its close, Webb, now nearing seventy, felt that the time had come for him to retire and settle in the country. It was Cockerell, energetic as always where the welfare of a friend was concerned, who found what he believed to be the perfect cottage. In May 1900 he wrote to Webb from Newbuildings:

Dear Signor Filippo,
Near Three Bridges there is a hill, and on that hill there is a cottage, and in front of that cottage there is a Saxon Church and a forest where a dragon was killed. . . . The cottage is an oldfashioned thing without a bathroom or even a gasometer, but it could be made very comfortable, and the position is reputed the healthiest in the district. Mr. Blunt has kept it for himself of late, but he almost never goes there, and would be proud if you would

occupy it and roam over his portion of Worth Forest. . . .
The cottage is called Caxtons, a name of good omen for a
friend of the Kelmscott Press.

Webb was grateful, but hesitant. ' "Three Bridges",' he
wrote. 'As if *one* was not enough for my old hinder end. Well
as — say — a *pisaller*, Wilfrid Blunt's magnanimity should not
at once be "blocked". . . . Of course it would be considerably
bigger than I should want. . . .' So he went to see Blunt,
whom he found preoccupied and silent:

> He was not disagreeable, but I had to make all the run-
> ning; from which I more than gathered he would want
> the occasional use of the room downstairs on the left of
> the 'keeping-room', and the bedroom over it to keep his
> things in at other times. . . . I believe he *would* like me
> to inhabit the place, but hardly that he would be able to
> understand my position as a constant resident, with no
> other housing for the 365 days in the year. I have had too
> much to do with born aristocrats of a really kindly turn
> of mind — even generous — not to know that they cannot
> understand the restricted ways of a poor lower-middle-
> class man. . . . And that is why, probably, I had better
> try for another kind of landlord and the freedom of action
> so necessary for my simple life.

In fact, Cockerell had been playing the dangerous role of
matchmaker, where neither party was over-eager. But finally
the matter was agreed, and neither lived to regret the arrangement. Though Webb talked from time to time of moving to
something smaller and cheaper elsewhere, in fact he remained
at Caxtons until his death in 1915.

Webb lived the simple life, chopping wood and drawing
water when he was well enough, walking in the woods, watch-
ing the first daffodils open, reading, meditating. Cockerell
visited him constantly — usually once and sometimes twice a
month. He sent him books, and *daily* postcards when he was
abroad. He brought his friends — Walter Cobbett with his

violin, and Lethaby 'in fine plumage' — to cheer him. 'Dear P.W.' and 'the dear old man' occur frequently in his diary, with mention of happy evenings passed in discussion of French architecture and manuscripts, or in reliving the old days with Morris.

When war broke out Webb was eighty-three and his health beginning to fail. On 17th April 1915 Cockerell wrote in his diary:

> Very bright morning. Went to Three Bridges by the 9.9. Reached Caxtons an hour later and found dear Webb still alive but unconscious. Mrs. Dickinson [his housekeeper] and a very kind and helpful male nurse were with him. He had been in much the same state since 5 a.m. yesterday. . . . At 6.30 P.W. died peacefully, his breathing becoming weaker till it ceased. It was the first time I had been actually present at a death (when Morris died I was in the next room) and I found it, at any rate in the case of an old man, a natural event attended with no horror. . .

In July, in company with Emery Walker and St. John Hornby, Cockerell scattered Webb's ashes 'within the bounds of the ancient camp on the wind-swept wholesome down above the White Horse' at Uffington. There was little cause to grieve: 'He had lived manfully and finished his work,' wrote Cockerell. 'Morris said he was the best man he ever knew.'

'W. R. Lethaby was an architect and student of antiquity who occupied a place apart by reason of his remarkable insight, his varied learning, and his unique personality.' So wrote Cockerell in a tribute in the *Sunday Times* on 19th July 1931. But in his diary he spoke more informally:

> *William Richard Lethaby*. Next after Emery Walker my dearest friend, whose acquaintance I made 4th May 1890. . . . I suppose it was not until about 1893 when I was for nine months Lethaby's neighbour in Gray's Inn

that we became fast friends. . . . He had certain limitations and some prejudices but he seemed to me to be as
nearly as possible a flawless man — of the rarest kind with
amazing rectitude of conduct and vision. It was a great
honour to be admitted to his affection.

The son of a frame-maker at Barnstaple, and born there in
1857, Lethaby had been from the first a steadfast disciple of
Ruskin. As a young man he worked with Norman Shaw, who
in due course entrusted him with important tasks until he was
ripe to set up on his own. Lethaby helped to found the Art
Workers' Guild, and as a Committee member of Anti-Scrape
was soon on intimate terms with Webb and Morris. 'He won
the older man's [Morris's] respect,' wrote Cockerell, 'and they
talked on equal terms,' and with Webb, his neighbour for a
time in Gray's Inn, he 'used to thrash out artistic and political
problems in discussions that lasted far into the night.' Though
Lethaby was for many years a practising architect, he is
chiefly remembered as a teacher, author and critic. As surveyor
to the Dean and Chapter of Westminster Abbey he set a
standard in the care of ancient monuments which had a wide
influence.

After the death of a close friend it was Cockerell's habit to
reclaim the letters he had written to him. Five bulky packets
of letters that passed between Lethaby and Cockerell testify to
a deep friendship of forty years standing, and it is interesting
to contrast the dapper calligraphy of Cockerell with Lethaby's
straggling and barely legible scrawl. The letters deal largely
with architectural and other technical matters: the dating of a
stained-glass window at Lincoln, the interpretation of a
damaged inscription, the extent of Moorish and Spanish
elements in Romanesque architecture, and so on. There is also
much about dear old Philip Webb, the state of his health, and
the memoir of him that Cockerell — always a past master in
the art of getting other people to give of their best — was constantly urging Lethaby to finish.[1] Two months before his

[1] It appeared first in 1925 in the *Builder* and was posthumously
published in book form.

death Lethaby wrote a last pathetic note to Cockerell, who replied:

> Dearest Lethaby,
>
> It gave me a great thrill to see your handwriting and to read your dear and loving words. I think of you often and often. It is more than forty years since our first meeting. I have looked up to you ever since. Your friendship has been a precious blessing that has helped me through life. I can never be sufficiently grateful for it. . . . No one knows better than I of what beaten gold (the words used by Ruskin of Morris) you are made. I grieve to think of you so ill. . . .

In a final summing-up of his friend, Cockerell wrote:

> Lethaby was a man of middle stature and spare build, moustached, of a delicate pallor, with a gentle and endearing manner. On many topics he held strong convictions, a little coloured by a strict evangelical training never quite outgrown. Happily he was blessed with that most essential corrective, a keen sense of humour. All his life he behaved with an unswerving integrity of thought, speech, and conduct.
>
> To sum up his qualities at short notice were, indeed, an impossible task. A certain childlike simplicity must be mentioned first. Then his nobility of outlook, his self-effacement, his learning, his wit, his penetrating vision, his industry in research, his fairness in discussion, his sympathetic encouragement of young students, his general loving-kindness, and his scorn for all that is shoddy, pretentious and base.

After the death of his wife Lethaby had been devotedly tended by his sister-in-law, Grace Crosby, who worshipped him. Many of her letters to Cockerell express her gratitude to him for his devotion to Lethaby and his constant kindness to herself. Some years after Lethaby's death she wrote, 'Your faithfulness, and thoughtfulness, and kindness know no bounds. It is no wonder that Richard loved you so dearly.'

In the autumn of 1898 Lethaby had introduced to Cockerell a young man named Edward Johnston, whose health had obliged him to abandon a career in medicine. This meeting was to have a considerable influence on the development of the art of lettering of every kind in England, and indeed throughout the world.

'Calligraphy,' said Cockerell, 'is certainly a part of myself. Calligraphers, like cricketers, are born, not made. I was interested in handwriting almost from the cradle.' His father had a fine scholarly hand, and at an early age Theo and Sydney were already writing neat, incredibly small and very similar scripts which in time became finely personal. 'I was critical of the handwriting of the masters at my private school,' Cockerell said. 'One wrote beautifully, and I treasured his scraps. At the City of London School, where I went for a very short time before winning a scholarship at St. Paul's, there was a fellow who taught a perfectly beastly handwriting to a class of forty. At St. Paul's it was better, and the classes were smaller.'

Though William Morris's interest in calligraphy was chiefly directed to formal script, Morris much admired Cockerell's cursive hand, which had by then settled down to the beautifully flowing, microscopic calligraphy whose quality never varied. Cockerell, for his part, produced but one attempt at formal writing—an Omar Khayyam of which, at a later date, he was not very proud.

It was two years after Morris's death that Lethaby took Johnston to see Cockerell. Johnston wanted to 'take up art;' Lethaby suggested a craft. Cockerell led Johnston to the illuminated manuscripts in the British Museum, showed him his own Morrisiana at Richmond, and thus kindled the flame that was to make Johnston the pioneer of the revival of formal writing.[1] 'You drew my attention to specific MSS.,' wrote

[1] See *Edward Johnston*, by Priscilla Johnston, Faber, 1959.

Johnston to Cockerell later, 'particularly the tenth century Winchester Psalter, and so the Ideal came—to make *living letters* with a formal pen.'

But Johnston's first essays in calligraphy were far from impressive. Lethaby was kind and encouraging in his criticism; Cockerell was severe. When, many years later, Cockerell was again shown some of Johnston's early attempts, he said, 'If a young man came to *me* with work like that, I should tell him there was no hope for him.' Events were to prove that Lethaby was right. He appointed Johnston to teach formal writing at the Central School of Arts and Crafts, of which he was the first Principal. Incidentally, Kate Kingsford, the future Lady Cockerell, was among Johnston's pupils.

While Johnston, ever dilatory, was slowly compiling his now famous *Writing & Illuminating, & Lettering* (1906) he frequently consulted Cockerell, who on its publication declared it to be 'the best handbook ever written on any subject.' Later he wisely modified this 'rash claim that could only be made after a perusal of all other handbooks on all other subjects,' to 'a masterpiece, immensely instructive and stimulating.' 'Johnston has had numberless pupils, but not one of them has attained to his degree of accomplishment. Nor do I think that it is possible to rival him by technical skill without an accompanying range of imagination equivalent to his.' And to Katie he wrote at the time of Johnston's death in 1944, 'It is wonderful to consider the enormous influence that weak pale consumptive had on lettering in this country and abroad. I remember a young man who had travelled from California just to set eyes on him. I liked and admired him greatly.'

From the turn of the century onwards, Cockerell was the *éminence grise* of calligraphy and the art of lettering in England. Robert Bridges (whose *Tracts on English Handwriting* appeared in 1926 and 1927), Graily Hewitt, Eric Gill and Mr. Alfred Fairbank were among the many who consulted him. 'I believe I was responsible for getting Gill his first commission,' Cockerell said, 'but I cannot be certain about this.' Graily Hewitt spoke gratefully of Cockerell's encouragement—'the first I ever had . . . I never forget it;'

but ultimately the two men drifted apart. On being asked about this, Cockerell said, 'We quarrelled about immortality;' but a letter to him from Hewitt (23rd December 1935) suggests that Hewitt had no idea that his religious views had caused the breach. He thought he must have failed, in Cockerell's eyes, as an artist:

23 Dec. 1935

Dear Cockerell,

. . . Quite humbly I would like to know where we are, perhaps I should say where I am. For you are a great man. But you are not the man I used to know; who meant more to me in relation to what I tried and try to do than any-one else. . . . For it is some (almost many) years now since I felt I had lost your countenance — ever since I sent you my essay in the Treyford Type. Since then I have published my book on Lettering, and there have been 2 or 3 Arts and Crafts shows and also my show at Bumpus'. As to none of which you allowed me a word of criticism or friendliness . . . I have felt I am one of those you spoke well of and encouraged once, who have failed to come off, one of the geese who did not turn out swans — and so needed to be dropped gently. Well that is of course reasonable enough. Only why with never a word these years? if only of warning that you thought my attempts mistaken, and 'illumination' out of place?

You have puzzled me indeed. . . .

It is possible that Cockerell also resented Hewitt's criticism of Edward Johnston, who in Cockerell's eyes could now do no wrong. Hewitt wrote:

In Johnston I have lost confidence. Despite all he did for us at the beginning of this century he has undone too much by forsaking his standard of the classical Roman Alphabet — giving the world, without safeguard or explanation, his block letters which disfigure our modern life. His prestige has obscured their commercialism and vulgarity. And latterly he has given us the calligraphic firework of the panel, which is the modern equivalent of the seventeenth century writing master's tours de force; beautiful no doubt, but not the true business of the scribe —which to me has remained, as I learnt it at first, that of the *scriptor librarius*, not the conjurer.

It was always rather rash to suggest to Cockerell that his idols might have feet of clay.

10

SOME FRIENDS

AMONG the many famous people whom Cockerell came to know around the turn of the century were Kipling, James Barrie, Francis Thompson, Samuel Butler, Swinburne and Charles Doughty. But though these and other illustrious names occur fairly frequently in the earlier volumes of his diaries, only too often the entries are brief and unilluminating.

It was while Cockerell was spending a week-end, in October 1897, with the Burne-Joneses at Rottingdean that he first met Kipling and Barrie, who came for the day bringing with them 'Crom' Price, Kipling's old headmaster at Westward Ho! (Kipling was, of course, a nephew of Lady Burne-Jones.) The occasion was memorable. Kipling read a school story, *In Ambush*, turning from time to time to Price with a 'Do you remember that, Sir?' Price said to Cockerell, 'Kipling remembers many things that I have forgotten, and I remember some things that he would like me to forget.' 'Yes,' said Kipling in an aside to Cockerell; 'and the dear fellow never gave me away.' There was much 'boisterous laughter' till the evening drew to a close with Lady Burne-Jones's reading of Keats's *Ode to Autumn*. The only blemish to the day had been the complete silence of Barrie — 'a little anaemic black man with a large head and forehead.'

'I believe that Barrie was already on bad terms with his wife,' said Cockerell. 'After he had left, Burne-Jones said, "I don't think it's good manners for a man to come to my table and not contribute to the conversation." But Barrie was like that. One evening at Cambridge he found himself next to

96

Housman at dinner in Trinity, and neither uttered a word throughout the meal. Next day Barrie wrote to Housman to apologize, saying that he sometimes had these fits of silence. "So do I," Housman replied; "and now you have made it worse by spelling my name wrong."'

Cockerell described Kipling (in 1897) as 'a man of rather less than average height, but broad and manly, in knicker-bockers and a brown coat and soft brown hat, very bushy black eyebrows and pronounced chin, unassuming and high-spirited.' At the time of Kipling's death (in 1936) he wrote:

> I had seen him at Burne-Jones's funeral, and ten years later when he received a doctorate at Cambridge, as well as at the funerals of Phil. Burne-Jones and Thomas Hardy [at which he was one of the pall-bearers] and now and again at the R.A. and elsewhere, but had not again met him intimately until I spent a night at Batemans on 15 Aug 1933, and a good part of the day there less than 4 months ago, 27 Sept 1935. On these two occasions he received me with great cordiality as though I had been an old friend, no doubt because we had so many friends and memories in common. On both occasions he read to me some recent prose (on the last occasion part of a new Stalky story) and recited very witty unpublished verses. He was a man of great charm, intensely genuine and lovable, full of eager interest in very many things. Though I have seen so little of him I feel his loss acutely.'

Cockerell adds in a postscript that he had forgotten a meeting in 1932 when he had 'a good talk with him about Lady Burne-Jones, a tribute to whom I implored him to write. He admitted that he owed to her more than he could say as he was in her keeping when he was a child and his parents were in India.' But Kipling could not bring himself to do it. He wrote to Cockerell (6th October 1932):

> This here biography and 'reminiscer' business that is going on nowadays is a bit too near the Higher Cannibalism to

please me. Ancestor-worship is all right, but serving them up filleted, or spiced, or 'high' (which last is very popular) has put me off.

Of Barrie, Cockerell wrote, 'At the time of Hardy's death we saw a lot of each other. I stayed at his flat in Adelphi Terrace on several occasions. . . . We thus became intimate and I sometimes dropped in to tea and a great talk . . . Barrie could be embarrassingly silent, but when at his ease he was the best of whimsical company.'

Cockerell had continued to see a good deal of the Burne-Joneses after Morris's death, which they felt very deeply. One extract from his diary may be quoted:

30th December 1896. Went to lunch at the Grange. Saw E B-J painting one of the Perseus series—P. and the 3 maidens. He said he dreamed last night that he was sitting astride of a roof with W.M. thatching it with beautiful green reed thatch. A very nice talk with Lady B-J about W.M. after lunch.

Cockerell was much attached to Lady Burne-Jones (the 'Bartess'), who used to call him 'the Friend of Man'. He spent a week in her company in France in 1897, and was among the first to visit her after her husband's death the following year. 'She had that air of determined resignation that she wore after Morris's death. She was very thankful, she said, to have known these two men as she had known them—and "we must pay for the wine that we have drunk."' One day, at the time when she was working on her biography of her late husband, she read to Cockerell the first four chapters of her manuscript.[1] Lady Burne-Jones lived on until 1920; the last letter that she wrote was to Cockerell.

Of Sir Philip Burne-Jones, their son, Cockerell said, 'He was a good artist; but he was a gadabout and didn't work. If he got an invitation from a lady of title in the country, he

[1] For the rather effusive, but none the less genuine, letter of gratitude that he wrote to her afterwards, see *Friends of a Lifetime*, pp. 118–19.

went off at once. Lady Burne-Jones told me that her husband had had a very unhappy childhood, and wanted Phil to have a happy one.'

Cockerell first met Francis Thompson at Newbuildings in 1898 —'an undistinguished weak little man with nothing about him to show that he is so fine a poet.' Five years later he saw him in Chancery Lane 'attired in dirty rags, and looking the picture of ruin—a very sad sight.' In October 1907, only a month before Thompson's death, he found him 'very thin, but looking far more like a poet than ever before when I have seen him—like some Spanish ascetic with dark hair and a little thin grey beard.' 'He was the greatest enigma I ever encountered,' Cockerell said. 'He seemed so insignificant and feeble; I could never imagine how he could have written *The Hound of Heaven*. He was interested in cricket—but he couldn't have hit a ball across this room.' Many years later, Cockerell asked Wilfrid and Viola Meynell whether either of them had ever heard Thompson say anything worth while. 'They both declared that they hadn't, but that Patmore had found his conversation interesting! Nor had they seen any letters of his worth reading—or at any rate worth printing.'

But Thompson's poetry moved Cockerell deeply, and he was entirely in agreement with his friend Lady Helena Carnegie, who wrote to him:

> When I read the introduction to the poems I was struck with surprise at the odd little incident mentioned of Burne-Jones's having dressed and undressed twice in absence of mind at first reading *The Hound of Heaven*: for I, after seeing *In No Strange Land* quoted a week ago in the *Times* review, had been so haunted and absorbed that I found myself brushing my hair with my tooth-brush which I was dipping into a spoonful of the tonic I ought to have been swallowing!

Samuel Butler was a close neighbour of Cockerell and Emery Walker's in Clifford's Inn. One day in 1901 he called in to see them, in much trouble because Longmans had declined to publish *Erewhon Revisited* on the grounds that it might give offence to their High Anglican connection. Butler took Cockerell to lunch with Bernard Shaw, who had invited Grant Richards to meet them. Richards eagerly undertook to publish the book, which appeared that autumn.

'Butler was excellent company,' said Cockerell, 'and he had a keen sense of humour. He complained bitterly of his Papa — but when Walker and I looked into it we found that Papa was generally right. Butler told me during his last illness that it was hard luck that the sins of his youth had pursued him. He had to take mercury for syphilis. My own theory is that it was because of his syphilis that he threw everything up and went out to New Zealand — just as he was beginning to make a name for himself.' Here Cockerell's memory is certainly at fault, for Butler at the time had published nothing.

Cockerell's last visit to Butler was in May 1902, a month before Butler's death. He wrote: 'Looked in on S.B. who seemed to me worse and very weak. He quoted fervently from the 145th Psalm, "The Lord is gracious and full of compassion; and his tender mercies are over *all* his works."'

In his diary for 19th October 1896 Cockerell wrote: 'In the evening to dinner with Theodore Watts and Swinburne. S. a little man, very deaf, and very polite. He spoke enthusiastically about [Morris's] *The Well at the World's End*. After dinner I saw no more of him, but sat talking with Watts about Morris and Rossetti, and the proposed publication of T.W.'s poems at the K[elmscott P[ress].' This was the first of four or five visits that he paid to the poet at the Pines, Putney.

There is a fuller account of another visit, in 1904:

> September 29th. Went with Walker to dine with Watts-Dunton and Swinburne at the Pines . . . Watts-Dunton talked well at dinner, but Swinburne being very deaf (he looked very well and younger than I remembered, his beard still with a tinge of red in it) said nothing until we

were half way through when he suddenly burst out with a eulogy of *The Two Noble Kinsmen* and expressed his wonder that it had never been acted. He also spoke of his reading *Arden of Feversham* at Oxford and coming to the conclusion that if not by Shakespeare it was by someone capable of even greater things than he was capable of at the time when it was written. After dinner we went up to his room and he delighted us by reading out two fine scenes from his new unfinished play on the Borgias. He read in a loud and dramatic manner, with much nervous movement, enforcing every sentence.

Cockerell had brought with him from his own collection a Bembo and a Catullus manuscript, and a book bearing Ben Jonson's signature. These greatly interested Swinburne: 'He said that Catullus was the first Latin literature to please him at Eton, Virgil and Horace having obviously been written with the sole object of tormenting schoolboys, and that Bembo's Latin verse and Italian prose were surprisingly fine. We finished the evening downstairs, talking with Watts-Dunton about Morris, Rossetti, and others.' Cockerell subsequently gave Swinburne the book signed by Ben Jonson, and received a manuscript of Swinburne's in return.

A further visit to the Pines took place on 16th January 1906:

In the evening went to see Swinburne and Watts-Dunton at Putney. Talked about Lord Lovelace's *Astarte*, which they have not yet read. Swinburne very much down on Lady Byron for confiding in Mrs. Beecher Stowe. W-D very glad to have the matter settled. He told me afterwards that Swinburne could not take much interest in Byron, his whole admiration being given to Coleridge, Shelley and Keats. He could not stand B's slipshod writing. But W-D thinks very highly of some of B's poems, including *Manfred*. After S. had retired W-D talked about his recent marriage and the happiness it had brought him, and told me all the details. He then discussed sympathetically the ambitions of Germany, and her necessity for expansion. Watts-Dunton may be and no doubt is a second-rate poet and novelist, but he is a most thoughtful man and an excellent observer and talker.

Swinburne died three years later, and Cockerell did not see him again.

Charles Doughty's *Travels in Arabia Deserta*, published in 1888, was a favourite book of Morris and Burne-Jones, as well as of Wilfrid Blunt who had directed their attention to it and who used to say that he would rather have written it than any prose work of the nineteenth century. Cockerell caught their enthusiasm and introduced the book, then little known, to Edward Garnett. This led to the publication by Duckworth in 1908 of the abridged version, *Wanderings in Arabia*, which made its author's name generally familiar.

It was not until a year after this that Cockerell actually met Doughty. 'I am very glad to have seen what manner of man he is,' he wrote to Blunt, ' — very dour, seldom smiling, sense of humour much in abeyance as it seemed to me. This may account for his poetry, if not for his prose.' The diary adds: 'a tall upright man with thick red beard and thick greyish hair, 66 years old . . . very serious and self-contained, with a voice laden with sorrow — but a splendid head and fine manners. . . . He lives the life of a hermit at Eastbourne and knows scarcely anyone.' Their mutual friend Dr. Bonney of Cambridge, who had examined Doughty for his tripos, recalled to Cockerell his regret that he had been unable to give Doughty a first because 'he had such a dishevelled mind. If you asked him for a collar he upset his whole wardrobe at your feet.'

Cockerell cultivated the acquaintance until, after the First World War, he could count himself among Doughty's principal friends, his older friends being by that time mostly dead. In 1921 it became known that Doughty was in very straitened circumstances. T. E. Lawrence and Cockerell acted at once. The manuscript of Doughty's *The Dawn in Britain* was bought from its author for £400 by a group of friends and admirers and presented to the British Museum, and Caius and Downing College[1] jointly purchased, for the same sum, the notebooks of his Arabian journeys for the Fitzwilliam. The following year, largely through Cockerell's energetic canvassing, Doughty was awarded a Civil List pension of £150. But barely had the pension been granted than he found himself possessed, quite unexpectedly, of an annuity of £2000; he therefore renounced the pension.

When Doughty died in 1926, Cockerell wrote again in his diary of Doughty's 'expression of great nobility, like that of a prophet of old. His courtesy, humility and gentleness were also of another age. He avoided company and publicity of any kind. . . .' Mrs. Doughty lived on until 1950, always deeply grateful for the many kindnesses that continued to be showered upon her by her husband's old friend.

Needless to say, Cockerell never ceased to battle on behalf of Doughty's literary reputation. When Shaw wrote disparagingly of Doughty,[2] Cockerell rushed to his hero's defence and drew from Shaw a recantation which he gratefully acknowledged; indeed, Shaw was now ready to admire Doughty's verse, which Cockerell had never quite succeeded in enjoying:

My dear Shaw,   7th December 1944
    I cannot tell you how pleased I am with what you have now written about Doughty. I am myself little more than a pigmy — and pigmies dote on giants and heroes. Morris is one of my giants, and Doughty is another, and you are a third — and it positively hurts me when one of them is unjustly decried, especially by one of the others. You used hard words about your fellow hero ('a bigoted Evangelical lout,' 'a crude savage,' 'brainless' etc.) which were perhaps not intended to do more than make me sit up, but which actually made me miserable. Now you take most of

[1] Doughty was first at Caius, then at Downing. He told Cockerell, 'They bothered me so much at Caius with lectures and chapels and things, and I knew that at Downing I could do just as I liked.'
[2] *The Best of Friends*, pp. 140–42.

it back and see great qualities in Doughty's verse, which others have proclaimed but to which I have been rather blind. I have no prejudice against blank verse. I am distressed when the early Shakespeare makes his characters drop into rhyme, and among the relics of my schooldays that I cherish most are certain passages of the *Iliad* and *Odyssey* which I learnt by heart in the original Greek. I quite frequently repeat them to myself in bed, along with English verse that I have not remembered so well. But to my mind Doughty's verse is too aggressively antiquarian. Manifestly I am prejudiced and mistaken, since you give it and him such tremendous praise. I feel exultant, as Doughty's giant stature is actually enhanced. Your own gianthood was a little diminished in my eyes by what I thought a false judgment. Now it is re-established, and I look forward to finding a eulogy of Doughty, or at any rate an absence of condemnation, in your new preface to *Back to Methuselah*. . . .

Yours always,
Sydney Cockerell

Can you find me a piece of your shorthand to go with my treasured Shaviana?

There were other famous friends also, whose names crowd the pages of his diaries: Cunninghame Graham, H. W. Nevinson, Roger Fry, 'Goldie' Lowes Dickinson, Ricketts and Shannon, W. B. Yeats, Charles Holmes, Ezra Pound, Chesterton, Galsworthy, William Rothenstein, W. H. Hudson, Desmond MacCarthy, Sargent and Sir Shane Leslie. There was a young man named Isaacs whom many years later he met again as Lord Reading.

There was Dr. M. R. James, whom he was to succeed as Director of the Fitzwilliam — 'one of the finest, kindest, nicest, as well as the most learned of men,' and a close friend for forty years. There were Henry James ('slow and weighty in speech, with an interesting head, shiny-topped and rather sallow') and Arnold Bennett ('his appearance gives no inkling of his power as a writer').

There were his aristocratic women friends, met when he stayed with Wilfrid Blunt at Newbuildings: the 'bewitching' Lady Margaret Sackville, the 'heroic' Lady Constance Lytton, Lady Helena Carnegie ('she would have married me, I think') and a dozen others.

Some of these he saw on a few occasions only; others, such as 'dear old Arthur Hughes,' Wilfrid and Alice Meynell, W. M. Rossetti and other members of his family, and Hilaire Belloc ('excellent company; he used often to come to lunch on Sundays with Mr. Blunt'), are mentioned often and affectionately but with little precision. Cockerell's lifelong friendships with Bernard Shaw and Dame Laurentia will be discussed in a later chapter. There was also his never-to-be-forgotten visit to Tolstoy:

In the summer of 1903, Mr. and Mrs. Robert Hunter, two American friends of Cockerell's who were on their way to visit Tolstoy at Yasnaya Polyana, suggested that he should accompany them; it was an opportunity not to be missed. Travelling by way of Uppsala, St. Petersburg and Moscow they reached Tula on 11th July, only to learn that Tolstoy was unwell. It was a rude blow; but the following day he pronounced himself sufficiently recovered to receive his guests.

In a letter to Blunt, written from Tula on 13th July, Cockerell describes the visit:[1]

I promised to write to you when I had seen Tolstoy. He lives in a country house about 8 miles from this town, and we drove out yesterday afternoon and stayed till about 10 p.m. He is the finest old fellow that could be, seventy-five years old but strong in body and mind, very gentle in manner, reminding me of Ruskin more than of anyone else that I have known. He speaks English perfectly.

When we arrived he was with his large family at tea, and after an interchange of civilities he went to lie down, and three of the party, including his wife and eldest son,

[1] For a fuller account see *Friends of a Lifetime*, pp. 78–86.

conducted us over the estate, which has a certain rugged Russian beauty but, like the garden, is very unkempt according to English notions. By the time we got back to the house dinner was spread at a long table under the trees, and Tolstoy was down again and ready to talk as much as we pleased. The Countess is seventeen years younger than he — she was seventeen when they married and he was thirty-four. She is now fifty-nine and although she has thirteen children, and innumerable labours in connexion with the management of the estate, the copying out of her husband's books (*War and Peace* she is said to have copied out seven times!), etc., she looks quite ten years younger. She is a capable woman and a kind hostess, but not, I think, of an idealistic temperament, though she is very proud of her husband's fame. We talked much of Ruskin and Morris. I told Tolstoy that Ruskin had wished that he had renounced his riches. 'That interests me very much,' he said, 'for it is my case also.' He had read *News from Nowhere* but not much else of Morris's, and I promised to send him some of his other prose writings. Like Morris and Burne-Jones and Ruskin, he has a boundless admiration for Dickens. He has always known Shakespeare, but without caring for him. Only lately something written by a friend has given him a clue to this indifference. It is that Shakespeare despised the peasant class, and only introduced them to make fun of them — all his heroes being lords and the like. This struck me as a very just criticism.

He took me to see the village near his house and it was like a Morrisian dream — the men and women splendidly dignified and handsome, and dressed in beautiful garments. Their reception of Tolstoy — he spoke to everyone we met — was respectful, but without an atom of servility in it. . . . The peasants near here are well off, and the communal village life is an exceedingly satisfactory one. I could not help feeling how enormously inferior we are to these Russians, whom we are in the habit of regarding as only half civilized. Tolstoy said that the peasant speech

was the best there was, and that he had learnt his power
of language from them — 'unlike your peasants,' he said,
'who drop their h's. In other parts of Russia they are of
course much more pinched . . .'

On his return to England Cockerell sent Tolstoy some
volumes of Ruskin and, later, an English translation (made by
Lady Anne Blunt) of a long letter[1] of appreciation and encouragement, addressed to Tolstoy by Sheykh Mohammed Abdu,
Grand Mufti of Egypt. Tolstoy, acknowledging the receipt of
the Mufti's letter, informed Cockerell that it was 'so orientally
laudatory that I find it difficult to answer. But I will try to do
it and am very glad to communicate with such an interesting
personality.'

[1] The text of the letter will be found as Appendix 1 in Wilfrid Blunt's
Diaries, vol. II.

11

BLUNT AND LADY ANNE[1]

IN the spring of 1904 Cockerell was again the guest of the Blunts at Sheykh Obeyd.

He now felt brave enough to abandon his donkey in favour of a mare of guaranteed docility — 'the angel Yashmak, whom I hope eventually to ride in heaven,' as Blunt's daughter, Judith, called her. 'You would not have recognized your partner,' Cockerell wrote to Walker, 'speeding over the desert at full gallop on an Arab mare, and in Bedouin garb;' and to Philip Webb, 'If Yashmak and I do not absolutely constitute a centaur, we are on the best of terms and there have been no accidents.' He also sampled a camel and found it satisfactory.

In the middle of March Cockerell went with Blunt, Lady Anne and Miss Lawrence by sea to Beirut (where, as first-class passengers, they were spared compulsory fumigation) and thence to Baalbek. Blunt considered the ruins 'the most splendid in the world. They have been to a certain extent *remis à neuf* for the Emperor William when he was here,' but he considered the restoration in general successful. Only man was vile: 'there are the usual American tourists . . . the most senseless type of human nature, being quite insensible to beauty or decorum and with the manners of shop-boys,' he wrote characteristically. 'They should be kept at home, for they have no business in these ancient lands.'

There followed a week in Damascus, where Blunt still owned a house that he had bought in 1881. Damascus now

[1] The Author wishes to make it plain that he is only a rather distant kinsman (a second cousin twice removed) of Wilfrid Scawen Blunt, and that he has tried to treat objectively the family quarrels, discussed in this and two subsequent chapters, in which he was never in any way involved.

pleased him so well that he was half-inclined to reclaim a portion of the building from Sheykh Saleh Tillo, who rented it, and spend a few weeks there every year. Life was incredibly cheap, rents a tenth of what they were in Cairo, and the bazaars the best in the world. 'There are no modern shops or Frank innovations, or bye-laws, or other Christian tom-fooleries. . . . Newspapers of all kinds are forbidden, the post is unsafe and irregular, and at the central telegraph office there are no printed forms.' So to Blunt, who loved the primitive ineptitude of oriental administration, Damascus was charming; Cockerell, with his orderly mind, found it far less satisfying. The two men visited the Great Mosque, and walked together up to Salahieh to enjoy what Blunt declared to be 'among the first half dozen great views of the world.'

By 30th March they were back at Sheykh Obeyd.

Ten days later, Cockerell sailed with the Blunts and Miss Lawrence for Naples, where there was time for a quick visit to Pompeii, and Genoa. Here the Blunts were invited to spend a few days with the Duke of Aosta; Cockerell therefore made the journey to London alone.

Throughout the winter of 1904–5 Blunt was in Egypt, where since November he had been seriously ill; indeed, for the rest of his life he was frequently ill, and often in great pain.[1] When spring came and he was no better, he decided to return with Miss Lawrence to England. The sea journey, wrote Blunt, was 'a terrible experience of fever and pain.' Cockerell (with a copy of *Anna Karenina* in his pocket) rushed to Venice, where he found Blunt sick, weary and depressed; it seemed impossible for him to travel further for the present. An English doctor was summoned, who recommended a starvation diet but could not discover the cause of the trouble. Cockerell divided his time between the galleries and the patient, sometimes sitting up all night with him in order that Miss Lawrence could get some rest. When, after several

[1] Towards the end of his life much of the pain was due to his refusal to have the (at that time very risky) prostate operation.

weeks, there was no improvement, the decision was taken to risk the return to England. Blunt was carried on a stretcher to a gondola and so to the station, where he was lifted into the train. He reached Chapel Street thirty hours later, having travelled the whole way without dressing or setting foot to ground. Malta fever was now diagnosed, and subsequently a tubercular spine which kept him on his back and in agony for three more months.

To the anxiety about his health there was now added the prospect of the final break-up of his marriage after thirty-six years. There had been discord for a long time past, and many faults on both sides. It was said of Lady Anne that she had 'the heart of a child, the brain of a scholar, and the soul of a saint.' 'She was a remarkable woman,' said Cockerell, 'and a much better Arabic scholar than Blunt. It had been a love match, and Blunt was also very much attracted by the Byron blood; he once told me that if she had refused him he would have proposed to Lady Mary von Hügel — and that would have been a far more successful match. Part of the trouble was that Lady Anne had absolutely no sense of humour. Blunt also told me that there had been no disagreement of any sort until Lady Anne became a Catholic in 1880.' It appeared to Blunt, so he told his wife in a letter, that by taking that step she put God first in her life and himself second: 'I have felt ever since that you were, so to say, serving another master, acknowledging another king, worshipping another god. It seemed to free me by so much of my responsibility to you. Your happiness did not any longer depend on me — at any rate not solely.'

It is a lame excuse. But is it even the truth? Was Blunt unfaithful to his wife because she became a Catholic, or did she turn to religion because he was constantly deceiving her? The latter is much the more probable. Of his unfaithfulness she must have been aware long before 1880. There was the notorious Zouche divorce case in 1876, in which Blunt narrowly escaped being cited as co-respondent. Lady Lytton was no doubt referring to Lady Anne's generous behaviour on this occasion, when she wrote to her from Simla on 20th August of that year: 'You are a good plucky little woman and such a true loyal friend to your dear husband that nothing I hope can really come between you . . . but Oh the pain he has given you, it is hard for your friends to forgive. . . .' And in another letter of about the same date Lady Anne asks her husband what is to become of herself and 'our child' (Judith) if the worst comes to the worst.

And can it really be that Lady Anne had no sense of humour? In an illustrated letter, undated but almost certainly written in 1874, Lady Anne has shown her husband being met at a London railway station by a bevy of female admirers holding bouquets. One of these women arrives at the last moment in a hansom cab, and beside her picture Lady Anne has written, 'She is too late.' In the foreground sits the infant Judith, keeping her mother tied by the 'prosaick reality' of baby-sitting. If Lady Anne, when Cockerell first came to know her, seemed to have no sense of humour, may it not be that by that time there was little left for her to laugh about?

Two letters written to Cockerell from Egypt early in 1905 by Judith and Neville Lytton suggest at all events some of the causes of daily friction. Judith supports her father, whom later she was to attack so vehemently:

There were some very characteristic scenes yesterday. At lunch rockets flew and cannons roared. Mother was in the state of mind when nothing was right. She arrived with a very stern expression and luncheon opened with a fire of invective against the servants. . . . Then I was foolish enough to ask for something which wasn't there, and the storm with the servants began again with a violence which made me repent my rashness. Any attempt at lightening the conversation with cheerfulness was immediately killed, and Neville had only to open his mouth to have his words snapped and twisted and flung back in his teeth. Miss Lawrence sat quaking. . . .

There follows a list of further alleged enormities, including the havoc that Lady Anne was said to have wrought in the garden. Judith concludes, 'I am dreadfully sorry for my father's sake as well as my own as I know what he feels about it. Mother has an amazing lack of sense of proportion. She is quite capable of cutting down a tree 300 years old because she thinks the shade will interfere with drying a pocket hand-kerchief.'

Neville Lytton, writing to Cockerell, laid a part of the blame on Miss Lawrence:

> Miss Lawrence is wonderfully devoted in her constant attentions. I wish however that there were less sentimen-tality in her affection. I think this sentimentality is annoy-ing (very justifiably so) to Lady Anne. Also I think Miss Lawrence is apt to forget that Lady Anne has nursed Mr. Blunt through many dangerous illnesses, and has been of service to him such as *no* other woman could have been. At times she seems to me a little lacking in deference and to take a certain amount of pleasure in rubbing in the fact that she is now the constant companion in sickness in health etc. The situation is a most delicate one. . . . No doubt if the heart did not play some part in the affair, Miss Lawrence would not be the devoted servant she is; on the other hand the heart being for a good deal in the matter, the atmosphere is always a little volcanic. I think few people realize the amount of bitterness it must be to Lady Anne to have been supplanted in this her last domestic happiness, namely of being a domestic essential.

After his return from Venice, Cockerell, on his own initiative and without Blunt's knowledge, had cabled to Lady Anne that Blunt was dying. Thinking that her husband had summoned her, she returned to England at once. Blunt, in great pain, and angry at Cockerell's well-intentioned interference, was (he admitted to his wife later) 'rude . . . but really there was some excuse.' In June, when Lady Anne tried to visit him at Newbuildings, she was turned away from the door.

Cockerell was incensed when he heard; he offered to mediate, and in a brave letter to Blunt he begged him to be reasonable:

I am too fond both of you and of Lady Anne not to be very much disturbed by the state of affairs to which you alluded tonight. And what worries me most is that I cannot help feeling that you are chiefly to blame. No wife with an atom of spirit would stand the humiliation of being denied admission to her husband's house — especially when he is as ill as you have been. And I believe that in your heart of hearts you would think the worse of Lady Anne if she were to take such treatment with submission. She loves you dearly, and the manner that irritates you is partly the result of nervousness caused by the failure of her efforts to get you to speak to her with the old kindness. I pray you to think of this and not to let the breach grow irreparably wide after so many years of dutiful companionship. I feel miserable about it.

Blunt's answer showed neither gratitude for Cockerell's good intention, nor appreciation of his courage in speaking so frankly. 'Don't worry yourself about these domestic arrangements,' he wrote. 'They will work their own way to a new modus vivendi. And above all do not talk of them. . . .' Nor did Lady Anne seem to realize that Cockerell had a genuine desire to help her, although he could not blind himself to the fact that only the ministrations of Miss Lawrence could ease Blunt's pain. To her daughter, Lady Anne wrote (2nd July 1905): 'Mr. Cockerell arrived about midday. Of course if there is any question regarding me he will do more harm than good. I can feel it in his manner, even without anything being said, that he assumes I am always unwelcome and . . . should be kept out of the [i.e., her husband's] room.'

The marriage was, however, beyond saving, and a year later the Blunts agreed to live apart. '21st July 1906. W.S.B. told me of the arrangement that had been come to, to have a division of the stud between Lady Anne and himself and for them to live apart—which is no doubt the best solution of their long-standing disagreement. The immediate consequence is that they seem on better terms than they have been for a long time. Lady A. very affable at dinner.' '22nd July. Had some talk with Lady A. about the separation. It appears that it is to be a final one and that she will never again set foot in Newbuildings after leaving it next week, while her husband is alive.'

Ten weeks later Blunt's kinswoman, Miss Dorothy Carleton, whom he now 'adopted as his niece,' came to live at Newbuildings as his 'secretary.' If, as Blunt stoutly maintained, Miss Carleton was not responsible for the separation, she certainly became the major obstacle in the way of a full reconciliation. The present Lord Lytton, at the age of nine, was told by his grandmother that Miss Lawrence was the cause: 'She was put in my place at the head of the table,' she said, 'to pour out tea.'[1] At all events, Miss Lawrence and Dorothy Carleton were both infatuated with Blunt. They were also intensely jealous of one another. After Blunt's death they were destined to live for a time under the same roof: 'They hate one another so much,' said their doctor of them, 'that they cannot bear to be separated.'

Lady Anne did, in fact, revisit Newbuildings in 1915, at Judith's suggestion. The meeting with her husband was cordial: 'Lady A. was charming, liked all the improvements at Newbuildings and W.S.B. was extremely pleased,' wrote Cockerell. But there was no question of her returning to live there.

[1] See Lord Lytton's biography of his grandfather, pp. 293 ff.

12

FAMILY AND FRIENDS

IN the pursuit of Cockerell's friendships with the famous, and of his work for Morris, Blunt and Yates Thompson, we have passed over the changing fortunes of his own family and the course of his more intimate affairs.

In his diary for 1890, Cockerell sums up the events of the previous year:[1]

> Another year has hurried past, and has left me as it found me, only more so — selfish enough, conceited enough, thoughtless enough of others — yet not quite heartless or ungrateful. . . . The family pack has undergone some shuffling. Theo is back from Colorado, Una from Boulogne, and Douglas, the first to go to America and the last to leave it, is now on his way home. Leslie returned from Canada in the spring, but after spending six months with us, went off to Theo's quarters in Colorado to gain strength, as his health will not yet permit of his undertaking work in London. . . .

During the nineties Theo and Leslie were mostly in America. Theo married in 1891, but his wife died soon after the birth of their son, Martin, and Olive went out to look after the boy. It was a rough life for her and a difficult one, she wrote to her brother Carlie (19th July 1895):

> I'm not going to break down . . . I'm not *ill* at all. . . . The chief trouble for me is Theo — *please don't tell the*

[1] These summaries are to be found in all the diaries from 1886 to 1916.

following to anyone: I hate grumbling — but you know he
never thinks for me in anything: never helps *me* in anything: he lets me do just as I like in the house: but takes
absolutely no interest in any of it. You don't know how
hard it is to work for him — how discouraging — I never
get a word of encouragement or affection. It's his nature
of course, and he is, as you know, absorbed in his work.
He's wonderfully clever, and has splendid theories — and
a grand character, but oh! he's hard to live with!

But Olive adored the boy, and for his sake stayed. When she
had the leisure she worked, professionally, at book-illustration;
she had great talent and her letters home are delightfully
illustrated. While in America she became engaged to a worthless young man, but was saved, just in time, from what would
have been a disastrous marriage. Martin died of diphtheria in
1901, and she, unmarried, in 1910.[1]

Una, who also drew very well, adopted the stage as a profession and worked on and off with Tree, at the Haymarket and
on tour, until her marriage to Captain Charles Low in 1900.

Cockerell himself had settled in Richmond in 1894. After
sampling two very unsatisfactory sets of furnished rooms he
moved in June to excellent lodgings in Rosemont Road. In
1902 he moved 'with the same perfect landlady', Mrs. Blas-
dale, to Friars Stile Road, where he remained until 1908
when, for the first time in his life, he possessed, at Cambridge,
a house of his own.

The chief problem that faced the family during the closing
years of the century was that of their mother, and the principal
trouble with Mrs. Cockerell was that she had become bored
with life. She had lived for her husband and her children; but
her husband was dead and her children had grown up, and she
could find no substitute for the family life that she had lost.

[1] Cockerell wrote in his diary: 'My brother Douglas and I took her
ashes to Coniston, and from Ruskin's boat consigned them to the sombre
depths of the crystal-clear lake, where mine will some day join them.

Enormously sociable, she unfortunately lacked the money to move freely in the social circles that might have diverted her. Already in 1890 she was writing to Leslie in America 'melancholy almost distressing letters with no actual complaints but with a general aspect of tiredness, headache, backache, etc.' Olive, Una and Cockerell were all at one time or another involved in the thankless task of trying to keep her amused. For long stretches she lived abroad, chiefly in Switzerland and Italy, moving from cheap hotel to cheap hotel, dieting here, drinking the waters there, but complaining everywhere. At Grindelwald it was 'dreadfully dull; I have never in my whole life been so miserable and dreary as during the last six weeks,' and she would gladly have exchanged the foreign food for 'a good bloater and an onion.' In England it was worse, for the mere sight of her father gave her 'spasms'.

A letter from Una to Cockerell, written at Bagni di Cascina in the summer of 1896, gives a fair picture of the situation:

> I am going to bother you again! I want to know what you think we had better do. Because this place is dull, and there are no interesting people, Mother is bored — and when she is bored she gets ill. A fortnight ago, in Florence, she was as well as I have seen her for months, but directly she gets away from outside interests she broods and gets ill. This is worrying Olive and making her ill too. When Mother is ill she always wants to come to England. She saw the doctor yesterday (a clever man), who said *nothing* was the matter with her *at all* except nerves. Of course nerves are serious, but I hoped it would soothe her to know that nothing was the matter *really*. I dread England for her. . . . The country would never do for her . . . and in London she would not be happy if she couldn't join in things and dress well — and you see, over here that doesn't matter so much. . . . As far as I can see she wants constant change. She longs for London now, but I am afraid that Auntie and other things would upset her . . . I feel so that Mother needs someone *strong* to manage her; even Olive can't do it. . . .

Theo being in America, the whole responsibility of coping with the various family troubles, or at least of organizing those who must cope with them, fell upon Cockerell. No one could possibly have behaved better: he dealt shrewdly with each crisis as it occurred; he wrote long and affectionate letters regularly to everyone; he constantly made little gifts of money, which he could ill afford, to the most needy member of the family at the moment; and he never complained. He was, throughout, the perfect son and the perfect brother. 'Carlie dear,' wrote Olive from Santa Fe, 'I don't know how to thank you enough for all your goodness to me. You have no idea what a comfort your letters are to me: to feel that I can never drop out of *your* life, however long I may stay away out here.'

In June 1900, just before Cockerell was due to start work with Emery Walker, news reached him that his mother was seriously ill at Wörishofen, Bavaria. Olive set out immediately for Germany, and a fortnight later Cockerell and Una followed her there. Mrs. Cockerell was taken to a hospital in Munich, and a week later Cockerell returned alone to England. There had been a silver lining to his melancholy journey, for it had enabled him to see galleries and libraries in Munich, Cologne, Nuremberg, Mainz and Brussels.

In July Mrs. Cockerell was considered sufficiently recovered to attempt the journey to England. Olive and Una brought her to Dover, where for a time she rallied. But a relapse followed, and in September she died. Cockerell noted in his diary that an acute attack of neuralgia between the shoulder-blades, which had struck him at the time of Morris's death, recurred at this moment. Mrs. Cockerell was buried at Mountfield; she was only fifty-five.

Meanwhile Cockerell had his own life to live.

'As a young man I was, I think I may say, neither repulsive nor too attractive,' he said. 'It is a great misfortune for a young man to be too good-looking.' Early photographs suggest that his estimate of himself was just. The most characteristic, but not perhaps the most attractive, feature of his face was the mouth. By 1899 this had been partially concealed by a drooping moustache and, as has already been mentioned, a beard was added in 1904. Thereafter his appearance was distinguished and scholarly.

As might be expected, Cockerell's women friends — and there were plenty of them, for he was something of a flirt — were usually intellectuals; on his side, at any rate, the head ruled the heart. There was, it is true, the very pretty girl, Marguerite Beaucantin, whom he met in the diligence at Veules in 1885 and accompanied as far as Arques. 'She lived at Rouen,' he said, 'I never saw her again, but we corresponded for some time and she sent me a book — Daudet's *Lettres de mon Moulin*, I think it was. I still have it upstairs somewhere.'[1]

There was a Miss Wilks 'who, so far as I have been able to judge [says the diary], has more virtues than any other girl I have met.' In the summer of 1886 he stayed with her parents at Veules, near Dieppe — 'an earthly Paradise and I am in perfect bliss.'[2] Nell Wilks, who was four years his senior, remained a lifelong friend and more than a thousand letters passed between them.[3]

In the nineties he made several further close and enduring friendships with women. There was Jane Duncan — 'much prized', thirteen years older than himself but 'always very young for her years.' 'She was very clever,' said Cockerell. 'We went to picture exhibitions together. She knew much more than I did: I didn't know a Reynolds from a Gainsborough. She was very poor and her sister was a midwife. She had lived in France.' She was also his constant companion on

---

[1] On 4th April 1892 he wrote in his diary, 'Received an announcement of the death of Madlle Marguerite Beaucantin . . . thus sadly ends that little romance.'

[2] Two pages of the diary, covering the period from 29th July to 11th August 1886 have either been removed or have fallen out. These are the only leaves missing from all the seventy-seven volumes, though here and there a few words have been erased.

[3] In 1915 she married Colonel Worthington, who pre-deceased her. On her death in 1950, Cockerell, her sole executor and residuary legatee, inherited a substantial sum of money.

evening walks in Richmond Park, where 'the nightingales did their duty' and the moon seemed always to be full. That she was deeply attached to Cockerell is shown by the fact that on more than one occasion she accompanied him on quite long train journeys for the mere pleasure of his company, returning alone by the next train. And that he came very near to marrying her in 1907, the year that he married Kate Kingsford, is revealed in a letter that he wrote to his fiancée at that time: 'Miss D. does not reproach me—neither do I reproach myself. We should have been utterly miserable as man and wife;' and in Kate's reply, 'it is dreadful for us to have made anyone so sad.' Jane Duncan died in 1932.

Sara Anderson, also twelve or thirteen years his senior, was, said Cockerell, 'the woman I really liked most of them all. We were friends all the time till her death at the age of ninety. She was secretary to Ruskin, then to Kipling, and a very great friend of Burne-Jones. Kipling told me she was "a woman apart; all the others were just secretaries. She knew by the way I pronounced the word 'damn', just how to answer any letter. And she was utterly discreet." But my mother said, "too old for you".' In March, 1922, after her mother's death, he went to see her and wrote in his diary, 'Though we have known each other for thirty-five years and have been very close friends for most of that time, I had never before been to her home—for reasons that are hard to define. I think principally a fear that I should find it inartistic and her relations uncongenial and that this might affect our friendship.'

Eleanor Burnett taught singing, and was always prepared to sing to Cockerell. In 1894 it was,' In evening to dine with Miss Burnett, who sang Lucia and other songs very nicely.' The following year she was singing Grieg's *Ich liebe dich* and he was teaching her Greek. But she settled in Florence and thereafter he saw her only occasionally.

There was Katharine ('Katie') Adams, afterwards Mrs. Edmund Webb, who became one of the best bookbinders in England. 'I would have married her,' he said, 'but she was five years older than I, and by the time I could afford to marry we could not have had a family.' Their friendship, which lasted until Mrs. Webb's death in 1952, is recorded in nearly sixty years of correspondence; it was of the greatest value to both of them, and an inestimable comfort to Mrs. Webb in the closing years of her life when sickness and poverty were her lot.[1]

Lastly there was his sister's friend Amy Carruthers (Mrs. Tozer). 'Olive wanted me to marry her,' he said, 'but I was protected by poverty from marriage until I was forty.' Doubtless there was some truth in this; but doubtless, also, ways and means would have been found if passion had been stronger. The fact was that other interests came first in his life.

So the new century dawned with Cockerell, now in his thirty-fourth year, still unmarried. But a few months earlier he had met the woman, Florence Kate Kingsford, who seven years later was to become his wife. The diary records his first meeting with her: '31st July 1900. Miss Kingsford called about the illuminated and written pages that she has been doing.'

'She was one of a large family,' said Cockerell, 'and she was descended on her mother's side from Oliver Cromwell's sister, Jane Disbrowe. There were five or six sisters and a brother, and there was always great poverty. Her father had died; I can't remember his profession—perhaps he was a merchant. I bought her books before we were married, and so helped to keep her alive.'[2]

[1] After her death Mrs. Webb's letters were returned to Cockerell, who had the joint correspondence (upwards of 1,100 letters in all) bound in five volumes. These are now in the possession of his younger daughter, Mrs. John Laughton, who is Mrs. Webb's god-daughter.

[2] Mr. Christopher Cockerell, S.C.C.'s son, comments on this: 'The Kingsfords came from Canterbury and were millers. My grandfather was a great fisherman, gay, and very musical (he played the violin). There were six daughters who adored him, and a son who died young. My grandfather also died young and, having somewhat neglected his business, left his family penniless. The girls all sang or played the piano or drew; but they were quite unequipped to earn a living.

'I remember my grandmother as a tiny little Victorian lady with a hooked nose, a string of black and white onyx beads, and very carefully dressed in grey and black silks. She always sat bolt upright on her chair, and never allowed herself to be late for breakfast. She had very clear ideas on how a young boy should behave.'

Kate (as he called her after their marriage) was twenty-nine when Cockerell first met her: handsome rather than pretty, a talented and imaginative artist with a special gift for illumination. Like all the Kingsfords she had great courage; on her own initiative she had succeeded in entering the Royal Academy Schools (the only girl student of her day), and thereafter kept herself at just above starvation level by her work. She had the soul of an artist: beauty was everything to her, and she lived through her eyes. She could not spell or add or plan, and it had never occurred to her that such things were of the slightest importance. She found the world a strange place, and could not take life, or herself, quite seriously. In almost all her paintings a little touch of humour breaks out.

Probably Cockerell fell in love with the paintings before he fell in love with the painter; 'if necessary,' he wrote to her, 'I will sell old manuscripts from my collection in order to get your new ones, which really give me more pleasure than all but the *very best* old work.' For on his side, at any rate, there was no sudden passion, but rather the gradual realization that he had found in her the fitting companion for life. In the years that followed he met her from time to time and got commissions for her from his rich friends in the manuscript world; there were occasional inexpensive little supper parties at Gatti's, followed perhaps by a visit to a friend or to a theatre; and sometimes she would come down to Richmond for an evening meal and a walk in the Park.

In 1904 Kate went to Egypt for eighteen months with her friend Miss Hansard, to make drawings of Professor Flinders Petrie's finds. Here they met Neville Lytton, who wrote to Cockerell, 'Of the two ladies I think Miss Hansard is the more intelligent. She is not shy and talks exceedingly well. Miss Kingsford though charming is very shy and does not add much pepper and salt to the conversation.' 'In Egypt they lived in holes in the earth,' said Cockerell, 'in fearful discomfort. Flinders Petrie was good company, and a good lecturer; but he had little sense of right and wrong.' While she was abroad Kate wrote to Cockerell about once a month, and doubtless Cockerell answered, as was his habit, by return.

In July 1906 Cockerell visited Mrs. Morris at Kelmscott and had a long talk with her about 'marriage, its pros and cons,' and a fortnight later he carried off Kate and Emery Walker on a long week-end to northern France. But no proposal followed, and in December he invested £480 — 'all the money I have in the world' — in a manuscript[1] that had once belonged to William Morris. Though it was to prove a very shrewd investment, its purchase was hardly the act of a poor man contemplating immediate matrimony.

Cockerell saw a good deal of Kate during the early months of 1907, and in July he went with her and Eric Gill to Bruges, where they were joined by Emery Walker and Katie Adams. Eric Gill[2] — 'a very shabby silent little fellow in a child's hat,' wrote Katie — was a good deal teased by the ladies of the party. They returned four days later by the night boat from Ostend — 'a disagreeable crossing, the ladies both very ill and myself nearly so. Got to Charing Cross at 7.' The diary entry for the same day (31st July 1907) concludes, 'Supped alone at Gatti's and saw Lady Dora [Rodakowski] and her children off to Inverness by the 7.45 train. After that went to see Florence Kingsford who consented to be my wife.'

The acquisition of a fine manuscript would never have been recorded in words as arid as those in which he noted down the acquisition of a bride.

[1] A fragmentary thirteenth-century Old Testament which recently changed hands for about £7,000.

[2] Cockerell wrote to Katie Adams in 1941, 'Gill was a more remarkable creature than he appeared to be at Bruges, and he wrote and drew exceedingly well. His tendency to be preoccupied with sex was, I think, a great pity . . .'

13

MARRIAGE

IT was no rash act,[1] Cockerell noted in his diary; 'in all *essentials* I think we are in complete accordance, and I count myself very fortunate to have won so gifted a wife.' And to Nell Wilks he wrote jokingly, 'She is penniless, which to me is rather an advantage than otherwise, as I shall be able to treat her with the ferocity which is so large a part of my nature.'

There was indeed general agreement that the match was most suitable, though Albert Fleming felt that since Cockerell seemed always to be living in castles[2] he ought to have married 'a Duchess at least.' Wilfrid Gibson,[3] a young poet whom Cockerell had befriended and encouraged, wrote, 'I don't think I know anyone who more deserves to be married than you do; and I hope you will get your deserts. I can only trust that it will bring you a ten-thousandth part of the happiness you have been the means of bringing to other people.' Sukie, the little daughter of Cockerell's friend Lady Dora Rodakowski, informed him that it was 'quite the most sensibul thing' he could do, and Katie Adams predicted 'a flutter among the 11,000.' Una wrote, 'I like your "Kate" very much indeed. I can't *tell* you what a relief it is to hear that she cannot *spell*.

[1] But in a letter to Emery Walker he called it 'a rash act, I know, on both our parts, but we are determined to make each other as happy as we can.'

[2] When working on the manuscripts of his rich patrons.

[3] The poet of two World Wars. 'I met him, his father and his sister in a train at Pisa in 1898,' Cockerell said. He and Gibson continued to correspond, and occasionally to meet, for fifty years.

I thought she would write her letters in gold ink, and be too exquisite to have anything to do with the likes of me.' Alone Ouida raised her Cassandra voice in warning:

> I am very sorry to hear the news you give me. Your golden hair will soon grow grey. You have such a charming life, and are so welcome everywhere, that it is really suicide. No woman, were she the loveliest of living creatures, is worth the sacrifice of a man's life. Remember the wise proverb: 'Dans l'amour il n'y a que les commencements qui sont charmants.' With sincere regret for the irreparable error I am
>
> ever your friend
Ouida

It so happened that, almost immediately after their engagement, Cockerell was obliged to go to Scotland for some weeks to work upon certain manuscripts in the library of Dyson Perrins at Ardross. The separation, painful though it was, provided the occasion for the exchange of love letters.

For Cockerell, the writing of these was no more than a new facet of a favourite craft. But poor Kate, though not in the least stupid, was inarticulate with the written word and found all letter-writing a torment; 'drawing (and that with very great difficulty),' she wrote, 'is the only mode of communication I have with the outer world.' She could not see how to turn the trivial happenings of the day into words that would please him, or to spread herself to that second sheet which, he tells her, 'I shouldn't mind now and then, seeing that your writing is not very small.' She never remembered to answer his questions, or to comment upon what he had written. She muddled everything. Her writing was bad and her spelling worse. She wrote 'as one might to a piano-tuner,' Cockerell informed Katie.

'Your good example,' St. John Hornby told Cockerell, 'will perhaps by degrees instil into her casual soul a sense of time and love of order, the lack of which you will perhaps say is now

one of her charms.' Cockerell said nothing of the sort; puncti-
lious always, at heart a schoolmaster and something of a
pedant, he considered her artistic vagueness mere inefficiency
and found it quite exasperating. He determined to begin
Eliza Doolittle's education at once, and the method he
employed was remarkably like that which his father had used
with Adah.[1]

Most of Cockerell's letters (and he wrote every day) open
with a little bantering lecture on Kate's latest sins of commission and omission, proceed to an account of events at
Ardross and his progress at diabolo (the current craze), and
close with protestations of undying devotion. But unfortunately the banter, which was ponderous and pointed, cut her to
the quick; the more he lectured her, the more incompetent
she became. 'If I were not such a good-tempered fellow,' he
tells her, 'I should chide you for not remembering to post the
other letter. . . . You are terribly impressionistic and vague in
your writing. No date on yesterday's letter. Probably to you
this seems of no consequence; but to old-fashioned fogeys of
business habits, like myself, it is of real importance—so you
must be good enough to humour me, however silly it may
seem . . . I am a precise beggar, Kate, and I think that is what
will annoy you most about me.'

Kate seizes her pen to apologize, in her flurry dates her
letter 'October 92nd', and by misspelling his name exposes
herself to further badinage, 'If you decide to call me Sydney',
he replies, 'may I have it spelt with a *y*?'

Her spelling is, indeed, a constant source of trouble: 'There
is no such word as "alright", which comes in your three last
letters . . . do *try* to remember, and not persist with "alright"
as you persisted with "Teusday" . . . and about the bogey
portrait (N.B., only one 'g' in bogey). . . .' So poor Kate is
reduced to writing 'the day after Monday' and to testing
various possible spellings—'wate', 'wait', 'waite', 'wayte',
'whate', etc.—before making her final choice.

He tells her to write 'Dear Mr. Perrins' and not 'Dear Sir',
and to address Mrs. Napier as '"the Hon. Mrs. Mark Napier"

[1] See p. 14.

—I am not sure whether you know that she is entitled to this little complimentary addition, as her husband is a peer's son — and for all that the very best of fellows.' To this she replies:

> You have hurt my feelings a little by teaching me how to write to Mr. Perrins. Because I am forgetful you think I must be quite ignorant. I suppose all men are born with the idea that wives are children, just as women are born with the idea that husbands are unreasonable creatures to be indulged and endured—which is the tone they generally adopt when discussing together the lords of creation. It is sad if we can no longer be friends on equal terms. Dear one, I am quite willing to pretend that I think you reasonable for 40 years if you will pretend that you think I am your equal. How will that suit us?

Cockerell clumsily attempts to justify himself. 'I like you to be as silly as you really are,' he adds, and so makes Kate, who longs for love, not logic or condescension,

> more miserable than ever, which is quite as it should be — and now you will always patronize me in your mind, which is degrading to me and pitiful for you and will put up a barrier between us. But all friendship is the saddest thing in the world because of our faults. I know you think I don't care a button about you or I should take more trouble; but that does not seem to be true, and I shall love you dearly long after I have wasted all your affection by my stupid carelessness.

It was Cockerell's aim, also, to make Kate 'become part of his slightly musty, slightly un-vital world of books and by-gones.'[1] I hope to kindle in you some interests that have not had much opportunity of development,' he informs her in another letter. So he orders her to visit some of his fine and famous friends, and is saddened when she panics ('I know how selfish it is to be shy') and makes an excuse ('What lies did you

[1] Mr. Christopher Cockerell, in a communication to the Author.

tell?') to cancel her visit to Kelmscott. He prescribes her reading, and reproaches her when she does not instantly obey his orders: 'Show me that you do care a button by doing it [i.e., reading Lady Burne-Jones's life of her husband], and by being more careful about those little things that you know are of more importance to me than they are to you.'

'No, I am not angry,' he writes after she has wrongly copied (from his exquisite block capitals) two of his three names in her application for the banns; 'not angry—but just a little saddened that you should seem incapable of doing the smallest errand without a blunder.'

The pathetic approach having failed, Kate now introduced what her fiancé called a 'saucy' tone into her letters. One such letter was provoked by an occasion when she failed to find a candle at his lodgings in Richmond. 'Don't you know where they're kept?' said his landlady. '*All the others know!*' So *that* was why he called her 'the *best* of Kates'! How many other Kates were there, she would like to know— 'my best but two of Sydneys!'

'We did not skin you alive so much as usual last evening,' she wrote after a visit to Katie. 'We now think it more appropriate to try to remember your good points. It is wonderful what you can do with determination and a little fancy!'

Cockerell was delighted. 'Hurrah!' he wrote. 'It is a Kate of spirit, and it is not going to give in or allow itself to be bullied! and that is just the sort of Kate I want. I have told you that I do not care for blind devotion.'

Katie Adams was a good friend to Kate through these difficult days, and it was probably she who urged Kate to hit back. She saw what was happening: 'I must say,' she wrote to Cockerell, 'the woman has a good deal to go through when she is first engaged.' Cockerell could not understand. He felt that he was being utterly reasonable and extremely patient. He felt sure that Kate was made of good material, and that when he had shaped and polished her she would be his worthy consort.

But Kate was thirty-five, and his treatment of her, which

might have succeeded with a girl of twenty, merely destroyed
the little self-confidence that she possessed and left her shy
and battered. It was quite extraordinary that the man who had
proved himself the perfect son and the perfect brother should
fail so completely in the role of lover.

'I steer smilingly towards the abyss,' Cockerell wrote to Blunt
as the wedding-day approached. But poor Kate became more
and more alarmed. She had 'stage-fright'; she was 'in a blue
funk.' 'I shall be a failure,' she wrote; 'I can't imagine anyone
choosing me for a wife, but you have done it now.'

She wanted to be married in London, where she and her
mother lived; but Cockerell preferred the little Norman
church with a shingled spire at Mountfield, in Sussex, where
his parents were buried, or, failing that, Oxford. 'I said, Go
to! — we'll choose the prettiest church in England, and we
needn't ask anyone but real friends.' So, by way of a compromise, he proposed Iffley, as lying between Oxford and
London (but rather nearer Oxford); and Kate was obliged to
yield.[1]

Cockerell decided upon 1st November for the wedding, then
changed it to the day following and wrote to inform his friend
Dame Laurentia[2] of Stanbrook Abbey: 'There is this to be
said for November 2nd, that it is All Souls' Day.' But Dame
Laurentia was horrified: 'How could you, a student of Kalen-
dars, consent to All Souls' Day?' she replied. 'It is altogether
weird to me.' So the date was again changed — now to 4th
November. Dame Laurentia was satisfied: it was the festival
of the respectable if rather nebulous SS. Amantius and
Modesta, and she had no doubt that they would take 'a lively
interest' in events at Iffley. Presumably Kate was satisfied

---

[1] A few years earlier, in a letter to a friend, Cockerell had written that
when, if ever, he married he would either choose 'a small unrestored
church among the fields' or be 'prosaic with a vengeance' and go, as his
brother had done, to a register office.

[2] Cockerell had first met Dame Laurentia the previous January. Their
long friendship is discussed on pp. 224 ff.

also, for on 4th November Sydney Cockerell and Kate Kingsford were duly married at Iffley, Cockerell's old friend Detmar Blow being best man.

Blunt had offered his London house for the honeymoon. He had written to Cockerell in September, echoing Ouida's forebodings but sugaring the pill with a handsome cheque: 'As the day of doom is now near at hand and I suppose it is useless to remonstrate or bid you pause before sacrificing your golden locks upon the altar of Hymen, I do what I can to soften the blow for you by proposing that the sacrifice shall be made at Chapel Street and the honeymoon be there worked out.' But Cockerell had asked if they might instead spend a few weeks there on their return. The honeymoon was spent, first at Burford in a house lent them by Mrs. Morris, then with Lady Burne-Jones at Rottingdean, and finally in various old haunts of Cockerell's and at Winchelsea, where in the evenings Cockerell read Blunt's *Esther* to his wife.

Cockerell had, of course, bought Kate an engagement ring, but later he gave her a second ring: '19th December 1907. Bought an emerald ring for Kate, said to be sixteenth century, from Heigham & Co., 139 High Holborn, who gave me a written undertaking to buy it back at any time for £17 10s. if in same condition. There is an indentation on one side but otherwise it seems perfect.'

From Winchelsea the Cockerells went to Chapel Street, where they remained until they moved to Richmond in January.

Meanwhile Cockerell was still busy with his work for Yates Thompson and Dyson Perrins, and more particularly in collecting material and preparing the catalogue for an important exhibition of manuscripts at the Burlington Fine Arts Club. These labours kept him for much of his time apart from Kate, who therefore paid several visits to friends in Sussex.

The Burlington Fine Arts Club exhibition was the most splendid of its kind that had ever been staged, and Cockerell's sumptuous catalogue, with its scholarly text and its numerous plates engraved by Emery Walker, was possibly the most impressive of the seven *de luxe* volumes dealing with manuscripts that he produced between 1905 and 1930. Dyson Perrins was the principal contributor to the exhibition, but Cockerell himself lent fifteen manuscripts and two loose sheets; with his very limited means he had already managed to get together the nucleus of a collection that was later to become famous and which was particularly rich in work by named scribes.

There were two features of Cockerell's collecting which are so uncommon as to deserve to be placed on record. Though he was shrewd in his purchases and probably bought little or nothing which did not enormously increase in value over the years, he thought of money primarily as something which would buy works of art, not of works of art as something which could be manipulated to make money. Also he looked upon his books as something he could offer to his friends. His rich acquaintances could offer comfortable houses, good food and fine wines, shooting and fishing; Cockerell drew kindred spirits to his house by his manuscripts: they were the tools of his trade.

As he told Emery Walker, neither poverty nor his new responsibilities as a married man could keep his collector's instinct in check: 'I am like Morris. It is no use my swearing never to buy another thing. The moment I am sufficiently tempted I fall!' In the world of manuscript he was, said his friend W. M. Ivins, 'a mighty hunter before the Lord.' But with a wife and the prospect of a family, Cockerell saw clearly that it was essential for him to find a steady job. The Directorship of the Fitzwilliam Museum at Cambridge had fallen vacant through the resignation of Dr. M. R. James, and Cockerell, though told on all sides that the successful candidate would inevitably be a Cambridge man, decided to try his luck; the salary (£500 *per annum*) was so meagre that he hoped that competition would not be strong.

He immediately began an energetic campaign of canvassing. Fortunately he possessed many good friends in high places, but other important people had to be approached indirectly. Rothenstein was set to work on various Darwins, Lady Helena Carnegie and the Meynells on Baron von Hügel, Blunt on George Wyndham. The Duke of Devonshire and Arthur Balfour, though they had never met Cockerell, were urged by friends of friends to use their influence. Before long Cockerell had assembled a formidable pile of testimonials; from these he extracted the ten most potent and had them exquisitely printed by the Chiswick Press on handmade paper.

But for the fact that he had not been at a university Cockerell's credentials were magnificent — so magnificent, indeed, that (he told Katie) he felt he ought also to publish a collection of 'anti-testimonials' in which his most candid friends put his 'various shortcomings in as odious a light' as they could. His uncle Sir Douglas Powell, President of the Royal College of Physicians, testified that he was 'a man of high rectitude of character, thoroughly trustworthy and exact in his work, of great business capacity, and of tactfulness, so far as this can be combined with perfect straightforwardness.' Lord Plymouth, George Frampton, R.A., Roger Fry, Charles Hallé, W. R. Lethaby, D. S. MacColl, C. Fairfax Murray, Henry Yates Thompson and Dr. G. F. Warner — all men of high standing in the world of art or scholarship — were in agreement that no better man for the job could be found in all England. On 30th May Cockerell learned that he had been appointed. He rushed to Cambridge, shook hands with everyone, and found a house — the first house of his own — which was vetted by Kate the next day. On 21st June 1908 the furniture, closely followed by Kate, arrived at Wayside, Cavendish Road (with a fine view over the cornfields and the Gogmagogs — rent, £32 per annum).

Cockerell's forty years of wandering in the wilderness were over, and he embarked upon the work which was to make him both happy and famous.

PART TWO

[1908—1937]

1

THE FITZWILLIAM

We Cockerells must be hell to live with:—so *unrelaxing*.

(*Mr. Christopher Cockerell, in a communication*
to the Author, January 1964)

THE Fitzwilliam, when Cockerell became its Director,
was in a deplorable condition.
Writing in 1932, at a time when he felt that the
major part of his work of rehabilitation had been completed, he
described the state of the Museum as he had inherited it:

When I was appointed, 24 years ago, the arrangement
was utterly barbarous. Good and bad pictures, all schools
and countries mixed, were packed together on the walls
to a ridiculous height and the Greek and Egyptian
departments were a complete and repellent muddle, such
little oriental china as there was being housed with other
irrelevant objects in the main Greek room and the cases
in the Egyptian rooms being mostly deplorable improvisa-
tions. Of the 102 watercolours and other drawings just
hung in Gallery III, 99 have come in my time, and
so have all but one of the pictures in Gallery V, as well
as nearly all the miscellaneous works of art in the place.

'I found it,' he said, 'a pigstye; I turned it into a palace.'
Undue modesty was never one of Cockerell's faults, but what
he here says is no more than the truth. Bernard Berenson, in
a letter to his wife after he had visited the Fitzwilliam in 1936,

135

wrote, 'Cockerell has transformed it from the dismal miscellany it used to be, into one of the finest museum buildings existing, with lighting and arrangement, not to speak of contents, every bit as good as the so famous one at Rotterdam.'

Since its foundation in 1816, the Fitzwilliam had received no money bequests whatever, though pictures and other objects had been added; in the thirty years of his Directorship Cockerell collected bequests and gifts of money amounting to over a quarter of a million pounds.[1] It was an achievement of which any man might be proud.

Dr. M. R. James, Cockerell's predecessor, was a scholar of international repute, after Léopold Delisle the greatest authority of his day on manuscripts. 'He had an enormous knowledge of medieval Latin,' said Cockerell. 'He'd smell a page of a manuscript and say, "St. Augustine" — and it *was* St. Augustine! But he had absolutely *no* taste whatever (you had only to look at his house to see that), and he hadn't the *least* idea how to run a museum. He just looked in occasionally to see if there were any letters. But I was very fond of him; he had a good sense of humour, and he was an excellent host.'

A photograph of the Central Gallery of the Fitzwilliam, though taken in 1887, shows the state of the Museum much as it was when Cockerell inherited it twenty years later. This crowded and tasteless method of displaying pictures was, it must be remembered, the common practice of the day. Masterpieces and very inferior paintings jostled one another for wall space; and strangely inappropriate objects, accepted as gifts by rash Directors in the past, littered the cases. Almost everything might be found there except fossils, for which, Cockerell once told Katie Adams, the dons were a very adequate substitute. 'There was a fearful model of the Taj Mahal,' he said. 'I told the Director of the Victoria and Albert Museum that if he

[1] This included the money given for extensions to the building. The acquisitions alone would no doubt today fetch many times this sum were they sent to the saleroom.

was very good he could have it on permanent loan for his
Indian Museum, and he was delighted.[1] I also planted out a
few portraits. I often wished I'd got a machine-gun mounted
at the top of the stairs, to mow down the people who tried to
make me accept second-rate and third-rate objects.'

The Fitzwilliam was closed on Sundays, and on Fridays to all
but Members of the University and their friends ('who never
came'). Overshoes had to be worn on wet days. Ropes kept
visitors at a respectful but inconvenient distance from the
pictures, which were rarely changed. There were few temporary exhibitions or loans. The whole place was little better
than dead.

Cockerell also had a very real grievance. At the time of his
appointment, no mention had been made of the disagreeable
fact that, for his meagre salary, he was also expected to take
charge of the Museum of Classical Archaeology — a gloomy
institution which did not in the least interest him and which
was, he considered, an unreasonable and perpetual drain on
the slender grant that he administered.

If the University authorities were under the impression that
they had appointed a 'yes-man' — one who would toe their
line and maintain the *status quo* — they soon discovered their
mistake. Cockerell had vision, energy, faith. He was afraid of
nobody. And he had a clear purpose which he proposed to
carry out in the face of all opposition: to make the Fitzwilliam
one of the finest and best arranged museums in the world. 'I
was not fearfully popular in Cambridge,' he said, 'because I
was determined to get my own way.' It was not for nothing
that he had jotted in his diary the couplet:

Thrice is he armed who has his quarrel just,
But four times he who gets his fist in fust.

Cockerell usually did.

[1] But apparently it took him sixteen years to get rid of it: '8th May
1924. A great day. Our model of the Taj Mahal dismantled and to be
taken (on loan) to the Indian Museum tomorrow.'

Within a year of his appointment, Cockerell and his
Museum had become 'news'. 'The undergraduate has discovered the Fitzwilliam Museum,' wrote Archibald Marshall
in the *Daily Mail* (15th March 1909), 'and he owes his discovery to the new director, Mr. Cockerell.' Marshall continued:

> Knowing something of the amount of knowledge and
> self-sacrificing labour that has for years been at the
> service of the Fitzwilliam, from the directors and the
> members of the syndicate, I could not quite understand
> how so great a change as I had heard of could have been
> brought about by one man, and in so short a time. . . .
> But a morning spent with Mr. Cockerell in the museum
> has solved the problem. He has knowledge and enthu-
> siasm and an attractive personality. But these would not
> have availed him unless he had taken definitely in hand
> the task of making the collection a living and growing
> thing. In other words, the Fitzwilliam Museum is being
> talked about in Cambridge now, and being visited,
> because something is always happening there.

The *Morning Post* (15th June 1909) was also impressed by
the 'missionary work' that Cockerell had already accomplished. Mentioning Baedeker's advice to the foreigner
anxious to see the treasures of England's two great university
cities: 'If pressed for time, Cambridge may be omitted', it
hinted that, thanks to Cockerell, this might soon cease to be a
sensible recommendation.

The Syndics who ruled the Fitzwilliam stirred uneasily in
their sleep and began to view with alarm the zeal and energy
of the new Director. Some of his immediate innovations,
however, proved to be reasonably acceptable, or were at all
events unlikely to involve them in trouble. He inaugurated the
'Friends of the Fitzwilliam', the first of the now innumerable
institutions of this kind in England, though modelled upon the
'Amis du Louvre' which was already proving a success in
France. (The idea occurred to him after he had bought an

object without the money to pay for it). He appointed Honorary Keepers for the various departments of the Museum, who freely gave of their specialized knowledge and often of their money and of objects from their private collections. He obtained the permission of the King to borrow six Old Master drawings at a time from Windsor Castle, the drawings to be changed at the beginning of each term;[1] and the Duke of Devonshire agreed to a similar loan from Chatsworth. There was a great increase in the number of pictures and other works of art lent to the Museum, and in the quantity of objects presented.

But other proposed changes were more controversial, and Cockerell soon found himself at war with Ridgeway, the Professor of Archaeology, with whom he had had 'a rather heated discussion' within a few weeks of his arrival. 'Another disagreeable letter from Ridgeway' soon becomes a familiar entry in the diary. 'Though Ridgeway was very obstreperous, and though we had great battles,' said Cockerell, 'when I'd won he bore me no grudge and we remained good friends.' It was Ridgeway who most strongly, but unsuccessfully, opposed Cockerell in his campaign to abolish 'that idiotic Friday arrangement,' and he was still more vigorous in denouncing the dangers and wickedness of throwing the Fitzwilliam open on Sundays.

'Ridgeway appeared to think that young men and maidens would make assignations in this dangerous Museum,' said Cockerell. 'The motion was put to the open vote of the M.A.s, and parsons were whipped up from all parts of the globe to vote against it. It was Canon Hutchinson, of Worcester, who saved me; he said in a Church newspaper that Sunday opening was desirable. I only won by a few votes.'

The affair of the Museum of Classical Archaeology was no pitched battle; it was a bitter campaign that lasted for several

[1] To the Vice-Chancellor, who made the formal request, King Edward VII said with a chuckle, 'It might deter the young men from going over to Newmarket.'

years and which ended, as did most of Cockerell's wars, in victory for Cockerell. The Fitzwilliam obtained a divorce from its unloved partner, though it was obliged — and with what reluctance! — to pay £500 a year alimony. The chief opponent of the separation was Professor Cook who, as Reader in Classical Archaeology, now became *ex officio* Director of the Archaeology Museum and who might, one would have thought, have welcomed his independence. Two letters explain the divergent points of view. Cook writes to Cockerell on 26th May 1911:

> I parted from you abruptly and in some irritation yesterday; for which I am sincerely sorry. Please regard bygones as bygones. . . .
>
> You hold that the Fitzwilliam has spent £30,000 on the Museum of Classical Archaeology and should therefore spend no more. I hold that, having called the Archaeology Museum into existence, and having once undertaken its equipment and maintenance, the Fitzwilliam Syndicate is legally and morally bound to see the thing through — unless and until it is relieved of its obligation by the University at large. In this, as in so much else, we are not — I fear — likely to agree. Let it stop at that.
>
> Of one thing at least I am really glad — that my place on the Fitzwilliam Syndicate will soon be occupied by another. I do not pretend to a knowledge of fine art in general. I much prefer to peg away at my own subject. I hate the policy of push. And I do not care to help in running a shop which keeps its blinds half-drawn on Sundays. Added to all this, it is a perpetual vexation to hear the department that I represent slighted and — as I maintain — unduly neglected. No, I am heartily glad to be out of it. So, I venture to predict, will you be one day, when the great change comes.

And he signs himself, 'Yours on the old footing.' Of Cockerell's reply, only an incomplete draft survives:

> Thank you for your letter. Surely you know by this time

that I do not easily take offence. If I were as thin-skinned as some of my friends are here I should have started sulking long ago, and should have either gone elsewhere or have adopted the policy of inactivity and easy morning hours which many people would prefer to 'the policy of push' and double or treble the attendance laid down in the regulations. I agree with you that I may be driven to it yet, and that I may even be as glad to leave Cambridge as Cambridge will be to get rid of me, though I do not know what you refer to as 'the great change.' Meanwhile I intend to do my duty to the Museum and the University according to my lights, as I have done for the last three years.

You ought not, however, to forget that Thursday's vote was the result of 'the policy of push' which you hate, though the pushing took nearly two years and a half; and that on Jan. 1st you will be able to approach the Museum of Classical Archaeology with a new sense of semi-proprietorship, which ought to make an immense difference both to your personal comfort and to the efficiency of the Museum, since you will be able to arrange and label it in accordance with the latest discoveries and generally, I hope, to bring it up to date without feeling the incubus of an ignorant and neglectful Director from round the corner. In all you say about the present relations between the two Museums you seem to be utterly forgetful both of our financial limitations and of the leeway that the Fitzwilliam had, and still has, to make up. In this matter we must evidently be content to think each other prejudiced and even blind . . .

While these battles were in progress, Cockerell was also in hot pursuit of benefactors to the Fitzwilliam. 'To beg,' said *The Times* subsequently of him 'he was not ashamed;' and when a friend called him to his face, 'a scrounger of genius,' he chuckled contentedly. On being asked how he succeeded in acquiring such magnificent gifts and bequests, he said, 'It was quite easy: I never admitted the possibility of a refusal. I would select my man — somebody with a lot of money, of course, and no children — and get myself invited to dinner with him. Then, over the wine, I would say, "What's going to happen to your collection when you die?" or "What will you do for your old University?" They hardly ever refused to help me. Yes — I enjoyed that wheedling.' To Dame Laurentia, of Stanbrook Abbey, who wrote to him, 'Can you teach me how to collect money as you do?' he replied, 'My answer, though it seems a strange one for the likes of you, is always the same — that it is simply a matter of faith!' He studied the millionaire market so carefully that he was able, at a moment's notice, to provide Sir Charles Stanford with 'a list of millionaires who might be approached' for contributions towards the foundation of a Musical Centre in Cambridge.

It has been alleged, and not without some reason, that Cockerell's methods of extorting pictures, *objets d'art* and money from his millionaires were brutally direct if not actually crude. 'There is no collector in the world,' said the Chancellor of Cambridge University when Cockerell came to retire, 'who feels his treasures safe so long as Sir Sydney is in the land;' and Thomas Hardy once wrote, 'How you managed to squeeze £1,000 out of a dinner table passes my understanding. It is . . . better than big game shooting.' It used to be jocularly said in Cambridge that, if any wealthy man received a call from Cockerell, he suspected that his end was near; and a present Fellow of Jesus has a vivid recollection of the first words he ever heard Cockerell utter. They were, 'So I called on the Duke: he was a dying man then.'

No doubt many of the stories current in Cambridge at the time — for example, those of his sudden appearances, pen in hand, at the deathbeds of the very rich — are exaggerated or perhaps purely fictitious; it would not have been in character for him to have left matters of such moment to the eleventh hour. But the facts are remarkable enough. 'A man named Power,' said Cockerell, 'gave me £500 to buy rugs for the Fitzwilliam. I said it was not enough, and he sent me another £500. A little later I wrote to him again: "There is a sad lack of *rugs* in my Museum; I want more money." He sent me another £500, saying, "Go to hell! But before you go, cash this cheque".' 'I call that a bit cool,' Cockerell is related to have said when he showed the letter to Dr. James. People gave to the Museum, said Lord Knutsford in a letter to Cockerell, 'because of their admiration for your devotion to it, and to shut up your damned mouth in asking for more . . . I congratulate you.'

Cockerell attached a good deal of importance to Cambridge men supporting their old University, and once returned a handsome cheque from an Oxford man because he had decided that a particular manuscript should be the gift of Cambridge men to Cambridge. He succeeded in touching Mr. J. P. Morgan for £600 for this manuscript on the very day on which he received an Honorary Degree at Cambridge and so qualified as a donor. Yet in a crisis—as, for example, when he had acquired an expensive object on credit and found he could not pay for it—he was glad enough to raise money from any source and by any means. The following entry from his diary would seem to suggest that at times he was not too proud to pass round the hat: 'Went to Selfridges and saw one of the Directors, Mr. Cowper. He was very civil, but I failed to get any money.' (The previous evening, it may be mentioned, he had touched Oppenheimer for £100 and the following morning he extracted £250 from Mr. Chester Beatty before the end of breakfast).

Cockerell was expert in the 'a-little-bit-of-bread-to-finish-up-my-butter — a-little-bit-of-butter-to-finish-up-my-bread' technique. 'What's the use of pictures,' he would say to a donor, 'when I've nowhere to put them?'; or, 'What's the use of this gallery when I've nothing to hang on the walls?' Potential benefactors were lured to Cambridge and given, like Sir Horace Timberlake in Sir Charles Snow's *The Masters*, the 'V.I.P.' treatment. Loan objects had a mysterious way of ending up as gifts. Sometimes Cockerell would bait a hook, accepting with much show of gratitude a poorish picture in the hope of extracting better ones later on. It is said that on one occasion, when a collector indicated several objects which might possibly be left to the Museum, Cockerell immediately wrote 'For the Fitzwilliam' labels and stuck them on the backs. Among the waste paper left behind one day after a Syndicate meeting in 1934 was found a doodle that was happily saved from destruction; it is entitled, 'St. Cockrellius RELIEVING a poore traveller of a manuscript.'

Nine times out of ten Cockerell's vigorous policy reaped a harvest. '*You* won't be any good,' he (quite mistakenly) told the present Director, Dr. Carl Winter; 'you aren't *aggressive* enough.' But there were occasions when he struck too hard and so defeated his object; times when 'the bullying and wire-pulling for which I am so justly famous' did not work. Of course he studied his victims, sometimes preferring the velvet glove to the mailed fist. Then he would resort to guile, flattery, cajolery. He would appeal to the man's generosity, vanity, patriotism, sense of duty, sense of gratitude, sense of shame, or whatever appeared most likely to touch his heart and loosen his purse-strings. In the compilation of these coaxing letters he was unrivalled; yet even the velvet glove was known to fail. There was, for example, the sad case of the Yates Thompson manuscripts.

As far back as 1898 Lethaby had expressed the hope, doubtless shared by Cockerell, that this important collection would be kept together. In a letter that is almost as illegible as it is illiterate, Lethaby had then written to Cockerell, 'Don't let Y.T. dribble away his MSS. they must get lost sight of one in a place they are better in big collections: you cd talk him over "famous collection" sort of thing better big.' When Yates Thompson was about eighty he became almost totally blind with cataract in both eyes; he therefore came to the conclusion that he would sell his collection. Like the Goncourts, he had derived great pleasure from buying in the sale-room, and like them he decided that his manuscripts should pass to those whom he called 'les héritiers de mes goûts.'

Cockerell was indignant when he was told. On 24th January 1918 he wrote to Yates Thompson:

Since I saw you and last heard from you, what you have told me of your intention to sell your manuscripts has been a constant weight and dragging oppression on my mind — a sort of wound of which I am almost never unconscious. Each day I have meant to write to you, but have not had the heart. You may suppose that this feeling of sorrow and dismay is due in part to personal disappointment in connection with this Museum. But it is not so.

It is true that I regard the Fitzwilliam as an ideal destination for such a collection as yours — by reason of its being already recognized as a place offering singular advantages to students of manuscripts, because bequests to it are free of legacy duty, and because of the lucky chance that I can undertake for myself and my successors to build a handsome and suitable room for its permanent exhibition in cleaner air than that of London — and I think that the Fitzwilliam has some claim to your favourable consideration, seeing how largely your manuscripts have been elucidated by two of its Directors. Yet I have not seriously cherished the hope that you would bequeath them to us.

I had assumed that you would leave them to Mrs. Thompson, who has shared with you the pleasure of collecting them — which would be in the highest degree natural and appropriate — or perhaps to Trinity College, or to some other institution with which you have been closely associated. Your collection as it stands, gathered together with rare taste and judgment during a quarter of a century which has been rich in opportunities, is now splendidly complete. In its way it is quite without a rival. Kept together it is one of the great artistic and spiritual assets of England. That you should be willing to scatter it, unless for good reasons that you have not disclosed, seems to me — and would seem to others, were I at liberty to speak of it — lamentable in the extreme. Neither I nor anyone else who has helped in the shaping of it has ever contemplated the possibility of your knocking to pieces in your lifetime the unique edifice which has been put together with such enthusiastic pains.

I say that I have helped in the shaping of it. With what pride and zeal I have done so and have sought out facts concerning it I do not think you have ever realized.

It was through me that you obtained the glorious Lancelot du Lac. Neither from the seller nor from the buyer did I seek or receive any remuneration. I may have expected thanks, but I got them from neither side.

It was through me that you obtained the Isabelle Psalter (and its missing leaves), the Yolande of Flanders Horae (and its additional leaves), the Brantwood Bible. I can show you a letter from Mrs. Severn offering me a commission that would have amounted to £500 on the sale of the first of these. This I declined—but it is right to add that I bought from her for the price that Ruskin had given a Bible that was at that time worth a higher price, so I certainly received on this transaction a 'consideration' of an indirect kind, though not a large one. On the other three transactions I declined any kind of commission. Moreover I discovered and drew your attention to the St. Cuthbert MS., the Ste. Chapelle Epistolar, and the first volume of the Duc de Berry Vincent of Beauvais. It was also on my recommendation that you bought the Hegesippus, and I think the Sherbrooke Missal.

I say nothing of the Dugesclin and of the Sinibaldi Horae, for the purchase of which you paid me, or of the three books that you bought from my own collection. Setting these aside there are eight or ten of your hundred MSS., and these among the best, that I have enabled you to procure. There is another, the Salvin Horae, that you owe to Dr. James.

If you are not to be shaken from your present intention to sell these, I appeal to you, in the name of your old University, to put them in a class apart, and to give me the chance of raising the money and securing them for the country and Cambridge at the price you paid for them. I do not say that, in these increasingly difficult times, I can be certain of doing this — but if you will give me the chance and a time limit I will at least try my utmost to save them from the hands of ignorant millionaires who do not know how to handle or appreciate such inestimable treasures.

Yates Thompson replied:

When in strict confidence I told you my intentions with regard to the 100 MSS. I hoped and thought I should hear no more on the points you raised.

Also in strict confidence I now add that in regard of one of the MSS. which I had by bequest I propose that its final destination shall be the Fitzwilliam Museum on conditions which I shall I hope arrange satisfactorily with you if you become reasonable and not too purely Cockerellian on the subject. I think you will understand my views on the matter more clearly when you have dwelt 30 years longer on this planet.[1]

Conscious that he was defeated, Cockerell accepted the promise of this manuscript, the Metz Pontifical — 'in some ways the most interesting manuscript in your collection' — with as good a grace as he could muster. He concluded his letter, 'But as to being Cockerellian, I am that, for good or ill, because I am myself and can't be otherwise, and I shall remain so to the end of the chapter.'

Yates Thompson arranged that most of his manuscripts should be disposed of by Sotheby's in three sales; these duly took place and very big prices were realised. But shortly before the last sale, and too late to stop its being held, he had an operation for cataract and recovered his sight; he therefore bought in some of his own books and started to collect again. This new collection he bequeathed to his wife.

[1] Yates Thompson was born in 1838 and was therefore nearly thirty years Cockerell's senior.

Mrs. Yates Thompson had long been irritated by Cockerell's domineering manner and by his tacit assumption that it was for him to decide where her husband's collection should go; she therefore pointedly left it, not to the Fitzwilliam but to the British Museum. Meanwhile Cockerell had taken his revenge by refusing to write an obituary notice of Yates Thompson for *The Times*. 'He treated me decently on the whole,' he said, 'and we were mutually indebted. But I wasn't going to be bullied by a man with a lot of money; I couldn't do it without more affection for him. After his death, his wife wouldn't have anything to do with me, and I think that was the reason.' It was a sad ending to a long association with the woman whom he had once described as 'Yates Thompson's wonderful wife'.

And sometimes there were failures for which he could not be held responsible. There was the wretched affair of the bronze-gilt statuette of David by Donatello that Fairfax Murray had lent to the Fitzwilliam:

14th February 1918. Went to London by the 3.51 taking with me Mr. Fairfax Murray's exquisite little statuette by Donatello. He told me last Friday that he would sell it for £10,000 to a private buyer and for £6000 to the Fitz-william. I took it to Otto Beit who agreed to pay £6000 for it, to bequeath it to the Museum, and to lend it to us for three months in each year. Greatly pleased I went to Fairfax Murray with the news and he asked for a day for consideration.

15th February 1918. Fetched the statuette from Belgrave Sq. and took it to Albemarle St. to receive Murray's answer. To my surprise, disappointment and indignation he utterly denied that he had offered it to the Museum for £6,000. Unhappily owing to his state of health (he has had two strokes) his memory has gone to pieces, and he accused me of having no memory! I burst out of his room in a rage and went round to Bond St. to consult Lockett

Agnew. To my dismay I learnt that he had just died of angina pectoris. I went back to Murray and broke the news to him, Lockett Agnew being his executor and in charge of his affairs. We made up our quarrel, and agreed to say no more about the statuette. It is the greatest disappointment I have suffered since I came to Cambridge.

13th November 1919. Went to London by 9.5 with Fairfax Murray's little 'Donatello' statuette of David, which the executors had written for. Went to see Pierpont Morgan and Otto Beit in the city in the hope that they might help me to buy it. P.M. was very nice and said that he was 'good for a thousand or two.' Beit, who had made a very generous offer in Feb. 1917, declined to renew it. . . . Went on to Mr. Dorney, 5 Clifford St., to whom I delivered the statuette. He told me about his recent visit to Florence and of the threat of Fairfax Murray's Italian sons to dispute the will.

There can be little doubt that Fairfax Murray's ill health was the cause of this unhappy misunderstanding. Murray had for many years been a most generous (and often anonymous) benefactor of the Fitzwilliam. 'He was a very wonderful little man,' said Cockerell. 'He had bow legs—like that'—and he made a gesture with his hands—'so that he was always very visible in the street. His origins were very humble. As a boy he had worked in a draper's shop and slept under the counter. He taught himself to draw, and he was very well read. He was a worthy companion of Rossetti and Morris.'

But how few were Cockerell's failures in comparison with his many triumphant successes! Besides the Marlay bequest and the great benefactions of the Courtauld family, which will be described in due course, there came to the Fitzwilliam in Cockerell's time, and entirely through his energetic campaigning, the Leverton Harris maiolica, the Glaisher ceramics, the Charrington engravings, and splendid works of art from Charles Shannon, Charles Ricketts, Thomas Riches, Charles Fairfax Murray and hundreds of other generous donors. The acquisitions of a single year, 1936, have been described as 'almost enough material to stock a respectable museum.' As somebody once said, Cockerell was not so much the 'curator' as the 'creator' of the Fitzwilliam as we see it today, and his eminent successors have been able to do little more than maintain what he created.

2

LIFE AT CAMBRIDGE

FROM what has been told of Cockerell's battles over the Fitzwilliam, it might be imagined that he had no friends at Cambridge. This was very far from being true. He was a man to whom people always reacted strongly. He made no secret of his opinion that 'Universities are all uncivilized; dons are specialists in one subject, but are otherwise largely uneducated,'[1] and not unnaturally there were some who decided that he was self-opinionated, cock-sure, brash. But he also had many devoted friends and warm supporters who admired his energy and enthusiasm, his integrity, courage and kindness.

Cambridge had shown its traditional hospitality to a newcomer. At the close of 1908 Cockerell wrote in his diary, 'Kate and I have been received with the utmost cordiality on all sides. I have been made an M.A. and have received abundant other marks of good will from members of the University. Cambridge seems full of nice people with whom it is easy to make friends.' He was invited to dine at high tables, to College feasts, and with Kate to private dinner parties; with his unerring instinct for gravitation towards the great ('always', he once said, 'try to be with people better than yourself'), he was soon able to count many of the most famous Cambridge figures of the day among his particular friends.

[1] More than thirty years later he said to a young man who was considering becoming a don, that the career 'had grave limitations, that the Universities were like aquariums cut off from the bracing rough and tumble of the open sea, and that at the average high table conversation had to be restricted to non-controversial subjects for fear of offending susceptibilities.'

Not long after Cockerell's arrival in Cambridge his first child, Margaret,[1] was born. 'We have been gladdened today by the arrival of a sturdy little daughter,' he informed Lethaby; and to Katie he wrote proudly: 'She is probably hideous to outside eyes, but we find her rather attractive.' A son, Christopher,[2] followed in 1910. and a second daughter, Katharine,[3] in 1911. The small furnished house in Cavendish Avenue was changed, and changed again, as the family grew.[4]

Kate had learned to adapt herself to her husband's little ways, and they were happy together. On the second anniversary of their wedding he wrote: 'We agree, Kate and I, that our marriage has been the greatest possible success.' The infant Margaret, at six months, was 'very fit and fascinating. She sits up and blows the whistle at the end of her bauble when told to do so.' A week later she swallowed (but restored) a ruby from her mother's brooch. '1st November 1909. Margaret tried to blow out the sun, but was fortunately unsuccessful.' Kate enjoyed the company of her children, though they made great demands on her time, and drew them as they played in the garden. But she could no longer concentrate sufficiently to carry on with her illumination;[5] she found an outlet for her talent, however, in designing the dresses for Cambridge operatic productions; those for 'The Magic Flute' won (wrote her husband) 'an extraordinary artistic success.' 'It was mounted magnificently,' he said, 'at a cost of nothing at all.'

[1] Married Mr. Anthony Minns in 1935 and has three sons.

[2] Inventor of the Hovercraft. Married Miss Margaret Belsham in 1937 and has two daughters.

[3] Married the Rev. John Laughton in 1937 and has three sons and one daughter.

[4] Mr. de Navarro wrote: 'When he was moving house I went to help him pack his books. "I am going to make you my waste-paper basket," he remarked; and I thus became the recipient of several volumes which I treasure to this day.'

[5] After their marriage, Cockerell had gradually prevailed upon her to abandon the painting of pictures (as opposed to illumination). Although she had become known as an artist under her maiden name, he insisted upon her signing her work with her married name—and thus lost her many commissions.

Kate also ran a little weekly drawing-class which was attended by a few local amateurs who took it in turn to 'sit'.

The Cockerells were very hospitable, and fortunately their maid, whose name was Mayzod Tryphena Wesley ('of course we have to pay her extra, but it is worth it'), was a treasure. Cockerell's old friends came in a steady flow to look him up and to be shown his latest improvements at the Fitzwilliam. Naturally Walker, Lethaby and St. John Hornby were among the first to appear. Wilfrid Blunt and Lady Anne came—on separate occasions. Thomas Hardy, Kipling, Bertrand Russell, Lady Burne-Jones, John Sargent, Roger Fry, Ricketts and Shannon, Charles Holmes, Doughty, Gilbert Murray, Laurence Binyon, W. B. Yeats and Walter Sickert all came to his house, and the Bernard Shaws paid him many visits. 'My wife was too shy to give dinner parties,' Cockerell said, 'but we became rather famous for our Sunday tea parties. I was nibbled at by all the young men at Cambridge interested in art.'

But it was not only shyness that prevented Kate from giving dinner parties. Cockerell was not sympathetic to the apparatus that a woman needs for formal entertaining. The house was cold and carpetless and ugly: there might be money for a book or a work of art, or for a friend who was down on his luck; but there was none for a new dress for Kate, a bottle of sherry, a lick of paint to the woodwork, or even for a hot-water system that worked. Kate was acutely conscious of this austerity and ugliness. Tea parties, however, could be managed. These continued to take place with little change of pattern throughout the thirty years that the Cockerells were in Cambridge, and Christopher Cockerell's description of them as he remembered them in the late twenties may therefore be given here:

> People just dropped in [he wrote], and we sat round a rather high table designed by Philip Webb, on Morris chairs with the bobbles of the turned parts sticking into one's back. Father sat at one end, Mother at the other amongst a multitude of tea-cups and an almond-iced cake from Hawkins'. If Mr. de Navarro (Toty), Dorothy Hawksley, Ethel Lindgren or certain other habitués whose names I

have forgotten were there, then Father soon had them talking and the whole table in fits of laughter. Or it could be a bit dull, with a table full of undergraduates trying to be even more highbrow than they really were. The rest of the family said nothing; and when one comes to think of it Father didn't say anything memorable either, but just kept poking the fire of conversation until it glowed. He could get anybody talking if he wished to; but heaven help us all if there was even a single person at the table who wasn't a kindred spirit.

Tea finished, he invited the various people he liked into his study to look at books, and the rest of us stayed with Mother — and relaxed.[1]

Among those who willingly accepted the bait and in the pre-First War days regularly attended the Cockerells' 'tea and books' were (Sir) Geoffrey Keynes, (Sir) Steuart Wilson, Leigh-Mallory and Rupert Brooke. Of Brooke, Cockerell said, 'I can remember little about him except that he was extremely beautiful. After taking his tripos he said he would never open a Greek or Latin book again.' Cockerell omitted to mention that he and Brooke jointly organized a lecture-demonstration of folk music and dancing at Cambridge, given by Cecil Sharp and Mary Neal with the help of the girls of their Espérance Club. Cockerell was always keenly interested in folk dancing and later became first President of the Cambridge branch of the English Folk Dance Society, his successor being Vaughan Williams.

With undergraduates Cockerell found himself very much at his ease, and they for their part appreciated the interest that he took in them. 'I love these young men,' he told Wilfrid Blunt, 'and gather them round me at the Museum and on Sundays at home.' But he was soon to learn what every don and every schoolmaster must learn: that friendships between the middle-aged and the young are like those board-ship romances which rarely survive the end of the voyage. After ten years at Cambridge he wrote to Katie:

[1] In a communication to the Author.

The young men that I get to know here can only give a tiny fraction of their affection to a man more than old enough to be their father. Now and then they lean on me a little — but the terms here are very short and when they go out into the great world something like mutual forget-fulness ensues. They are like waves of the sea, each wave breaking over the receding stream of its predecessor. Of the older residents in Cambridge there is not one that counts for a moment with the friends of my earlier days — you and Walker and the rest.

There were the young women too, and usually a reigning queen of the moment; one girl was not a little abashed at being informed that she was 'S.'s successor.' Miss Etta Addis (Mrs. Edmund Booth) recalls, in a letter to Cockerell, her visits to his house in the twenties, when she was at Newnham:

My three years at Cambridge . . . are for ever coloured by my association with 3 Shaftesbury Road. I remember the dining-room with the Blake drawing, and the study lined with books and hung with Morris curtains, and the garden with the acacia tree, where you and I used to play at bowls and you always beat me. On my first visit I arrived too early and you put me on a chair in your study and gave me an exquisite Roxburghe book of Henry VIII songs to look at. You showed me the reddish-gold hair of Rossetti's wife in a locket, and you let me look at Lady Cockerell's beautiful manuscripts and handle many of your books. I met Charlotte Mew[1] at your house, pale and withdrawn, and Mary Anderson with only her luminous eyes to recall her past beauty. And one cold day you wrapped me round in an Arab cloak, remarking that the last person who had put it on was Bernard Shaw. It was a very great privilege to be allowed free entry to

---

[1] In 1923, with the help of Hardy, Masefield and de la Mare, Cockerell secured a Civil List pension of £75 a year for her—a pension that she tried to relinquish because she found she could no longer write. She committed suicide in 1928.

your home, and I am more than ever grateful now that I realise more how illustrious were your real friends.

In the first two or three years of their marriage, the Cockerells were able to take a number of little holidays together, either on their own or as the guests of one or other of Cockerell's friends. But before long Kate became increasingly tied by the demands made upon her by a young family. Cockerell, however, often went away alone — to Blunt at Newbuildings or the Lyttons at Crabbet; to the Yates Thompsons at Oving, Lady Burne-Jones at Rottingdean, Mrs. Morris at Kelmscott, Hardy at Dorchester or Doughty at Eastbourne. The hospitable Leverton Harrises and Lambs were always available when he needed peace for the distasteful job of writing his annual report. Fitzwilliam business also took him to Chatsworth, Windsor and elsewhere.

One particular continental holiday of his deserves to be mentioned, because it reveals him in the curious and distasteful role of male nurse. His patient was Charles Butler, and his place of imprisonment Aix-les-Bains. 'Butler,' said Cockerell, 'was very rich, very old, very pernickety; he had a huge collection of books and pictures. He had treated me very kindly,[1] and when he became ill — or imagined himself ill — none of his family would go away with him. So *I* went.'

Butler and his unwilling companion arrived at Aix on 23rd July — 'C.B. none the worse for the journey, though he declared that he was dying. I got Dr. Rendall to see him, and he did his best to reassure the old man — whose state of self-centred misery is very pitiful. This huge luxurious hotel is quite full of rich overfed people, chiefly Americans. I don't know how I shall stand it for a whole month;' and to Nell Wilks he wrote that the fat visitors reminded him of Heine's remark that it was easier for a camel to enter the Kingdom of Heaven than for such persons to go through the eye of a needle.

'24th July. Mr. B. still full of complaint and most exasperating. . . .' '26th July. Mr. B. more dejected than ever. . . .'

---

[1] For some years past he had been giving Cockerell £100 annually.

'28th July. Mr. B. declared that he was weaker and in a state of unspeakable mental agony, but I thought him better. . . .' And so the miserable days dragged by. Sometimes Cockerell managed to escape for a few hours, either to walk in the surrounding countryside or to work on the catalogue for the Burlington Fine Arts Club exhibition that he was organizing. Then, on 11th August, Mr. Butler developed an ulcer on the neck and the doctor — 'to my intense relief' — advised his returning to England. On 16th August Mr. Butler, 'complaining as usual', was safely restored to the unwilling bosom of his family. He died the following June, in his ninetieth year.

In March 1910 Cockerell was elected to a Fellowship at Jesus, tenable for six years and not renewable.[1] He was, very naturally, delighted; not only did it afford him a proper status in the University, but it made it easier for him to give potential benefactors the kind of entertainment best calculated to encourage them to disgorge their treasures. It was, however, to have one grave disadvantage: it was to keep him much away from home in the evenings.

Had Cockerell been given a free choice, it is unlikely that he would have selected Jesus — an athletic College with a

[1] 'His surname provided an obvious target for the [Jesus] undergraduate magazine ["Chanticlere"] . . . which acknowledged his arrival in these appropriate verses:

> Thrice welcome, brother, to our run!
> The Fates to thee be gracious!
> For never have we hailed a one
> So truly gallinaceous.

> Thy fellow roosters may'st thou see
> To be of goodly breeding
> And thy election never be
> Adjudged a foul proceeding!

The author of these lines may or may not have been a member of the Jesus club called the Roosters, founded in 1907, with the cockerel as the centre of its curious ritual and vocabulary of later years.' (Arthur Gray and Frederick Brittain, *A History of Jesus College Cambridge*, Heinemann, 1960, p. 188.)

frivolous and hearty element among the younger dons. 'I am afraid we were rather a ribald lot, and we pulled his leg a good deal,' said one who was his contemporary there. 'He wouldn't enter into the spirit of it. I don't think he had much sense of humour; and he was always so sure that he was right. Later he had his name taken off the books.' 'But he earned his keep,' said another, 'by introducing interesting guests to the high table.' Probably Cockerell would have been happier with A. C. Benson and his intellectual friends at Magdalene. Certainly Benson appreciated him better than did the rowing men at Jesus, though he was far from being blind to Cockerell's shortcomings. In his diary (26th July 1911) Benson wrote:

> Cockerell came to lunch, and we have had a dignified duet about art and artistic things and artistic people. I took him round my various decorations. He half-approves, but not very cordially. He is rather a purist, of course, and doesn't like anything which is not authoritarian. But I always like a talk to Cockerell; he is simple, direct, rather *fierce*, very sure of his opinion, not sympathetic; he is like an old-fashioned Evangelist, with the difference that he worships beauty in his way.

It had long been apparent to Cockerell that the salary he was receiving as Director of the Fitzwilliam was ludicrously small by any standards. His Fellowship had temporarily improved his financial position, but in 1911, with the arrival of his third child, he once more found himself in difficulties. His diary for 23rd January 1912 announces the opening of a new campaign: 'Fitzwilliam Syndicate meeting. I raised my cry for an increase of pay.' Three days later he addressed the following letter to the Vice-Chancellor, *ex officio* Chairman of the Syndics:

> I regret to find that in my remarks to the Syndicate on Monday I made a small mistake as to the stipends at the Ashmolean Museum. There are two Keepers, one in charge of the Antiquities, the other in charge of the

pictures and drawings. The senior of these, whichever he may happen to be, receives £675 a year, the junior £575. At the present time they both hold Fellowships. . . . The visitors to the Ashmolean are about half as many as those to the Fitzwilliam.

It is obvious that Museums like those of Oxford and Cambridge demand the constant activity and pre-occupation of at least one man who is widely in touch with the world of artists, connoisseurs and collectors. Apart from questions of arrangement and administration, our endowments do not allow of any purchases worth mentioning and it is therefore the business of the Director to keep the Museum from stagnation by means of loans and gifts and by any other means in his power. During my term of office — i.e. in less than four years — I have been responsible for:

(1) Friday opening.

(2) Sunday opening.

(3) Appointment of Honorary Keepers of the Coins, Prints, Egyptian Antiquities, Pictures and Music — all doing excellent work on the collections.

(4) The establishment of the Friends of the Fitzwilliam, who have subscribed a sum of £760.

(5) Donations of pictures and other works of art of the value of many thousands of pounds.

(6) Constant loans of important works of art (often leading to donations), including terminal loans by the King and the Duke of Devonshire.

(7) Promises of bequests of very great value.

(8) The conversion of the featureless landing into a ceramic gallery.

(9) The exhibition of the McClean manuscripts.

(10) Cheap illustrated Catalogue of the pictures (now in preparation).

My hours of attendance have been more than double the very insufficient number fixed by the Regulations. It is in the afternoon, when I am under no obligation to be present, that my presence is most necessary.

It is not solely with a view to pressing my personal claims that I have given these details, but in order to show that there is much that can be either done or left undone and that it will be false economy on the part of the University to regard the present nominal stipend as sufficient to attract future Directors with the necessary equipment and with an experience of the art world that can only be gained away from Cambridge. Much as I appreciated what Dr. Waldstein was kind enough to say about my efforts on behalf of the Museum I could not help hoping that on reconsideration he would modify what he said about the payment of my successors.

On 30th April, at a meeting of the Syndicate, Cockerell was informed that the University 'regretted its inability' to increase his stipend. But it would appear that the Syndicate, and no doubt Cockerell himself, fought on, for on 4th June he wrote, 'Syndicate meeting. It seems likely that I shall get another £200 a year as a result of the action of the Syndicate and of an anonymous promiser of £100 a year for 5 years, whom I take to be Yates Thompson.'

It was now that Cockerell had one of those strokes of good fortune that so often came his way, though it was occasioned by the death of a friend. Less than three weeks after learning that his salary had been raised by £200 a year, the death of Charles Brinsley Marlay brought to the Fitzwilliam, not merely the greatest bequest that it had received since its foundation, but to its Director, as 'Marlay Curator', an additional £550 a year (to be reduced to £350 so long as he held his Fellowship at Jesus).

'It was *I* who *landed* this big fish,' said Cockerell. 'I had known Marlay for some time. He was an uncle of the Duke of Rutland; he lived in Regent's Park and he was very rich. But he was a bargain-hunter. Bargain-hunters are no use: you must pay top prices for the best, and ten years later you'll feel ashamed how little it was. However he had good things as well. He showed an inclination to leave his collection to the Fitzwilliam. I said I must have money to build a gallery to house it, and he promised me £50,000. "That's all very well," I wrote to him (I was staying with the Duke of Devonshire at the time), "but what about a staff?" He promised another £30,000 — and we also got the lease of his house, which we sold for another £10,000.'

Marlay was a man of catholic tastes, and his collection included pictures, drawings, engravings, furniture, manuscripts and printed books, and *objets d'art*. But, realizing that many of the objects were unworthy of 'my' Museum (as Cockerell always called the Fitzwilliam), Cockerell had cunningly persuaded him to authorize the sale of anything 'modern, imitation, or of too low a standard for an important museum,' the proceeds to be used for enriching the Marlay collection.

Unlike the Ashmolean Museum at Oxford, which was hemmed in on all sides by buildings, the Fitzwillian had ample room to expand. The adjacent Grove Lodge property was purchased from Peterhouse, and Messrs. Smith and Brewer invited to draw up plans for an extension. Then came the War, and an end, for the time being, to any possibility of building.

3

FAMILY AFFAIRS

LIKE many other towns in England, Cambridge expected
to find itself the first objective of an invading army. But
before taking steps to safeguard the contents of his
Museum, Cockerell rushed to Paris to rescue a group of his
wife's illuminated manuscripts which had been on exhibition
at the Louvre. Then he arranged for the smaller treasures of
the Fitzwilliam — the ivories, coins, gems, enamels and finer
manuscripts — to be stored away. The Museum remained open,
however, throughout the War.

About half the undergraduates and many of the younger
dons have taken officers' commissions [he wrote]. On
31st August wounded men began to arrive to fill a temporary hospital arranged in the broad cloisters of Trinity
College. An 'open-air' hospital has since been erected in
the King's playing field with beds for at least a thousand
men. They come and go in batches every few days and
are so familiar a sight in our streets as to be scarcely
noticed. In August the sixth Division — 20,000 splendid
fellows — was encamped in various parts of the town, the
officers dining in the College halls. We had at Jesus the
Durhams and the W. Yorkshires. Early in September
they left for the front and I suppose that more than half
of them have been killed or wounded. . . . The Colleges,
and all the members of the teaching staff of the University who are dependent on fees, lose heavily by the
reduced numbers of the undergraduates. Two of our

friends, Charles Geoffroy-Dechaume and Steuart Wilson, have been wounded. . . .

In November Cockerell resigned his Fellowship at Jesus 'in order that someone in poorer circumstances might take my place, and J. M. Edmonds, a good scholar and a nice man, was elected.' It appeared to be a generous gesture; but since Cockerell was allowed to retain his room in College and the privilege of bringing guests to the high table, and since the Marlay bequest made good the loss of salary, his circumstances remained unchanged.

Cockerell suffered some unpopularity in Jesus for his 'supposed pessimism'—or what he preferred to call his refusal 'to shut out all disagreeables and cling to every crumb of comfort in the newspapers, however worthless. . . . I try to envisage the situation in all its aspects and to know the worst as well as the best that can happen.' There is reason to believe that his confidence in the efficiency of the Germans did make him a defeatist, and doubtless he aired his opinions with a candour and a cocksureness that were irritating. Since he was forty-seven there was, of course, no question of his enlisting. For war work he conducted parties of wounded, chiefly Colonials, round the Colleges, and helped to compile a register of resident University men ready to offer their services to the Government.

He also took compassion upon one or two of the young officers who were training in Cambridge. Among these was Mr. Siegfried Sassoon, who wrote later:

I had known Cockerell since August 1915, when I was at Cambridge for a month's course with the Officers' Training Corps. Introduced by a letter from Mr. Gosse, I had spent several evenings at his house—evenings made memorable by the wonderful books he showed me—and from which I returned to my camp bed in Pembroke College in a trance of stimulation after having handled manuscripts of D. G. Rossetti, William Morris and Francis Thompson. From the first he had taken a strong and kindly interest in me. On those Sunday nights in the quiet candle-lit room he seemed a sort of bearded and spectacled magician, conjuring up the medieval illuminated missals and psalters on which he was a famous expert, and bringing my mind into almost living contact with the Pre-Raphaelites whom I had worshipped since my dreaming adolescence. Brusque and uncompromising, his light blue eyes regarded me somewhat austerely as he handed me yet another treasure to gloat over. People were sometimes offended by his plain-spoken manner; but to be contradicted by Cockerell was an education; and no doubt I offered him numerous opportunities to do so. More often than not, however, he received my incautious demonstrations of ignorance with a lenient laugh. . . . He was indeed a man who had been born to become, through his practical abilities, the trusted adviser of great writers. In this he might be compared with Henry Crabb Robinson, the diarist and associate of the poets of the Romantic Revival. But he will be better remembered for his directorship of the Fitzwilliam Museum, which he re-created, amplified, and enriched through thirty years of selfless service.[1]

On the last day of 1913 Kate had written to her husband:

Dearest,
A most happy new year to you and may your shadow never grow less. For my part I believe that this last has been about the most happy year of my life, so that it has often crossed my mind that something horrible *must* happen soon, so please mind the crossings as all the lamp of happiness would go quite out if you were made into a paper fashion plate by a motor bus. . . .

To Cockerell, however, nothing untoward happened; it was at the world in general, and at Kate in particular, that Fate

[1] *Siegfried's Journey, 1916–1920* (1945).

struck. One day in 1912 Kate had unaccountably fallen down in the street; but such things happen, and there had seemed no cause for anxiety. Before long, however, she fell again—and then again, till there was soon, wrote Cockerell, 'an abatement, amounting almost to a cessation, of her walking powers.' In the summer of 1916, disseminated sclerosis was diagnosed. She was only forty-four, and the mother of three young children.

Little enough is known, even today, of this terrible disease. Fifty years ago, arsenic, heat and light treatments were prescribed, but they were powerless to help. Sometimes there seemed to be a slight improvement in her condition; then followed the inevitable relapse. During the thirty-three years of life that remained to her, the overall pattern was one of increasing helplessness. The pain increased; there were times when she lost heart—'and no wonder,' wrote Cockerell. Though she came to learn how to live with her disability, and how to fill her long days with petty occupations, she could not blind herself to the fact that she had become a burden to the man she continued to love. . . .

Cockerell, so sure of himself as a rule, did not know how to face this crisis. He had his work to do—and might not the world be more enriched by the man who put his career before his wife or his family? He had his friends to visit, his hobbies to pursue. But as he went about his business or his pleasure, there was always the gnawing feeling that he was not doing enough for his wife. He fetched Hardy's bath-chair from Dorset, but the man he engaged to push it was knocked down by a runaway milk-float. He wheeled it himself—'but not quite so often as I ought to have done, as I afterwards thought,' he said sadly.

Kate felt her position acutely. On 4th January 1918 she wrote to her husband:[1]

When one is ill all the weakness gets the upper hand and one calls out unreasonably. Really when you come to the bottom of things all I want is a little sympathy and it is

[1] The letter from Cockerell to which this is an answer has not survived.

all you want either, and I know that very often I don't
give it you. About my not entering into your interests,
that has distressed me more than you know. In the first
years here I was quite swallowed up by trying to adjust
myself to a totally new life and to cope with arriving
babies. And perhaps you forget that when you were at
Jesus for 6 years you were not often at home for more
than twice a week, and then, what with guests and household details, there was little time for me to find out how
you really spent your life. And now it is very difficult for.
you to overcome habits of indifference or for me habits of
mental stagnation. You need not think that I don't know
your good qualities or my own innumerable blessings. . . .

In a letter to the Author, a woman who was up at Cambridge
in the twenties has vividly recalled an occasion when Cockerell
involuntarily betrayed the distress that his wife's illness
caused him. She wrote:

Mr. Cockerell had been showing me some of his treasures
one winter afternoon, when from behind the long
William Morris curtain, which divided his study from the
room where Mrs. Cockerell lay in bed, there gradually
came the sound of moaning. He took no notice, and it was
agonizing for both of us. I rose to go, and then a queru-
lous[1] voice came, 'Sydney, *when* is the nurse coming
back?' He answered almost brusquely, 'Not long now,'
and then, giving me a strange fierce look, kissed me. This
was such a new experience for me that I had no idea how
to take it. Not another word was said. I left the house, and
the incident was never repeated. I think, now, that it was
a sign of his intense unhappiness, and his inability to cope
with such misery at close quarters. . . .

One at least of Cockerell's children came to realize that Kate
was feeling neglected. In 1927, when Katharine (then aged

---

[1] Kate rarely complained, and never in the presence of her children.
She was more ill than usual at the time of this visit.

sixteen) was about to go with her father on a Mediterranean cruise, she wrote him a touching letter asking whether her mother might not come with them:

> I know of someone who would love to come too, and it would do her so much good. It would be such bliss for her not to think of housekeeping and meals, and so nice for her to enter in with us and not feel that she was being left out. She misses so much every day, so it would be so lovely. I will undertake to wait on her; she could see a lot from the ship. She would be alone while we were on shore but there are sure to be more people who do not go on shore every time. Well, just *think* it over. . . . I have not told her that I am writing and asking you this. Please don't think it horrid of me to ask (never harm in asking). I expect your answer will be 'no' but it would be nice to be 'yes'.

The answer was, alas! 'no'.

Four years later, Katharine was staying in Cornwall and wrote to her father:

> I hope so much that you will not discourage Mother from coming down. Oh don't please do not for even 6 weeks here for her, would be as much joy as 4 weeks for you and I on the 'Ranchi', see, if it were only the excitement of moving of going any ware. But it is not really for me to remind you of this for you must feel her position perhaps even more than I . . .

At that moment, however, Cockerell was engaged in a pitched battle with the Syndics about the reconstruction of the Central Gallery of the Fitzwilliam, and his diary does not record Kate's movements. Indeed, as the years passed, Kate's name occurs but rarely in his diaries (and hence in this book); sometimes he makes no mention of it for weeks, even for months, at a stretch, and, as several of his friends were to point out when his two volumes of letters were published, her portrait is only to be found in a snapshot group where Bernard Shaw is the *raison d'être*.

Through the years that followed, Kate struggled on. After her family, perhaps her greatest pleasure was her garden, in which her husband took little interest. Perched on a small stool, she managed to keep the more accessible weeds under control, and to tend the polyanthuses which were her particular favourites. Her shyness still tormented her; when Charlotte Mew, the poet, died in 1928 Kate wrote, 'She was one of the few people I have known, with whom I could be quite intimate without the fear of being laughed at.' 'I realize,' she wrote four years later, 'that most of my health and strength is bluff—and what a narrow margin there is between me and disaster.' Gradually the margin narrowed still further, till at the last she became totally bedridden.

'My life has been an intensely happy one,' Cockerell said. 'There was nothing in it that I would have wished otherwise.' He paused, then added—'except, of course, for poor Kate's illness.'

'Women,' he once told his son, 'are inferior to men;' and this may explain how he could say, with all truth, to an intimate friend, 'I have never understood my wife.'

On 10th November 1915 Kate wrote to her husband:

> It often grieves me very much that you don't try to see more of the children, because if you don't make intimate friends of them now you will never be able to, and it will make you awfully unhappy when they are bigger when you will want to help them and won't be able to get near them. I have still only to look at my father's photograph to feel courageous and you can be much more to these children than he could be to me.

It was, as we have seen, of Kate, rather than of his children, that he saw so sadly little. Cockerell may have had a low opinion of dons in general, but the high table at Jesus gave him a platform; he enjoyed dining there, and not infrequently stayed the night in College. In London, St. John Hornby and other friends were always ready to give him dinner and a bed. His diaries suggest that during the early years of the War he by no means neglected his children, whose little sayings he often jotted down:

> 29th November 1916. Margaret (aged 8) and Christopher (aged 6) walking with me before tea, showed that they were already perplexed by the great mysteries. Margaret asked who made God, and what there was before the world was made.
>
> Christopher asked whether when we are dead we should remember being alive, and they both said they were always wondering whether we had lived before and how we should live again. Margaret thought that we should perhaps live again as birds. Then she said that after we were dead we should be part of history. We should be talked of as 'the people who lived in the reign of King George.' Dined in Trinity . . .

But by degrees the first excitement of paternity began to wear off. Kate was to be proved right: Cockerell, though he was fond of his children and was later to be immensely proud of his son's successful career, never understood them. Whether he would have understood them better had he seen more of them must, however, remain an open question; when a man does not marry until he is forty, the age gap between himself and a boisterous young family is dangerously large. And they, for their part, never felt quite at ease with him.

Cockerell would return each evening from the Fitzwilliam and cry out, half jokingly, 'Out of my sight, you *horrible* little children!' Then, more gently, 'Where's my little Childie?' — meaning Katharine. Sometimes he might read to the children by the fireside, his shadow thrown gigantic on the ceiling; but after dinner, if he were not dining out, he would put on his Arab cloak and go to his study to write letters, stacking the envelopes methodically in a neat pile. ('Oh, those letters!'

said his son. 'How we hated letters! the whole house revolved aound letters. They were Priority Number One, whether Mother was ill or whatever else might be happening'). Then came the walk to the pillar-box to catch the last post, after which he would relax and talk with Kate.

In 1924 the three children suddenly announced that they wanted to be baptized, and, rather surprisingly, Cockerell put no obstacle in their way. Margaret was then sixteen, Christopher fourteen, and Katharine thirteen. Margaret had had doubts: 'I don't think I want to be christened yet as I haven't decided what to be,' she had written to her mother a month before. 'I would like to be a Christian Scientist very much or else nothing at all. Besides I may be a Jew because I don't know whether Christ was the true Messiah. These are awful things to write but I really don't know enough about it.' But at the last moment she decided to fall into line with the others.

Christopher was now at Gresham's School, Holt. It was a great disappointment to Cockerell that his son showed an interest in science rather than in the humanities; it seemed to him that the boy was deliberately being perverse. When offered a book, he asked for *The Boy Electrician* rather than a biography of Rembrandt; he wanted a motor bike, not a drawing by Muirhead Bone. When hope was momentarily aroused one holiday by his sudden daily visits to the Fitzwilliam, it was as suddenly dashed by the discovery that he went there only to watch a steam-driven crane that was being used in the construction of the new wing.

Moreover his school reports were none too good. 'I am depressed about my work! I do try! I am not too happy! I do concentrate on my work!' he wrote sadly to his parents. 'Do you really think I am not trying when I am being kept hear at a huge expense, and I know it, just because the French master does not think I try it is no reason to believe it: *I do*, I have slacked twice this term, in all about 10 minutes.'

Two years later the boy takes the offensive: 'You still think I have brains, I have not . . . it shows how unfair people can be. As for changing to Latin its a binge, I shan't get any more marks but probably less, and I hate it. The whole thing is a

binge. . . . It seems hard luck that you should have a son whos
so bad at work, when you, Father, won a schol, with *best* love
from Christopher. P.S. sorry about the writing (I am quite
cheerful you know).' Soon he is busy inventing 'a patent thing
for boiling the water for making tea, and even if you boil it for
an hour, will not make stewed tea.' Already the boy who (so
his father declared) was 'no better than a garage hand' saw
the path that he must take — a path that was one day to bring
him international fame.

It was decided that Christopher should go to Cambridge, and
Cockerell wrote to the Headmaster of Gresham's to say that it
would be a disgrace to the school if he failed in Latin in the
Little-Go. The Headmaster was, reasonably enough, indignant, and Christopher supported him. 'I don't think you can
realize what a dud I am at languages,' he told his father.
'You don't know what it is to be a dud.' One would have
thought that Cockerell, who after fifty visits to France was to
remain incapable of carrying on a simple conversation in what
he rightly called his 'execrable demi-French,'[1] might have
understood — and sympathized.

When Christopher was seventeen he wrote a letter that
should have touched any father's heart:

> I must say I think a person like you has a much more
> interesting life than an engineer can ever have, because
> the people you meet are so much nicer. I think that to be
> an author of good stuff is just about the top of everything,
> even more than a painter or poet. I wish I was built that
> way. I think that you know more interesting *people* than
> any other person that I have ever met. . . . I wish I
> could *talk* to you, I wish we had something in common.
> With best love from
> an admiring son.

Cockerell could not understand that his son was longing to

---

[1] Ruskin always referred to Chartres as 'Charters', and his protégé
may possibly have felt that there was little to be gained by pandering to
the Frenchmen's affected way of pronouncing their own language.

draw closer to him, but that he made this impossible. 'Christopher affected to be indifferent to art,' he said, 'because I was totally unaffected by his mathematical power. He did no good at Cambridge.' Again and again the boy makes overtures of friendship: 'I do want a friend in my Father, one who I can tell anything to and who doesn't scold but still has faith . . .;' 'Ridiculous! I want your friendship, you want mine, but being English it's the very devil to get started . . .'; 'I am longing to conquer shyness, to confide in you.' 'Accept me for what I *am* . . .', he begs. Sometimes there is a rapprochement: 'It's good to feel that in future we pull together. I take back all I've ever said or written against my home.' Then some fresh trouble arises, and the old barrier is back again.

But as the years pass and the children begin to lead their own lives, the tension lessens. When Margaret wishes to study pottery in London, her father, though doubtful of the wisdom of her choice, agrees. Margaret writes to him, 'I think you are wonderfully good, and too kind for anything. It is very generous of you to let me try when you have so little money to spare, and feel that it will not be a success. . . . You're the best father in the world.' Kate too is grateful: 'It is wonderful of you to go on paying for Margaret in town, especially in the face of your disbelief. I am so pleased, because lately I have been distressed by these misunderstandings, and last night I went to bed rather miserable thinking how unhappy you must be to have two philistine children whom you found it hard to like.'

Christopher too, at twenty-eight and recently married, is generously grateful: 'Perhaps the best thanks I can offer is to say that I find life a joy and the world beautiful and each year more thrilling and worthwhile than the last. I'm learning hard, lots of things, and one of them is the debt that I owe to my home.'

In 1940, Christopher wrote, 'It's funny, now I have got interested in beauty, one day I would like you to give me something that you consider beautiful that I can stick up somewhere in our house, shocking isn't it! And it mustn't be contemporary.'

In 1959, Christopher Cockerell's Hovercraft crossed the Channel and so, too late, made Cockerell the proudest father in England.[1]

What Mark Twain once said of Carlyle and the Americans might equally well have been said of Cockerell and his children: 'At bottom he was probably fond of them, but he was always able to conceal it.' In spite of so many misunderstandings he had always been a kind, but a Victorian, father. He was liberal with pocket-money, he remembered their birthdays. He read to them when they were ill ('When we were small,' wrote Katharine, 'it was always *The Wind in the Willows* — and he often said how he wished he had written it'). He took them abroad with him in the twenties — Christopher to see (in heavy rain) the cathedrals of northern France, Christopher and Margaret on a Mediterranean cruise, and Katharine twice on cruises. He took them to stay with his famous friends, gave them shrewd advice, helped them with their matrimonial problems.

But he had his blind side. He failed to understand that daughters need something more than education and an occasional cultural cruise: that they need dresses and parties and dances to launch them on the world. Admittedly money was very short; yet if he *had* understood he would probably have done at least something. But nobody — not even Kate — dared to tell him, and she herself could do so little. He failed to understand his wife. And where his son was concerned, how much unhappiness might have been avoided if only Cockerell had admitted the boy's right to have talents and interests and ambitions which did not happen to coincide with his own!

There is much about Cockerell's relations with his wife and children that it is painful to record, but a biographer enjoined

[1] Cockerell's death was announced in the *Evening Standard* under the caption 'HOVERCRAFT MAN'S FATHER DIES.' Within a few weeks he had become 'Sir Sydney Carlyle Cockerell, friend of William Morris and inventor of the Hovercraft. . . .' It sometimes amused Cockerell to refer to himself as 'grandfather of the Hovercraft'.

not to shirk the truth has no option but to record it. Against all this must be set Cockerell's endless kindnesses to his friends, his generosity, his integrity, his moral courage, his enthusiasm, and his brilliant achievement in transforming a sleepy provincial museum into something which has given, and which will continue to give, pleasure to hundreds of thousands of people.

4

BLUNT AND HIS DAUGHTER

COCKERELL had not allowed his duties at Cambridge to interfere with the maintenance of old friendships. Throughout the First World War, and in the years immediately succeeding it, he was many times the guest of Wilfrid Blunt at Newbuildings and always eager to be of help. He was allowed to read a part of the Secret Diaries ('Alms to Oblivion') which are now locked up in the Fitzwilliam Museum until 1972, and he often lent a willing ear to Blunt's reminiscences of his love life. These confessions he duly noted in his own diary:

21st April 1915. Had lunch with W.S.B. and a talk afterwards with him. . . . He said he did not mind anything that he had done or written, however delinquent, being known, but that other persons involved have of course to be considered. . . .

9th January 1916. I had a good talk with W.S.B. about his love affairs. He said that they had been numerous and that he regretted nothing and that he thought that he could say that he had added to the happiness of many women, and that he had made no woman lastingly unhappy. Many of those he had loved were dead, but those alive had remained his friends. He thought it possible to be in love with three women at the same time. He also expounded his religious views, and said that he had no belief in immortality, nor any desire for it. He had had a very varied and interesting life and now he would be content to sleep for ever.

3rd April 1920. Read the first two volumes of W.S.B.'s private memoirs, recording his love affairs with Catherine Walters (Skittles), Mrs. Baird, Mrs. Russell (d. 1870), and Mrs. Stuart of Buenos Ayres, and various others, up to the date of his marriage.

31st July 1920. I read some of his private memoirs about his building of Crabbet, the deaths of his brother and sister, and his love affairs with Mrs. S., Mrs. W., Mrs. P. (Juliet), Mrs. H., etc.

Several entries in Cockerell's diaries give details of 'Skittles' (Mrs. Baillie), the famous courtesan of the second half of the nineteenth century to whom Blunt addressed his 'Esther' sonnets:[1]

6th May 1909. Interesting talk with W.S.B. after 7 o'clock breakfast about the lady of his sonnets, whom he had seen yesterday at South Street and the day before in the Park. He made her acquaintance in Paris in 1863. She was the daughter of a Liverpool sea captain and an Irish mother. She has a sister married to a French Count and a pretty niece, but has never had a child. She was a fine horsewoman and was much in the hunting field and was mistress first of a Fitzwilliam and then of the late Duke of Devonshire, who was prevented by his family from marrying her in America and who had pensioned her off when W.S.B. made her acquaintance. She was also on intimate terms with the King, who now pays her doctor's bills, and with many other distinguished persons. She is now 70 years old and is dying of cancer.

8th August 1912. Went at Mr. Blunt's request to see some Old Masters belonging to Mrs. Bailey [sic]. . . . She is over 70 but immensely lively and young. She showed me all over her house and was amusingly communicative. . . .

[1] See Cyril Pearl, *The Girl with the Swansdown Seat*.

20th June 1922. Had an interesting talk with Captain Saumarez about 'Skittles', to whom his uncle Gerald was devoted for about 50 years. He is now 68. He made her acquaintance when he was a boy with a tutor and was with her when she died two years ago — a most romantic story. I had heard something about it from W.S.B. and had met Gerald Saumarez at Newbuildings. . . .[1]

Asked whether he had been aware, from the first, of Blunt's infidelities, Cockerell replied, 'I realized that there was usually a lady in the offing. But Blunt always behaved like a gentleman: he never told a dirty story.' It was a curious definition of a gentleman! Possibly Cockerell did in fact disapprove of much that went on at Newbuildings, for the 'great romantic passion' lay outside his experience; if so, then it was his personal loyalty to Blunt that made him accept what he could not understand. Lady Anne failed to appreciate this when she wrote to her daughter (5th May 1905) that 'S. C. Cockerell perhaps . . . has no particular regard for the tie of marriage.'

In the quarrels that developed between Blunt and his daughter,[2] who finally refused even to allow her children to visit their grandfather,[3] Cockerell always counselled moderation

---

[1] Cockerell kept careful notes of a conversation about 'Skittles' which he had with Gerald Saumarez a month later. 'Saumarez told me,' he said, 'that she was the only woman he would ever have married.'

[2] Lady Wentworth's version of the 'Great Quarrel' is recorded in full in her unpublished autobiography, and in a large collection of papers intended for use should her father's *Alms to Oblivion* ever see the light of day. 'My Mother's reputation and mine,' she wrote to a friend, 'depend entirely on the preservation of the letters and evidence connected with her tragic stormy life (and mine)'.

[3] Judith wrote to her mother in March 1916: 'As to the children, he is quite capable of teaching them the joys of morphia, just as he tried to teach me, and as Dorothy [Carleton] helps him to get morphia on the sly, Newbuildings is hardly a safe training school for the young.' Judith's principal objection to her children visiting Newbuildings was, of course, the presence of Miss Carleton there. She also feared that her father would alienate the children from herself and persuade them to take his side in the quarrels.

and forbearance. These quarrels came to a head in the spring of 1916, by which time Blunt and Judith had each come to the conclusion that the other was a little mad. This was not, as Cockerell told her, 'a good basis for sympathetic understanding;' and Cockerell was therefore dismissed as one who had gone over to the enemy.

To her father Judith now wrote what Blunt described as 'four foolscap pages of abuse and insult . . . accusing me of every baseness and almost every crime,' and her letter to Dorothy Carleton may be read in Lord Lytton's book[1]. This 'violent irritability,' Blunt told Lady Lovelace, was perhaps occasioned by her being 'not quite in her normal senses as her mother believes, through her time of life (she is forty-three) and her estrangement from Neville, or else to her having fallen under some very unscrupulous outside influence.'

But it was Cockerell, as so often happens with those who try to stop dog-fights, who was the most savagely bitten. Familiar as he now was with Judith's sudden changes of mood, he must have been surprised when she turned on him; for only two months earlier she had written to him in the friendliest terms: 'Your charming letter delighted me. You have always been such a good friend. . . .' We do not know the details of her direct attack; but in a letter to her mother she now denounced Cockerell as the villain of the piece: a lickspittle, a toady, an advocate of immorality, perhaps a fool, perhaps an unscrupulous adventurer. It is not fanciful to identify him as the 'Prig' of her Limerick sequence *The Prig's Progress*,[2] two of whose fourteen stanzas may be quoted:

> There once was a Person of Peace
> Who contrived all bad blood to increase.
> On a quarrelsome broil
> He would try to pour oil
> At the risk of untimely decease . . .

[1] p. 257.
[2] From *The Flame of Life*, John Murray, 1930.

When he lectured a man and his wife
And said, 'Pray desist from this strife,'
The whole of the clan
Rose up as one man
And gave him the fright of his life . . .

As for her father, Judith considered him to be 'as unscrupulous
a villain as could be found outside Dartmoor.'

Tension had not relaxed when, a year later, there came the
news that Lady Anne had died in Egypt. In 1919 there was a
sharp dispute between Blunt and his daughter over the
ownership of the Arab stud; this led to a legal action in which
Blunt was the loser. The dramatic details of Blunt's cross-
examination, at a court presided over by an official referee and
held while Blunt lay on his sick-bed at Newbuildings, may be
read in Lord Lytton's life of his grandfather.

Meanwhile Blunt's health was steadily deteriorating. '19th
March 1917. Had a talk with W.S.B., who spoke of himself as
an old tin kettle not worth the constant patching. . . .' '29th
June 1917. W.S.B. . . . yesterday afternoon declared that he
wished he were dead, but is a good deal better this morning.'
18th August 1919 (in a letter to Cockerell): 'There is nothing
so wearisome as what I have become, an ancient last year's fly
which can only buzz as it lies on its back and refuses quite to
die.' '5th April 1921. Had a very good talk with W.S.B. He
said that in view of all the world complications "he was glad
that he was dead," but that he had had as varied and interesting a life as anyone he could think of and that he would have
been very sorry to miss the last ten years of it.' '4th October
1921. W.S.B. sent Arab clothes for me before I was up and
asked me to come and talk to him. . . . We talked till a
paroxysm of pain came on. . . . He had had intense pain in the
night and said that he thought he should die in the next few
days. Seeing him so racked I could not but wish that the end
should come, but he does not look like a dying man. . . . His
brother gave him a permanent lease of Newbuildings on his

marriage, and when he came to look at it he exclaimed, "That is a house good to live in and good to die in".'

In February 1922 Cockerell was summoned to Newbuildings, where he found Blunt in great pain but clear in his mind. Blunt thanked him warmly for all he had done for him, especially for his (unpaid) work in connection with the Diaries 'which he says that he could never have written if I had not sorted and arranged his papers. It is extraordinary that he should have lived to see the world accepting and promoting his unpopular ideas on Ireland and Egypt,' though, as he told Cockerell, 'he could derive no pleasure from this, but only wondered whether all his strivings had been worth while.'

In June he was a little better, but full of remorse for 'a wicked selfish life' and with no desire for 'another incarnation as a human being.' The improvement, however, was not maintained. '21st July. Mr. Blunt growing feebler, they say, and continuing to suffer much pain. . . . As usual there are difficulties with the nurses which I am asked to overcome.' '22nd July. Talk with W.S.B. who said he was ashamed to be the sole care of five women (two or three of whom are near a breakdown) but that he could not cut his throat and end it. Talk with Gracie. Talk with other two nurses, both nice, one of whom he had declined to have near him. Talk with Miss Lawrence and with Miss Carleton, who are wearing themselves out with their devoted service. Went for a walk with the rejected nurse, Miss Stuart, and found her thoroughly nice. On my return had a talk with W.S.B. and he consented to treat her differently.'

Shortly before her death Lady Anne had expressed the wish that her husband should be reconciled to their daughter, and this reconciliation was now achieved. '12th August. W.S.B. wanted to consult me about a letter he had dictated for Judith expressing his forgiveness "for the unfilial acts which I believe you have acknowledged as such".' The letter was taken by Cockerell to Crabbet. After Lady Wentworth had read it she was 'full of thankful emotion and we had a most satisfactory talk in which she promised never to repeat her accusations and complaints and to bury all resentments.' Cockerell hastened to

Blunt's bedside to announce the success of his mission. 'I begged him to clinch the reconciliation by seeing her at once. He seemed to be afraid to do this, but at last he consented to let me fetch her tomorrow . . . Dorothy Carleton had . . . been active in promoting the matter.' The Diary continues:

> 19th August. Reached Newbuildings with [Lady Went-worth] at 11.15, after much satisfactory talk and repetitions of the promise to be submissive as we sped along. The interview between father and daughter took place in my presence alone and was longer than I expected and very affectionate. Then Judith came into the hall and kissed Dorothy Carleton and was reconciled to her, and then she kissed Miss Lawrence, and was carried home in the same car, after a visit which could not have been bettered in any respect. W.S.B. called me in after she had gone and thanked me for having been such a good ambassador.

But Cockerell soon discovered that Lady Wentworth's gesture was not quite so altruistic as he had at first imagined. The matter is referred to in a letter written by Neville Lytton to Cockerell in 1948. In that year, after Lord Lytton had broadcast a laudatory talk on his father-in-law, Lady Wentworth violently attacked her father's memory in three letters to the *Listener*.[1] Cockerell wrote to Lytton, who replied:

> You say in your letter and I said in my talk all the good that can be said of Lady Anne, but she was ordinary and he was extraordinary—that's why I made a broadcast about him. I have heard 'J' say hard enough things about her mother when she realized that money had been left to the granddaughters over her head, and you told me that when W.S.B. was on his deathbed, 'J' went over to New-buildings, much farded, and threw herself on her knees with protestations of affection—no doubt hoping to make

[1] Cockerell and others joined in. See the *Listener*, 9th and 16th September; 7th, 14th, 21st and 28th October; 4th and 11th November, 1948.

a last minute recovery of the inheritance of the Newbuildings estate. This present Goneril-like attitude is not pretty
and is certainly not consistent with that deathbed scene.

Cockerell was staying with the Hornbys at Chantmarle when,
on 11th September, a telegram arrived announcing that Blunt
had died the previous afternoon. He left immediately for
Sussex:

> Dorothy Carleton met me at the station. She had been
> awaiting my arrival before communicating with Crabbet.
> I sent a telegram to Judith from the station, but I had
> misgivings as to what might come of the delay — and I had
> hardly reached Newbuildings when Judith and Anthony
> arrived in a towering rage at having been left to learn
> the news from the papers. I did my best to pacify them,
> explaining that I had only just arrived and that the papers
> had learnt of the death from an unknown source. They
> then had amicable interviews with Miss Lawrence and
> with Dorothy Carleton. . . .

Chandler, the senior executor, was abroad. The others were
Charles Adeane, Miss Carleton, and Cockerell who at once took
charge of the situation:

> 12th September. W.S.B. had directed that he should be
> buried as soon as possible and in the simplest manner,
> without a coffin but wrapped in his old eastern travelling
> carpet, in a spot indicated by him in Newbuildings wood,
> without religious or other ceremony.[1] A very large grave

[1] About a month before his death Blunt had been visited by a Domini-
can Friar, Vincent MacNab. In a letter to a friend MacNab later wrote:
'It would not be fair to Wilfrid Blunt to say that I reconciled him to the
Church. I gave him the last Sacraments. I only hope I shall have at death
the same childlike faith that he had. I was in Ireland when he died. His
quite lawful desire to be buried in his own grounds caused some misunderstandings and he was buried without a priest. But when I next
visited his house I blessed the grave and justice-searching faithful soul
whom I had been privileged to tend. . . . You can make what use you like
of this letter . . .'

with steps down to it had been dug yesterday. This I had lined with boughs of oak, sweet chestnut, yew, elder and ivy. Judith came at about 12 with Anthony and Anne and knelt again at the bedside. We agreed to have the burial after lunch and word was sent to Belloc, Lady Burrell, Lady Hamilton, Mrs. Hawkins and Gerald Blunt. Just before lunch I went with Judith and her children and strewed everlasting flowers over the steps and scattered them over the green boughs and at 2 with Caffin I super-intended the sewing of the body into the carpet. It was then carried to the grave by six men from the estate. . . . It was a most beautiful and dignified burial, like that of an ancient Pharaoh. Miss Lawrence and Dorothy Carleton and Anne went down into the grave and heaped pot-pourri from Newbuildings roses about and on the swaddled body and a great fragrance arose. Judith next went down into the grave and knelt in prayer. Nothing seemed lacking. All was exactly as he had wished and the little company dispersed afterwards with full hearts.

Lady Wentworth, in a letter to Lady Lovelace, gave a very different picture of these happenings:

We only knew of his death by seeing it in the newspapers [she wrote]. D.C. prevented our being told and prevented Belloc sending for a priest and she and Miss L. only said, 'We could do nothing without Mr. Cockerell.' Both of them were entirely evasive about his end and would say nothing beyond that they 'couldn't remember' what happened. When A. protested against our being kept in ignorance of his death Cockerell only said, 'Oh don't make a fuss!'

The burial planned by H.F.[1] himself was theatrical, and like all the scenes of his life the unrehearsed amateur element made everything fall flat — Cockerell in a black tail coat with a huge light grey Trilby hat was an

[1] 'Head of the Family'—i.e., Wilfrid Blunt,

incongruous figure mixed with the Arabian carpet and the grave dug in the middle of a pathway behind the house. . . .[1]

I can't write more just now. We know nothing of his will but Cockerell took charge and ordered everyone about and I think D.C. will get everything (from his manner and hers). . . .

Doubtless Lady Wentworth had at first hoped that, after her reconciliation with her father, he had altered his will and would leave Newbuildings and Worth Farm, as he had once promised, to her son; she was soon to learn that her subsequent suspicions were only too well founded. '14th September. Wrote yesterday to Judith Wentworth to say that I would go to Crabbet today to give her details of Mr. Blunt's will and preparing her for disappointment, the Worth estate having been left to Lady Mary Strickland and the Newbuildings to Dorothy Carleton as life tenants.' But Lady Wentworth would not see him. When she eventually learnt the terms of the will she prayed 'that [her father's] soul might not rest until the wrong he had done had been righted.' Her son wrote, 'She felt at that moment that Blunt had cheated her love once again, and her bitterness returned to remain with her for the rest of her life — or at least until those last few hours when the soul is called to prepare for bodily death.'

[1] The grave is, in fact, in a charming ride in the woods, several hundred yards from the house.

5

COCKERELL
AND LADY WENTWORTH

WITH Blunt and Lady Anne dead, with Lady Wentworth antagonistic and her children still under her influence, it was only to be expected that Cockerell's ties with the family should become weakened.[1] A kind of armed neutrality between Cockerell and Lady Wentworth might, however, have continued indefinitely had not an American writer, Miss Edith Finch,[2] undertaken, in 1933, to prepare a biography of Wilfrid Blunt. Cockerell gave the book his blessing, and wrote to Lady Wentworth asking if Miss Finch might visit her. Lady Wentworth answered that she mistrusted a life of her father written by an American; she had already suffered enough from the Press. It was no recommendation to her that Miss Finch had been in touch with Miss Carleton, whose presence at Newbuildings had wrecked her mother's life.

Cockerell replied that Miss Finch was not a journalist, that her credential were impeccable, and that naturally she had had to visit Newbuildings where Blunt had spent much of his life. He offered to show Lady Wentworth the draft of the opening chapters, of which he was sure she would approve. He would never have sponsored an unworthy biographer of his old friend. He did not believe that a member of the family was the

---

[1] In following the course of Cockerell's friendships it will sometimes be necessary to carry the story beyond the period (1908–1937) covered in this section of the book.

[2] Now Countess Russell.

best person to write the book. The letter appears to have
remained unanswered, and four years later, in October 1938,
Miss Finch's book was published by Messrs. Cape.

Lady Wentworth wrote at once to Cockerell. She was, she
said, 'beyond measure distressed' at the false picture Miss
Finch had drawn of her mother. She had anticipated this when
she had refused to associate herself with a book sponsored by
Miss Carleton and Miss Lawrence. She continued:

> That *you* should incite biographers to hold my mother up
> to public ridicule and imply blame to me in order to
> whitewash him at our expense is surely unjustifiable
> hitting below the belt. You know quite well, unless you
> have no sense of justice left, that any woman of today
> would have divorced him and publicly disgraced the
> women in the case without mercy, the creed of free love
> for men, which you have always defended as so delightful
> and romantic, not having yet been sanctioned by the laws
> of the country, or free love for women either . . . I do
> feel that you, who ate her bread and salt and received so
> many and constant kindnesses at her hands, should have
> held her memory in more honour than to allow her to be
> falsely represented as a tiresome clog on the wheels of
> genius. She spent a lifetime being a galley slave to my
> father. Having finally cast her out, he was furious be-
> cause she at last refused to be whistled back to heel at his
> dictation. 'What he really cannot bear,' she wrote to me
> just before her death, 'is that I, being the worm, should
> have turned.'

Subsequently Lady Wentworth elaborated her attack on
Miss Finch's life of Blunt. 'Nothing,' she says, 'can excuse
the fantastic travesty of her book. . . . How Sir Sydney came
to sponsor such a tissue of falsehoods is beyond comprehension.'
If the biography is, in fact, a travesty, Miss Finch's chief
excuse is that Lady Wentworth refused to see her or to give
her any help whatever.

Cockerell, in his reply to Lady Wentworth's letter, defended the book, which had been a labour of love over many years. It was receiving excellent reviews, and Miss Finch had had many appreciative letters. Lady Wentworth renewed the attack, accusing Cockerell of being 'the prime instigator' and Miss Finch of having 'repeated her lesson dutifully, not knowing the facts. . . . You boast of twenty-five years as a privileged onlooker. I fail to see that being fooled for twenty-five years is a matter for self-congratulation. . . My father was a consummate actor[1] and you saw just as much of him as he intended you to see and no more. . . . By the way, how many years were you actually in his paid service?' The letter is signed 'Wentworth.'

Cockerell answered that he was 'a bit puzzled to know how to reply to a letter from a very old friend which was evidently written in the worst of tempers.' He reminded her of her letter to him from Sheykh Obeyd in which she had attacked her mother for her 'amazing lack of sense of proportion.'[2] He continued, '[Lady Anne] had splendid virtues, but this shortcoming was surely the cause of half her troubles. Was it not an inheritance from Lady Byron that she shared with Lord Lovelace? May it not be that a little of this inheritance, along with some of the virtues, has been passed on to you?'

But Lady Wentworth was not to be placated. She now demanded that two passages should be removed from all further copies of the book sent out by Messrs. Cape. She also insisted that Cockerell and Messrs. Cape should sign formal apologies. It is hard to see why Cockerell, though he had 'sponsored' the book, should have been held responsible: he was neither the author, nor the printer, nor the publisher of the alleged libels. The situation was further complicated by the fact that Miss Finch was in America. Messrs. Cape took legal advice and were informed that Lady Wentworth would be most unlikely to win an action. But much waste of time and, through delay, of money would be inevitable if they did not yield to demands that Cockerell and Messrs. Cape both

---

[1] 'Let no one forget that he *posed for posterity*.' Baroness Wentworth, *The Authentic Arabian Horse*, chapter II, 1945.

[2] See p. 112.

continued to consider unreasonable. So replacement sheets were printed, and apologies drawn up and signed. On page 358 of all subsequently issued copies of Miss Finch's book there appears the following footnote:

> It having been represented to the Publishers that passages on this page and elsewhere suggest that the estrangement between Blunt and his daughter Lady Wentworth and her mother was due to quarrels about the stud and to unreasonable conduct on her part, and that the necessity for the sale of the Crabbet Estate was caused by her mismanagement, and that she treated Blunt unfairly, these passages have now been withdrawn, and the Publishers acknowledge that any suggestions to the effect stated are without foundation.

Since many copies of the unexpurgated edition are still in circulation, the curious reader may easily form his own opinion as to whether or not the passages complained of were defamatory.

Three further letters may serve to complete this account of Cockerell's long association with Blunt — an association not marred by a single unfriendly incident and recorded in five hundred letters. In the first, Neville Lytton, writing to Cockerell in 1944, gives his opinion of his father-in-law:

> I quite agree with what Conrad says about [Blunt's] diaries[1] — to my mind they show up all that I disliked most in his character, humbug and insincerity, worldliness and even snobbishness. He was the great hero of my youth — somewhat like what Ruskin was to you. I don't think I have ever met a more gifted man — he seems to have been born with the right gesture and he oozed magnetism. I still admire his sense of adventure and daring and his romantic conception of life and his

---

[1] Quoted in *Friends of a Lifetime*, p. 324.

exquisite taste in art, but he was in some ways mon-
strously selfish as is proved by his reactions to the huge
tragedy of 1914–18. What worried him most was the
thought that he might be disturbed in his peaceful
atmosphere of Newbuildings. He had little thought and
no sympathy for those lads of the Royal Sussex (and
others) who were going through indescribable miseries to
keep the enemy away from the Seven Sisters. Also his
whole attitude to life was from above to below. He could
see all too clearly the faults of the average Briton (and
God knows there were plenty to see) but could he see
that sort of modest greatness which has been uppermost
in these two great wars?

This letter, says the present Lord Lytton,[1] cannot pass
without comment:

The writer, who had been divorced by Lady Wentworth
and was now married to a Frenchwoman, had just
returned from occupied France; he was writing with a
French detestation of the Germans and in a firm belief
that the Allies' cause was holy. Blunt, on the other hand,
had felt deeply for the Mahdi's people, 300,000 of whom
had been killed when *we* invaded *them*. To him it seemed
that England was only getting what she deserved, and
that nothing short of the invasion of this country by the
Germans would force her to liberate her Empire. That
Blunt's attitude to life was 'from above to below' is
blatantly untrue.

In the third letter, the present Lord Lytton, who had just
been reading Blunt's correspondence with Cockerell, pays
tribute to Cockerell's devoted service to his grandfather. It is
addressed to Cockerell and was written in 1958:

The letters contain also, taken all in all, a quite remarkably long and varied list of the commissions he laid upon

[1] In a communication to the Author.

you—commissions most promptly carried out and in measure full to overflowing. They included prolonged research into the history of horses and the acquisition of volumes of Strabo, Herodotus, Marco Polo and many another, ancient and not so ancient, English and foreign. I noted other requests for action perhaps more nearly in your line of interest—the binding of a book, the making of a book-plate, the buying of a picture, the selection of 18th century script. But it did not stop at that class of thing and I see you were summoned, or at least most pressingly invited, to take up your bed and visit him in Egypt where, so I understand, you made a desert journey and liked your camel-riding even less than Miss Lawrence did. Then you did many practical things during a shipwreck in the Gulf of Suez while W.S.B. lay abed with a fever reciting the 'Fatha' and displaying, with the consoling aid of Miss Lawrence, his disbelief in the Moslem as well as the Christian heaven and his confidence and trust in total extinction.

Whenever W.S.B. was on the point of death, which happened quite half-a-dozen times in the letters, Miss Lawrence never failed in getting you to the bedside to console her and him and to take the place of a physician whom he would never have anywhere near him till he was well on the road to recovery. . . .

As companion and chaperon whenever there was to be some visitor of particular importance or immense awkwardness, W.S.B. or Miss Lawrence or Dorothy [Carleton] or both or all three must have you there to make the reception easy and either more agreeable or less disagreeable.

When Counsel's opinion is sought (and it seems quite often), when a package must be delivered to the Secretary of State for Foreign Affairs (and receipt obtained), when a horse is to be sold, when a favourite young woman is to have a wedding present, when a quarrel is in the offing, when somebody's public utterances seven years ago must be checked, when an Editor must be cajoled, when the intentions of a publisher must be revealed, when a pamphlet must be printed and circulated to 100 victims, when printers' errors must be corrected, when fruit trees are needed for planting, when an architect is wanted to inspect the roof, when W.S.B. desires a meeting with a playwright, a poet, a radical, a horse-coper or some oriental rascal engaged in sedition . . . is it not Cockerell who is invoked on all such occasions? and never invoked in vain!

Certainly these letters reveal the great variety of the recipient's activities and a devastating speed of execution. This I certainly had not realized before, and I am left wondering if the many other men of letters into whose affairs you introduced order, method, precision and regularity were equally exacting.

Miss Carleton also appreciated Cockerell's many kindnesses. A week after Blunt's death she wrote, 'I am more grateful than I shall ever be able to say, for all you have done for us.'

6

THE ROXBURGHE CLUB

O F great interest to Cockerell, especially during the twenties, was the Roxburghe Club.

On 17th June 1812 the leading bibliophiles of the day had dined together at St. Alban's Tavern, London, to celebrate the sale by the Duke of Roxburghe, for £2,260 to the Marquis of Blandford, of Valdarfer's edition of Boccaccio—for which the Duke had originally paid a hundred guineas. At that memorable dinner was founded the Roxburghe Club, then as now the most select society of bibliophiles in the world.

The Club agreeably combined conviviality with scholarship: its members met periodically for a dinner, and each was expected, once during his membership, to produce at his own expense a choice book for presentation to his fellow members, at first twenty-four in number but today forty. Those who for one reason or another were unable or unwilling to prepare a volume themselves, employed the services of recognized scholars, a few of whom were in due course enrolled among the millionaires and aristocrats who formed the nucleus of the Club. In 1915 Cockerell was elected a member of the Club, which was at that time under the Presidency of Lord Aldenham, with John Murray as Treasurer. Cockerell's particular function was to join the Printing Committee, whose Chairman was Lord Aldenham.

Cockerell was, of course, immensely flattered at finding himself in this distinguished company, with not a few of whom he was already acquainted. But it did not take him long to realize that the Club dinners, agreeable though they were, had almost ceased to have any connection with the art of the rare book. He was not the man to remain silent in such circumstances: in 1918 he decided to take the offensive, and a letter to him from John Murray gave him the opening for which he had been waiting. The following correspondence, which speaks for itself, will illustrate Cockerell's impatience with stagnation and his moral courage in denouncing it whenever it came his way.

3rd June 1918   50 Albemarle Street
                                 W.1.

Dear Cockerell,
    There is at Sotheby's in Bond Street, a copy of Dibdin's Bibliographical Decameron fully and elaborately grangerized. One volume contains a page of signatures of the members of the Roxburghe Club and there are a few entries also referring to the Club. . . . It has been suggested that the Club should make a bid for this book. As you are aware, we have no home or depository of our own, but the minute books and a few others are kept for us by the Vice-President.
    We cannot hold a meeting before the Sale, and the question is—is it worth making a bid for the book of say £100? I do not feel sufficiently strongly about it to recommend this, but if you have an opportunity of going to Sotheby's and could let me know what you think I should be very much obliged.
                    Yours very truly
                    John Murray

8th June 1918   Fitzwilliam Museum
                                 Cambridge

Dear Murray,
    I went up to see the Dibdin yesterday. It is certainly a thorough and very interesting piece of grangerizing, and if the Roxburghe Club were what is ought to be, a Club of book collectors and connoisseurs—instead of consisting

largely of distinguished personages with little or no real
interest in the subject — and if it had any life in it and held
meetings of a reasonable kind for the discussion and
exhibition of rare and valuable books — I should say that
these volumes would be quite worth bidding for. But in
the circumstances I think the money would be thrown
away. . . .

                              Yours very truly
                              Sydney Cockerell

10th June 1918   50 Albemarle Street
                                       W.1.

Dear Cockerell,
    Many thanks for yours. I think that Lord Aldenham
proposes to make a bid for the book himself.
    Are you not rather hard on the Club? You unfortun-
ately joined after the war began. Till then we used to have
our annual dinners for the very purposes you name, and
gradually we had introduced the custom of getting the
members with large houses to give the dinners and show
us their books. Lord Rosebery, Lord Bath, the Duke of
Buccleuch, Lord Aldenham (Father and Son), Lord
Salisbury, Huth and others — had done this and others
would have done it, but ours, like all respectable Clubs,
must subdue these propensities in wartime. . . .
                              Yours very truly
                              John Murray

Cockerell's reply, which John Murray answered three days
later, is missing. Murray wrote:

13th June 1918   50 Albemarle Street
                                       W.1.

Dear Cockerell,
    Many thanks for yours, but I think you must have
overlooked the fact that most of the members of the Club
are doing national or war work of some kind and are far
too busy to come to such meetings as you propose. In the

old days when we dined at a restaurant even in peace
time, scarcely anybody came. . . .

Yours very truly

John Murray

St. John Hornby, to whom Cockerell had sent his correspondence with John Murray, wrote to say that he shared
Cockerell's opinions:

14th June 1918   186 Strand

London, W.C.2.

My dear Cockerell,

Many thanks for letting me see your correspondence
with John Murray about the Roxburghe Club. I took the
same view as you do about the Dibdin book. . . .

I rather despair of the Club ever becoming again what
it was originally. The present members are largely
inheritors of great libraries, or . . . heirs of a name once
connected with a great library, rather than book lovers.
The old style book collector of good family has apparently
almost died out. The enormous rise in the price of books
and MSS has made book collecting a rich man's hobby
rather than a book lover's hobby. There are very few
people like yourself who spend a considerable part of their
available capital on books. In any case if the Roxburghe
Club is to become once again a book lover's club and a
book-collector's club, it will have to largely drop its old
aristocratic connection, because so few of the modern
aristocrats love books and fewer still collect them.

What John M. says about the dinners before the war
'for the very purposes you name' is in the main ROT. I
went to several of them and quite pleasant functions they
were and the dinners beyond praise, fit for a Lucullus,
but as to there being any intelligent talk about books or
any real appreciation of them by the majority of those
present . . . well, one was almost afraid to touch on the
question of books at all, the atmosphere was so uncongenial to such talk. Further, a meeting once a year of a lot

of people who hardly know one another is not enough to
keep a Club alive. . . .

Ever yours

C.H. St J.H.

Murray wrote again to Cockerell:

17th June 1918   50 Albemarle Street
                                  W.1.

Dear Cockerell,

. . . I feel bound to write once more in justification of
the Club. I have very little doubt as to the source whence
your information comes, as I have heard a good deal of
the same sort before.

When Alfred Huth was alive we had many conversations about the meetings of the Club, and I think we did
a good deal to induce members with large enough houses
to entertain us. . . . Neither you nor your conjectured
informant was a member of the Club then. Lord Bath,
Lord Salisbury and others have got no libraries in London.

You write that it is not safe to assume that your
neighbour knows one book from another, and that some
degree of connoisseurship should henceforth be a necessary qualification. The Club was originally founded by
and for owners of large libraries, but for the very reason
you state it has of recent years extended its boundaries
and elected Sir E. M. Thompson, Sir G. Warner, Mr.
Fortescue, Sir F. Kenyon, Hagberg Wright and yourself
who do not own large private libraries but represent
them. Surely the Provost of King's, Hornby, Pierpont
Morgan (senr.), Michael Tomkinson, Perrins and Christie-
Miller are not classed among the ignoramuses! But these
have all been elected in the last 10 years. You cannot
expect men to talk shop all the evening if they have no
books before them. . . .

Yours truly

John Murray

On the top of this letter Cockerell has written:

> Replied 18th June admitting that J.M. had given 'a very
> effective and satisfactory answer to the questions I have
> raised' but urging that each member should be invited to
> bring a book or two to the meetings.

Cockerell put this suggestion to Lord Aldenham also, who
replied that the same idea had already crossed his mind. Very
probably it was carried out, for Cockerell now lapses into
silence. But within a couple of years there are signs in his
diary that fresh trouble is brewing:

> 20th February 1920. The meeting [of the Printing Com-
> mittee of the Roxburghe Club] absolutely ridiculous
> owing to the complete deafness of the two officers, Lord
> Aldenham and John Murray. . . .

The following year the situation is no better:

> 19th April 1921. The usual fiasco owing to the lamentable
> deafness of the two presiding members. . . .

Cockerell could remain inactive no longer. After giving himself forty-eight hours for reflection he wrote to Murray in
terms that were, as was his custom, brutally direct:

> 21st April 1921   Fitzwilliam Museum
> Cambridge
> Dear Murray,
>   . . . I wish to resign my membership of the Printing
> Committee as the unfortunate deafness of the two pre-
> siding officers makes all discussion impossible. Much that
> was said on Tuesday did not reach their ears at all and
> decisions were postponed in consequence. It is only my
> great respect for you and Aldenham, and my apprecia-
> tion of all that you have both done for the Club during a
> great many years, that has prevented me from taking this

step earlier, and it is the more disagreeable for me to take it as I believe that I was elected partly in order that I might serve on this Committee.

If for this reason it should seem to you desirable that I should leave the Club, I am quite ready to follow your advice in the matter. I am however in the awkward position of not having presented a book to my fellow members and of seeing no immediate prospect of my being able to present one.

I am

Yours Sincerely

Sydney C. Cockerell

John Murray was, not unnaturally, extremely upset and replied by return of post:

                                        JOHN MURRAY
22nd April 1921   50A Albemarle Street,
                                        London W.1.

Dear Cockerell,

Your letter has caused me much pain and surprise. . . . I believe I heard every word *openly* said at the last meeting,[1] and I came away with two other members and we discussed the proceedings. If your complaint is well grounded, it is not you, but the officers who ought to resign, and I have at once placed my resignation in Lord Aldenham's hands. I should have resigned my office long ago had I not believed that I could render some service to the Club in the drudgery of its work, which is much heavier than might be supposed. It is a great relief to be rid of it.

Yours very truly

John Murray

[1] A member of the Club comments: 'My recollection of Cockerell at the Roxburghe Club meetings was that he talked much, didactically, not very clearly and expected everyone to listen closely to him. It may be that John Murray heard more than Cockerell thought and did not want to hear more than he did.'

On this letter Cockerell has written:

> Replied Ap. 24. Exceedingly sorry that my letter, which
> must have been clumsily worded, gave you pain. Every
> member of the Club highly conscious of the debt it owes
> to you. Should there be a new Treasurer, Hornby would
> be an ideal successor.

It may be observed that Cockerell, for all his regret that he
has hurt Murray's feelings, has wasted no time in suggesting
a suitable successor to him. He also wrote to Hornby, who
replied:

25th April 1921   Chantmarle
                                   Dorchester

My dear Cockerell,

. . . I think you showed great courage in writing to
Murray as you did. At the same time I think it would be
a pity if he were to resign the Treasurership. He has done
a good deal for the Club and it might be difficult to get a
successor. What we want is a Chairman of meetings who
could hear. Then I think that we could put up with M.
It is having the two of them deaf which makes things so
impossible.

I had a letter from M. this morning, saying he had
received your letter and had at once sent in his resignation to Aldenham. I have written to him saying that I
think this would be a pity, though I have told him that I
entirely agree with you that it is hopeless to go on with a
deaf Chairman. I have suggested that Aldenham, while
remaining Vice-President, should make his deafness an
excuse for asking someone else to undertake the duty of
Chairman of meetings. If this were done, then members
could address the Chairman, and he could pass on to
Murray anything that it was necessary for M. to
answer. . . .

Ever yours
C.H. St J.H.

Cockerell sent his correspondence with Murray to Sir Frederic Kenyon, Director of the British Museum and also a member of the Roxburghe Club, who replied:

3rd May 1921   British Museum
                                     London, W.C.1.

My dear Cockerell,

. . . You have certainly hit rather hard, but in the interests of the Club, and I hope the results will be good. But you must not think of resigning, and there is not the least reason for you to stay away from the dinner. Murray spoke to me about the matter at the Athenaeum yesterday, and was quite nice about it. He had been taking the opinion of James.

                              Yours sincerely
                              F. G. Kenyon

Three letters from Yates Thompson conclude the correspondence:

9th May 1921   19 Portman Square, W.1.

Dear Cockerell,

Quite right. It is clearly a case in which the end will have (if it comes off) justified the means. . . .

                         Truly yours
                         H.Y.T.

8th June 1921   19 Portman Square, W.1.

Dear Cockerell,

I really must send a line of congratulation on your two Reports. Under all the circumstances the result[s] are first rate, indeed quite triumphant. I hope you will not fail to appear at the Roxburgh[e] dinner.

The only *apparent* result of the bombshell was that the Provost took the Chair apparently as qualified to *assist* Aldenham. But I think it may be said to have opened the question of a re-modelling of the Club. . . . I went so far as to express the hope that you might write another letter to Lord Rosebery as I think nothing effective will be done before we get a President who is not a useless cypher — e.g. Lord Crawford. But I don't think Lord A. heard this remark. . . .

Truly yours
H.Y.T.

10th June 1921   19 Portman Square, W.1.

Dear Cockerell,

No earthly *reason* for not coming to the Feast on the 20th.

There can be no discussion or nonsense about either your letter or Murray's proposal to retire, which latter was not intended or considered to be serious.

Truly in haste
H.Y.T.

Cockerell remained a member of the Roxburghe Club until his death, and there are many references in his diaries to splendid dinners in the houses of the great. Lord Aldenham died in 1936 at the age of ninety, after having been a member for more than sixty years and President since 1929. He wrote to Cockerell shortly before his death, 'My ninetieth birthday has given so much satisfaction to my friends that I intend to do my best to live for ever.'

During the twenties Cockerell prepared two volumes for the Roxburghe Club and joined Dr. James in the preparation of a third. The last-named dealt with two East Anglian Psalters in the Bodleian Library, Oxford — the Ormesby Psalter (described by Cockerell) and the Bromholm Psalter (described by Dr. James). The volume was issued in March 1927, though it bears the date 1926.

A far more considerable undertaking was *A Book of Old Testament Illustrations of the Middle of the Thirteenth*

Century, which Cockerell described for its owner, J. P. Morgan, for presentation to his fellow members. The manuscript was one of great beauty and importance, and the unravelling of its complicated history[1] involved much research. Dr. James contributed an introduction. Cockerell wrote in his diary:

> 10th February 1927. Returned the last proofs of the Morgan MS. for press. So ends a task the unfulfilment of which has been a haunting worry for over seven years! The delay however led to great discoveries and the book, thanks to these and to Dr. James's fine introduction, will be a permanently interesting and useful one.

And jokingly he wrote to Katie Adams of these two volumes, which appeared within a few days of one another, 'Jolly well done, both of them, but scarcely anyone will bother to find that out.'

Cockerell often spoke of the great generosity shown him by J. P. Morgan, who paid him £500 for his work and gave him a further £500 to buy, to present as from himself, anything he liked for the Fitzwilliam. It was J. P. Morgan, too, who came to the rescue when £600 had quickly to be found in order to secure the Isabelle Psalter for the Fitzwilliam.[2] It was fitting that it should have been he who gave Cockerell the opportunity of producing what will always rank as one of the finest of all the splendid productions of the Roxburghe Club.

The third book was Cockerell's own gift to the members, a monograph on the work of W. de Brailes, an English illuminator of the thirteenth century. He himself had discovered three

---

[1] Probably written and illuminated in Paris, it seems soon to have found its way to Naples. By the beginning of the seventeenth century it was in the possession of a Polish cardinal who, in 1608, presented it to Abbas the Great, Shah of Persia. Sold later by an Arab to a Greek for three shillings, it was sent by the latter to Sotheby's in 1833 where it was purchased by a firm of booksellers, Payne and Foss, for 255 guineas. Next it passed into the hands of that omnivorous collector and bibliophile, Sir Thomas Phillipps, and finally, by private purchase, to J. P. Morgan.

[2] See p. 143.

of the six then known manuscripts illuminated by de Brailles, so that his choice of subject was appropriate. The volume was well but economically produced, the text scholarly and concise; and the plates were admirably engraved by Emery Walker.

Members were expected to pay for the publication of their presentation volume, but Cockerell was of course in no position to do this. 'Though it was not considered "the thing",' Cockerell said, 'I got leave to print an edition of a hundred copies and to dispose of the remainder to Quaritch at eight guineas a-piece; so my costs were covered.'

One last episode in the history of the Roxburghe Club — and one in which Cockerell played a part — must be set down. In 1934 there appeared a book, by John Carter and G. Pollard, entitled *An Enquiry into the Nature of certain 19th Century Pamphlets*. In it the authors demonstrated, by a process of deduction as exciting as that to be found in any detective novel, that a large number of rare nineteenth-century pamphlets were undeniable forgeries, and that all these were in some way associated with the famous bibliophile, T. J. Wise, a member of the Roxburghe Club.

The book caused consternation among the other and highly respectable members, who immediately came together to discuss what action should be taken. It was finally agreed that Cockerell and Kenyon, who had jointly sponsored Wise's election,[1] should call on Wise and ask him to resign 'on the grounds of ill health'. Kenyon was very reluctant to take a part; but he saw that it was his duty to go with Cockerell and, as the senior of the two, to voice the embarrassing request.

Wise greeted his visitors with the greatest cordiality and gave them an excellent tea; the delegates grew more and more embarrassed, and Kenyon could not bring himself to speak. So at last it was Cockerell who said, 'You must know why we are here; we have come to ask you to resign from the Club.' Wise

[1] Though as early as 1924 Cockerell had noted in his diary that he had 'always been strongly prejudiced' against Wise.

realized that the alternative to resignation would be expulsion. 'I agree,' he said at last, 'but on one condition: *I admit nothing.*'

Cockerell went immediately to tell Lord Aldenham that their mission had been successfully accomplished, then he turned his steps towards Chelsea and the hospitable dinner-table of his old friend St. John Hornby. And perhaps, as he walked, he recalled with a wry smile a letter that he had written four years earlier to *The Times* on the subject of Byron forgeries by the impostor George Gordon Byron. One of these was in his possession, and he wrote: 'I have given it with many apologies to my friend Mr. T. J. Wise. He has thought it worth admission, as a disgrace and a danger-signal, to a back seat among the splendid company of his authentic Byroniana.'

7

MORE FRIENDS

"'"SIR!" said Dr. Johnson; "a man should keep his friendships in constant repair.'" Cockerell was in full agreement. On 10th March 1919 he drafted the following memorandum:[1]

> I leave my children a number of the best and kindest friends, both men and women, that ever man had. Gratefully conscious of all they have meant to me, I declare friendship to be the most precious thing in life. But it is like a plant that withers if it is not heedfully fostered and tended. It is only by constant thought, by visits, by little services, and by abounding sympathy at all times, that friends can be kept.
>
> I implore my children to remember this, in order that the blessings that have been mine may be theirs also, and, to help them to remember, I ask that each of them will read a copy of this memorandum on the anniversaries of my death.
>
> Sydney C. Cockerell

It was merely a reaffirmation of what he had said and written many times before — that friendship was 'affection combined with an infinite capacity for taking pains.'

The 'giving' in friendship, he told Sara Anderson (17th July 1904), was more blessed than the receiving: 'This being much

---

[1] In 1961 he had a slightly modified version of this memorandum printed by the Stanbrook Press. Copies, in envelopes addressed in his own hand, were sent to his special friends after his death.

to others is undoubtedly the greatest source of happiness. Strange that we all know this for a fact and yet seek happiness where it is transient or seldom to be found.'

Writing to Katie Webb in 1920 he discussed the qualities that he looked for in his friends:

> *I* like people of various kinds and keep my friends in different boxes. What I chiefly demand in them is under-standing and character—if they also have looks and wit and morals of some kind, however unconventional, so much the better.

And if they were also famous—then better still. He admired the great because he admired success; and the great were, by definition, successful.

To his already extensive collection of friends, Cockerell added many new ones during his Cambridge days. Not a few of these were, of course, men and women connected with the University; for though he always maintained that dons were narrow in their outlook, he was prepared to make exceptions or to forgive narrowness if it were offset by other virtues. He met Housman frequently but could not claim intimacy with one so notoriously reserved and difficult of approach. For Edward Browne, the Professor of Arabic, he felt deep affection and respect. 'Q', valued because 'he had the same sense of humour as I,' was often a guest at his house, and the only visitor who ever succeeded in smoking in his study ('No smoke, no Q'—and he won). There was also dear old Thomas Okey, the Professor of Italian, with whom he had visited Italy in the nineties.

Dr. Glaisher, Senior Fellow of Trinity, was a keen collector of ceramics. 'I collared him,' said Cockerell, 'and started special cases for the *loán* of his things; then he left them to the Fitzwilliam.' Another friend and great benefactor to the Museum was John Charrington, a coal merchant, who gave the Print Room and an important collection of engravings.

These friendships were all associated with Cambridge, but many others were formed outside the walls of the University.

What Cockerell's affection and generosity meant to a French artist, severely wounded in the First World War, whom he both helped financially and uplifted spiritually, is movingly told in the following letter, written in the early months of 1918:

Cher ami Cockerell,
J'ai toujours envie de vous voir, mais quand j'ai reçu votre affectueuse lettre l'autre jour, mon imagination m'a emporté avec plus de force encore d'habitude à travers ces quelques lieues de pays et ce bras de mer qui nous séparent depuis quatre ans; je volais à vous de tout mon coeur. J'aurais voulu vous serrer les mains, vous diré combien votre affection m'est précieuse, que ni le temps ni l'absence ne peuvent rien diminuer de mon attachement à vous, et que ce sentiment est une de mes richesses qui me font trouver la vie bonne malgré tant de tristesses, et des pertes si pénibles à supporter. . . .

It was in March 1922, in connection with Doughty's financial difficulties, that Cockerell first met T. E. Lawrence over luncheon at the grill-room of the Carlton:

Then finding that Lawrence was a great admirer of Bernard Shaw and had never met him, I took him with me to Adelphi Terrace where the Shaws were expecting me to come and carry off for the Fitzwilliam the larger of the two portraits they have by John. Lawrence's visit was a great success, and Shaw was in his most attractive mood. After half an hour we carried the picture off and taxied to 28 Mallord Street, so that John might touch up a white piece of the background. John, who had painted Lawrence twice, was very affable and showed us his works in progress, including a fine portrait of Suggia playing the 'cello. Then we went to the Hornbys for tea and dinner.

Of the thirty-nine letters written to Cockerell by Lawrence, sixteen of the most interesting may be read in *Friends of a Lifetime*. The two men met many times—most frequently at Max Gate with the Hardys, but also at Cambridge where 'Private Shaw' would turn up unexpectedly on one of the fast motor-bikes that were ultimately to be the cause of his death. With Florence Hardy Cockerell drove over one day to Clouds Hill, the cottage that Lawrence rented for half-a-crown a week:

> We spent an interesting hour in the comfortable upstairs living room. The cottage was more or less of a ruin, but he has made it watertight and attractive. It is about a mile from the camp. His brother has bought it with five acres of rhododendrons and heather. T.E.L. showed me some more sheets of his book. A great deal of it is set up, but none is yet printed. He pays his printer, Pike, £1 a day and has supplied him with the type. He has a gramophone with lots of good records, and a few nice books. He showed me a copy of *St. Joan* inscribed 'Private Shaw from Public Shaw.' Two young soldiers were with him. He welcomes any of them, I understand, but has a few special friends.

After reading Lawrence's Letters, Cockerell wrote:

> 28th March 1940. I finished reading Lawrence's *Letters*, with increased admiration for some of the many Lawrences. But these letters exhibit his self-centred nature to an unpleasant degree, as well as his generosity, wide interests and kindness and the desire for self-effacement which was so curiously contradicted by his vanity.

The two Italian trips that Cockerell made in the nineties in Bernard Shaw's company have already been described. Cockerell had first set eyes on Shaw (who was eleven years his senior) in 1886, when the latter was lecturing at Hammersmith. 'Fairly good, but nothing wonderful' was his verdict

of the talk, and of a subsequent one that Shaw ruined his case
by overstating it; he did not at this time foresee his future
fame. Three years later the two men met and there began a
friendship that was to last for more than sixty years.

This friendship, though it not unnaturally figures far more
prominently in *The Best of Friends* than in the biographies of
the dramatist with the world at his feet,[1] was yet of some
importance to Shaw also. Cockerell was twice with the Shaws
in France; there were many meetings in London and at
Malvern and Cambridge; and many letters passed between
them. It was Cockerell who introduced Shaw to the incomparable Dame Laurentia, Abbess of Stanbrook,[2] to Lord Ruther-
ford and to Sir J. J. Thomson. It was Cockerell, too, who
helped to sort out the various difficulties that arose in the
forties between Shaw's secretary, literary executor and biblio-
grapher, each of whom in turn poured out his or her troubles
and suspicions to him. 'I listened attentively,' he wrote after
one of these interviews, 'but kept most of my opinions to myself.' Cockerell saw Shaw for the last time when he went with
Lady Astor to lunch at Ayot St. Lawrence in 1949.

Shaw sometimes discussed his work with Cockerell, who
wrote (3rd June 1938):

I asked him how many times he usually wrote his work.
He said that his method was to write it in shorthand. It
was typewritten from this by his Secretary, Miss Patch.
He corrected the typescript considerably. Then it was set
up and he did a good deal more correcting of the proofs.
He never bothered his head about style but aimed at
getting his meaning set down in the fewest and most
appropriate words. He thought things out beforehand but
did not compose in his head. He did not know till he came
to it what was going to be on the next page.

[1] For example, in the index to Archibald Henderson's 870-page life
of Shaw, Cockerell's name occurs once only, is wrongly spelt, and is not
to be found on the page mentioned.
[2] See *In a Great Tradition* by the Benedictines of Stanbrook (John
Murray, 1956; chapter entitled 'The Nun and the Dramatist').

'Shaw came from a very musical family,' said Cockerell. 'He used to maintain that his education through music was as good as a University education. He could play and sing very agreeably; I remember him on one occasion imitating a gramophone record of himself.' 'I had a deep esteem for him,' he wrote at the time of his death. 'He had all the attributes of a gentleman — unswerving integrity, consideration for others, generosity on the sly. I think I am his oldest living friend, except perhaps Gilbert Murray.'

Cockerell, who had been one of Shaw's executors before the Public Trustee replaced him, joined in the dispute which arose as to the disposal of Shaw's ashes:

> 31st October 1950. I looked through my letters from Shaw and found several bearing on the subject. I then rang up the Public Trustee and had a long and sympathetic talk with him, and gave him information as to the absence of relatives (except Judy Musters) . . . I afterwards found a card in which he says that his ashes mixed with his wife's 'are to be scattered or inurned in our garden here if no public claim is made.' Such a claim *ought* to come from St. Patrick's Cathedral in Dublin, where Swift lies, in which very improbable case it should have priority.

But Shaw's will forbade any service that might be taken to imply that he was an orthodox Christian, and to Cockerell he had written that no monument to him should take the form of 'a cross, or any other instrument of torture.' Cockerell 'worked hard' to obtain permission for the ashes to be placed in Westminster Abbey, 'by seeing both the present Dean and his predecessor about it, by getting Masefield and Gilbert Murray to write to the Dean in favour of it, by telephoning to *The Times* asking them to advocate it, and by various consultations with the Public Trustee and Lady Astor.' But though the Abbey and St. Patrick's both for a time wavered, the anti-Christian clause proved in the end an insuperable obstacle.

Cockerell went to Golders Green for the cremation:

> There was no religious ceremony. The organist played Elgar's *We are the Music Masters* (from the Enigma Variations)[1] and *Libera me* from Verdi's 'Requiem', in accordance with a wish expressed by Shaw to Lady Astor, and between these performances I read (very badly) the final words of Mr. Valiant for Truth from *The Pilgrim's Progress*, a book greatly admired by G.B.S. all his life, with the following passage ending 'and all the trumpets sounded for him on the other side.' I think nothing could be more appropriate for the occasion.

Shaw's ashes, mingled with those of his wife, were scattered, at very short notice, in his garden at Ayot St. Lawrence by the Public Trustee:

> The Public Trustee said he was forced to be rather precipitate when he learned that the custodian of the two urns at Golders Green was being offered bribes of from 1/- to £5 for small samples of the ashes.... He told me of a second fracas that had taken place at Golders Green during the cremation. A journalist had forced his way upstairs and had assaulted a typist who tried to intercept him. She called for help and two painters who happened to be working near by threw him out, not once but twice.

[1] Cockerell presumably means one or more of the Enigma Variations. In 'The Music *Makers*,' a long work for contralto, chorus and orchestra, Elgar makes use of some of the 'Enigma' material.

8

THOMAS AND FLORENCE
HARDY

IT was, as it happened, the Fitzwilliam Museum that
led to Cockerell's acquaintance with Thomas Hardy.
In the autumn of 1911, Cockerell, who was planning to
form a collection of manuscripts of famous authors, wrote to
Hardy to ask him to contribute. A visit to Max Gate, Hardy's
house in Dorchester, followed, during which Cockerell made
so favourable an impression that he was invited to arrange for
the free distribution of Hardy's manuscripts among various
libraries. To the Fitzwilliam there came *Time's Laughing-
stocks* and *Jude the Obscure*. Thereafter Cockerell became an
habitué of the house, visiting Hardy on no less than forty-two
occasions. Other guests — Barrie, T. E. Lawrence, St. John
Ervine or Siegfried Sassoon — might also be there, and when
William Strang was staying there were 'hilarious evenings.'
But more often Cockerell was alone with the Hardys.

There was, of course, 'plenty of nice talk' about 'men and
books', with Cockerell always attempting to lead Hardy on to
speak of his early life:

> 12th January 1927. Much good talk with Hardy until
> bedtime at 11. . . . [He] told me again that as a child he
> had been so delicate that his parents said in his presence
> (not intending him to hear, but his hearing and sight
> were always extremely acute) that they did not expect
> to rear him! He said also that at the age of 5, when the
> Corn Laws were repealed he had a little sword and used
> to go about crying Free Trade or Blood! As usual there was
> talk about Shakespeare, Keats, and Shelley. I asked him

whether he would sooner meet Keats or Shelley and he said Shelley, as we know so little of his appearance. He reflected that he might have known not only Joseph Severn and Trelawny, but Claire Clairmont.

Speaking one evening of the art of the novel, Hardy said that 'one of the first rules for a writer of fiction was that it must not be made so strange as fact.'

Memorable also were the expeditions which Cockerell made with his host to various places associated with his life or described in his novels:—the cottage in Bockhampton where he had been born; the old tithe barn at Cerne, 'which Hardy had moved ten miles in *Far from the Madding Crowd* and described so magnificently as the scene of the sheep shearing;' 'Mellstock' (Stinsford), with the Hardy gravestones under the big yew; and Puddletown—'the Weatherbury of the novels.' At Puddletown 'we spent a long time in the beautiful church, which has a fine minstrels' gallery dated 1635, in which T.H.'s grandfather often played the 'cello. . . . The entrance to the gallery from outside the church, through which Sergeant Troy entered in *Far from the Madding Crowd*, has been removed. The passage was through a window in the W. end of the S. Aisle.'

On 30th June 1926 Cockerell wrote in his diary:

We went after breakfast for a motor drive, first to Stinsford Church, where T.H. pointed out the place where he sat in a pew as a boy under the skull at the base of the monument to Audeley Grey. The skull used to frighten him on dark days, and from the Angel Grey mentioned in the inscription he took the name of Angel Clare. He pointed out the graves of various Mellstock worthies, including that of 'Penny' whose real name was Reason. We drove on to Upper Bockhampton and went on the heath, now most delicious with new bracken. T.H. pointed out a pit in which the smugglers used to hide their casks, many of which his father used to harbour. We passed the school of Lower Bockhampton on our way back. T.H. was the

first pupil and it still looks much the same as it did when
he went there at 8 years old, still in a frock. He was such
a weakling that until he was 8 he was never allowed to
walk as far as Lower Bockhampton. At 10 he started walking into school at Dorchester and that made him strong.

'Hardy was the most modest of men,' said Cockerell. 'No
one could be more simple or more charming.' Cockerell was
helpful to him in a variety of ways. He provided the perfect
audience when Hardy talked, rehung his pictures after the
drawing-room had been repainted, and had the courage to
persuade him to stop waxing his moustache. He promised to
prevent the publication of any of Hardy's early letters that
might come to light after his death, and to protect his widow
from being 'sponged upon'. He even, for Hardy's sake, toler-
ated Florence's unspeakable dog 'Wessie', which ruled the
house and whose 'putting to sleep' in December 1926 was—
though it ruined the Hardys' Christmas—a matter of almost
universal rejoicing in the literary world. And needless to say it
was Cockerell who came to Florence Hardy's support when her
husband became infatuated with a local actress named
Gertrude Bugler, the wife of a Beaminster farmer.

Mrs. Bugler had entered Hardy's life by way of the Dorchester Players. At one time or another a good deal of drama
took place at Max Gate or in Dorchester. The Balliol Players
came over on a number of occasions to give performances of
the Greek tragedies, and the Dorchester Players staged drama-
tized versions of some of Hardy's novels. In one of the latter
Mrs. Bugler played the part of Tess with, wrote Cockerell,
'reserve, pathos and charm.' His diary tells the sad story of
Hardy's passion for the attractive and talented young actress:

10th January 1925. Max Gate received me very kindly,
but there is a cloud over the house as T.H. is absorbed in
Mrs. Gertrude Bugler, the leading lady of the Dorchester
Players, who has recently enacted Tess. F.H. greatly disturbed about it. She says T.H. is offhand with her, a sorry
business.

11th January. After breakfast for a walk with F.H. and Wessie and she told me her troubles. He is 84½ and I begged her to try to look on the situation from outside as a comedy. She said that that was what she was trying to do, but that he spoke roughly to her and showed her that she was in the way. . . .

12th January. Walked into Dorchester with F.H. in the morning. She told me that she had been in such a fret in the night that she thought she would go mad. It was her birthday (45) but he had not alluded to it in any way. She wondered whether she could be in such a state of nerves on account of her age. All the company of players were talking about it. Mrs. Bugler came to lunch to discuss a proposal from Frederick Harrison that she should play 'Tess' at some matinées at the Haymarket. On the face of it there does not seem to be much harm in her . . . F.H. was very civil to her and offered to put her up for the New Century Club if she should be rehearsing in London. T.H. went through the new scenes of Tess with her. F.H. had begged me to stay to make things easier, or I should have left in the morning. She went at 3 and I drove off at 4.15. . . .

Florence Hardy's concern over Mrs. Bugler is mentioned in the diary for the last time on 23rd August of the same year:

Went for a walk with Mrs. Hardy and Wessie. She said a good deal about his infatuation for the local Tess, Mrs. Bugler, which had been the subject of much gossip in Dorchester. But as she lives as far off as Beaminster . . . and they neither meet nor correspond, I did my best to allay her uneasiness.

All this time Mrs. Bugler had been completely unaware of the tension she was causing in the Hardy household. After reading the rough draft of this chapter she wrote:[1]

[1] In a letter to the Author, 18th February 1964.

'Oh what a cloud there must have been at Max Gate! And I knew nothing then of this 'infatuation for the local Tess'. As I read those words a line from *Tess of the D'Urbervilles* came into my head: 'It is in your own mind what you are angry at, Angel: it is not in me.' It was only in the mind of F.E.H. Yes, I am happy and proud of the perfectly innocent pleasure that T.H. found in my company, and proud of his friendship.

'I well remember my visit to Max Gate on 12th January. Thomas Hardy was in a happy mood that day and, as Mr. Cockerell writes, Mrs. Hardy was very civil to me; yet all the time I felt Mr. Cockerell's cold disapproval and wondered how I could have offended him. And it is only now, after all these years, that I know he was defending Florence Hardy — or the Florence Hardy he then thought her to be — from the woman she mistakenly thought me to be.

'A few days later there came a wire from Mrs. Hardy: she was coming to Beaminster to see me. She arrived, terribly upset and agitated, and said at once that her husband must not know of her visit to me. Then I listened with incredulous amazement to what she had to say. She concluded by asking me not to go to London. So I wrote to Thomas Hardy and to Frederick Harrison to that effect. I never saw Hardy again. His last words to me had been, 'If anyone asks you if you knew Thomas Hardy, say, "Yes, he was my friend."'

'The last time I saw Mr. Cockerell was at the unveiling of the statue to Hardy. I did not recognize him but he came forward with outstretched hand and asked if I remembered him. We spoke of the memorial service which had taken place at Stinsford, and in answer to some remark of mine he said, 'You see, I am not a churchman.' Then he looked at me, seemed about to speak, hesitated, and changed his mind. Someone came to speak to me, and no more was said. I see from what you have written that by that time he had changed his opinion of F.E.H. Perhaps by then he saw me too with different eyes.'

*　　　*　　　*

In a letter written to Cockerell by Katie Webb in August 1920, Mrs. Webb, who had been visiting Hardy, gives her impressions of him and his wife:

I looked at him with curiosity. I think it is 30 years since I saw and talked with him before, and the impression that was with me was of a rough-looking man, dressed very unlike his fellows, with a very keen alert face and a decided accent of some kind. Now I see a refined, fragile, gentle little old gentleman, with a rounder-looking head, as he has but little hair, a gentle and smooth voice and polished manners. He was very charming to me. We talked a little about his books, rather more about the performance of *The Dynasts* at Oxford which seemed to have pleased him very much, and a good deal about people whom we both knew and some whom I didn't know, and one whom I love and whose ears doubtless burned. . . . Mrs. Hardy was much younger than I expected to see and the most melancholy person I have ever seen. I think she smiled once, but the smile only expressed sadness. She said she longed to go to America — 'but I never shall,' she said with a deep sigh; and with a still deeper sigh she said, 'this place is too depressing for words in the winter, when the dead leaves stick on the window-pane and the wind moans and the sky is grey and you can't even see as far as the high road.' Does she find out too late, think you, that youth and age cannot be mated?

Dear old Hardy [Cockerell replied], I am glad you have seen him in his serene old age. Mrs. Hardy is as you say. She takes things very seriously, sometimes worries about what doesn't matter, and naturally feels the great restrictions of her married life. For years she has needed to get right away into a different atmosphere if only for a couple of weeks. But he always keeps her at his side and puts difficulties in the way of any plan. Of course he is devoted to her — but married people ought always to get away from each other, especially when they belong to different generations. She

is no less devoted to him and would probably start worry-
ing at once if she left him, in however excellent hands.
I have tried to plan it once or twice, but have failed.

Cockerell continued to visit the Hardys regularly several times
a year. In July 1927 he found Hardy 'very well indeed, it
seemed to me, and we had an even better talk than usual.' But
early the following January he received a telegram from
Florence Hardy, 'Come at once'. He reached Max Gate the
same afternoon to find Hardy dangerously ill, and though he
seemed to rally he died two days later.

Cockerell took charge of everything. He obtained permission
for burial in Westminster Abbey, overruling the objections
raised by Hardy's brother — 'a roughish kind of a man with no
literary leanings.' He helped Mrs. Hardy's sister, Eva Dugdale,
wrap the scarlet doctor's gown of Cambridge round the body.
He interviewed journalists, made arrangements for cremation,
chose the urn and had it engraved, and comforted the 'brave
unselfish widow.' During the spring he was much at Max Gate,
sorting and burning papers, arranging and labelling books,
helping Florence with her life of her husband that had mostly
been dictated to her by Hardy, and ultimately, after all his kindness, finding himself subjected to her reproaches.

Though he did not realize it at the time, the trouble
actually began with something that occurred on the very day
of the funeral. After the service, Mrs. Hardy, Miss Hardy and
Cockerell went with Barrie to Barrie's flat in the Adelphi
where, at Mrs. Hardy's request, Cockerell wrote the following
letter to *The Times*:

As proposals are likely to be made for various memorials
to Thomas Hardy, and one scheme for a window in
Stinsford Church has already been widely announced, it
may be well to state that he had a particular objection to
what he called 'utilitarian memorials.' In this phrase he
condemned the common practice of making the death of a
famous person the excuse for raising money for drinking-
fountains, lecterns, village halls, and other useful purposes, however commendable they might be on general

grounds. He preferred a monument to be commemorative, and nothing else. As an example he often pointed with approval to the column raised to his famous namesake [Nelson's Hardy] on a Dorset hilltop within sight of Max Gate. I have heard him admit, when the topic came up in conversation, that if any local memorial were to be raised to him he would like that column to have a fellow. If such an idea were adopted an appropriate site for many reasons would be Rainbarrow, on the heath behind his birthplace at Bockhampton.

The letter, Cockerell noted, was read out before posting, and Mrs. Hardy said she was 'glad that we had her husband's views on the subject.'

There was some discussion in the columns of *The Times*, and on 27th October Cockerell wrote a further letter in which he mentioned an expedition he had made with the Hardys to Rainbarrow: 'I asked [Hardy], in Mrs. Hardy's presence, whether his ghost would be pleased to see there a tower that would be a fellow to the well-known and conspicuous memorial to Nelson's Hardy. His reply was a wistful affirmative.'

The following spring Mrs. Hardy addressed two letters to St. John Hornby. Cockerell's first letter to *The Times* had been written, she said, 'without any consultation with me. To anyone who knew my husband well the whole idea is preposterous. He was so modest a man and would have shrunk from discussing with anyone — even with myself — the idea of a memorial to himself.' Of Cockerell's second letter she said, 'I do not know whether you have reflected upon what reply a highly sensitive old man of over eighty was likely to give when he was asked in an abrupt and domineering manner whether "his shade" would be satisfied with a tower raised to him on Rainbarrow.' Of a helpful and disinterested letter[1] to Cockerell from George Clausen, suggesting (at Cockerell's request and with Mrs. Hardy's cognisance) possible sculptors if the memorial should take the form of a figure, she said, 'I was not deeply impressed by this letter, it being so obvious to

[1] Actually there were two letters, but Mrs. Hardy treated them as one.

me that it was written by request, for the purpose of defeating
any wishes I might have concerning the memorial to my
husband. Barrie, to whom it was of course shown, called it
an impudent letter, which it was.'

The trouble continued. T. E. Lawrence produced evidence
that flatly contradicted not only the views expressed by Hardy
to Cockerell, but also Mrs. Hardy's assertion that her husband
would never have discussed the subject of a memorial with
anyone. Mrs. Hardy asked Lawrence to give the facts, in
writing, to St. John Hornby:

> We were driving past the Down [wrote Lawrence] and I
> was pulling his leg, gently, by telling him that everyone
> strange to Dorset naturally thought that the monument
> was his. He dissented, rather shocked that his fame should
> be so magnified as to begin to obscure the Admiral's. I
> insisted that already it was so: and that 100 years hence
> the mistake would be in print, and incontrovertible —
> 'unless they put up a ditto column to you, and there are
> two on the Downs.' T.H. woke up at that, and said very
> firmly 'No, that won't do at all.' I pointed out that I
> myself was dangerously near the public-monument class:
> and that he would infallibly have several monuments.
> He said that of course while he lived there would be
> nothing: and that he would be very sorry if they made
> the mistake of putting up anything large to him after he
> was dead . . .

There were other difficulties. Henry Hardy wanted a tower,
and was prepared to contribute towards its cost the whole of
his brother's legacy to him, provided, Mrs. Hardy told
Cockerell, 'he could have it done by himself, and according to
his own ideas. He had no intention of subscribing to a tower
designed by someone else.' A Puddletown landowner who was
just carrying out a scheme of afforestation for the Government, objected to the most promising of the possible sites on
the ground that there would be trespassers on his plantations
and the danger of fires from dropped cigarette ends; he was
'a power in Dorchester,' said Mrs. Hardy, and a dangerous

antagonist. She added that she considered it 'absurd to talk of a *National* Memorial if more than two-thirds of the cost is borne by the widow and sister, and paid for by money left by the one to whom the memorial is to be raised.'

The position for a statue — if statue it should be — also presented problems. 'Kate Hardy,' wrote Mrs. Hardy to Cockerell, 'objects strongly to the proposed site. . . . There is an underground convenience there which would have to be cleared away and rebuilt somewhere, *out of the fund*, and a very picturesque group of trees cut down. . . . The idea of a statue standing where a lavatory used to be is unpleasant to her, and to me, perhaps absurdly, but there it is.' Further, the Town Council was 'difficult,' one member of the Committee acted rashly and without consulting his colleagues, and Lord Shaftesbury was said to be 'vexed' because he had not been asked to issue the appeal.

Finally it was agreed to erect a statue — a life-sized seated figure of Hardy by Eric Kennington — at a point in Dorchester known as Top o' Town. This involved the removal of nothing more offensive than a horse-trough. Cockerell, who had compiled a memorandum of the disputes, added, on 21st July 1929, a postscript to what he had written, and withdrew into silence:

> *Note.* Mrs. Hardy seems to imply that my inability to regard a statue in Dorchester as the best form of memorial to Thomas Hardy was dictated by some hostility to herself and a desire to 'defeat her wishes.' This is a complete error. She forgets that my objections (shared by some other friends of his) were expressed to her (and acquiesced in) long before any question of a statue arose. A decision having been arrived at by the subscribers I have now no more to say.

But before the statue had been set up, American admirers of Hardy, led by Mr. A. Edward Newton, the well-known Philadelphia book-collector, erected a ten-foot Cornish granite column near Hardy's birthplace. Mrs. Hardy wrote to Cockerell to inform him, and enclosed photographs. Cockerell replied (28th March 1931):

Thank you for the photographs of the memorial. The lettering is (from my specialist point of view) very bad, but the wording is very satisfactory. All the same I cannot but regard it as another of the extraordinary 'satires of circumstance' that I have noted since T.H.'s death that a memorial on that particular site should be set up by Americans, and not by his friends or even by his countrymen. I have never seen Mr. Newton and I do not think that I have ever heard from him.

Six months later, Kennington's statue was unveiled by Sir James Barrie.

It would be tedious to follow in detail the disputes that continued, intermittently, until Mrs. Hardy's death in 1937. A final letter, written by Cockerell in March 1935, will indicate the nature of much of the trouble. In it he abandons the informal 'Dear Florence . . . Yours always' and reverts to Dear Mrs. Hardy . . . Yours sincerely':

Considering that your husband appointed me one of his literary executors I think that I ought to have been consulted before the printing of *An Indiscretion in the Life of an Heiress*; quite apart from the fact that you solemnly promised, after that unfortunate American publication, that you would never do such a thing again without seeking my views. I have not seen this publication, or even heard of it until this morning's announcement in *The Times*, and it may be something of the printing of which your husband would have approved. Nevertheless I am astonished that you should not have thought it your duty to let me see it.

'Mrs. Hardy,'[1] said Cockerell, 'was dull beyond description — an inferior woman with a suburban mind, but very ambitious to

---

[1] *Friends of a Lifetime* contains no letters written by Mrs. Hardy after her husband's death, it being at that time too soon for his disagreements with her to be made public.

be well off. I helped her a great deal in her life. Hardy left a
very large estate; she found herself suddenly with £50,000 and
wanted to shine. She thought Sir James Barrie would marry
her. Barrie *did* propose — in a moment of emotion; but, to her
great chagrin, he backed out. I regarded her as second-rate,
though she started by greatly improving Hardy's comfort.'[1]
And he wrote, 'She led a lonely and difficult life with her
aged husband, especially in winter when there were few
visitors.'

In 1938, a year after Florence Hardy's death, Cockerell was
just in time to prevent the publication of a 'contemptible
attack' on Hardy's sisters, one of whom was still living:
'4th June. I have been much disturbed by an extract from a
book called *Kulchur* by Ezra Pound which Viola Dallyn made
for me yesterday from a review copy that came into her hands.
It is a scurrilous and abominable attack on Hardy's "stinking
old sisters" who are alluded to as "aged hens".' Cockerell
immediately got into touch with one of the partners of the
publishers: 'I expressed my indignation in no uncertain terms,
threatened legal action &c, &c, &c. I read the passage out
to him. He had not seen it and appeared horrified. He promised
that the book, which is announced for publication next
Thursday, should not go out with the passage in it.'

The various troubles that Cockerell had to face as Hardy's
literary executor have been dealt with at some length, in
order to show the difficulty of his assignment and the tenacity
with which he fought on behalf of Hardy's reputation. As late
as 1961 he was writing to *The Times* to refute inaccuracies
that had recently been published. Cockerell's breach with
Mrs. Hardy had very likely been due, in the first instance, to
her overwrought state after her husband's death; probably she
had no clear recollection of what had occurred in Barrie's flat.

No doubt there were faults on both sides.

---

[1] Florence Hardy told Cockerell 'what a complete failure T. H.'s first
marriage had been, and that when the first Mrs. Hardy died they were
in the midst of a bitter quarrel and were about to separate. All the poems
about her are a fiction, but a fiction in which their author has now come
to believe.'

9

DAME LAURENTIA

EVEN more astonishing, perhaps, than the quantity of Cockerell's friendships was their variety. What could seem more improbable than that one should have been formed with an enclosed nun, and cultivated through the disconcerting barrier of a grille? Yet of his many friends in all walks of life, few became so dear to him as Dame Laurentia of Stanbrook Abbey.

It was in 1907, while Cockerell was acting as 'Mr. Perrins's hired man' (as he called himself), that he first met Dame Laurentia McLachlan,[1] a member of the Benedictine monastery of Stanbrook, of which she was later to become Abbess. Fate (or 'our respective guardian angels,' wrote Dame Laurentia) played no small part in this meeting, for it was a fool's errand that brought Cockerell and his friend Dyson Perrins[2] one chill January morning to Stanbrook Abbey, where Dame Laurentia was at that time in charge of the choir. The purpose of their visit was to examine the fine thirteenth-century Oscott Psalter, which had been lent to the monastery for the purpose of study; they arrived to find that the manuscript had already been returned to Oscott College.

The two guests were received by the Abbess (Dame Caecilia

[1] Margaret McLachlan (1866–1953), professed at Stanbrook in 1885 and renamed Laurentia. Elected Abbess of Stanbrook in 1931. For the life of this remarkable woman see *In a Great Tradition: Tribute to Dame Laurentia McLachlan by the Benedictines of Stanbrook* (John Murray, 1956), and also *The Best of Friends*, pp. 234–301. The material for this chapter is drawn mainly from these two books. The 750 letters exchanged between Dame Laurentia and Cockerell are now at Stanbrook.

[2] The collector of manuscripts (see p. 125).

Heywood) and Dame Laurentia, and over a discussion of the
Oscott Psalter Dame Laurentia's great liturgical knowledge
soon became apparent. She for her part instantly recognized
Cockerell's expertise in manuscripts, and a friendship of
'mutual benediction and recompense' was begun from that
moment. A bargain was struck:

> Any book I have is yours to borrow, '*mihi et amicis*' [he
> wrote]. I trust you implicitly not to put it in the hands
> of anyone who does not know how to turn over the leaves
> or that the paint and gilding must not be touched. Ladies
> of the world are terrible defaulters in these respects —
> and the monks (I say nothing of the nuns) of old days
> were little better. . . .

She for her part offered 'any little help I can give you . . . I
shall take due advantage of your kind offer regarding your
books.' But Cockerell's kindness and generosity were not to be
limited to the loan of a handful of his manuscripts. He immediately offered to help

> in the revival of the spirit of craftsmanship which exists,
> but needs direction, at Stanbrook, and which I have found
> to be so painfully absent in other religious houses at home
> and abroad. Of course there are heaps of difficulties on
> account of your seclusion and the remoteness from
> proper teachers and from the stimulus of seeing actual
> things instead of merely pictures in books — but some of
> these difficulties we must try to overcome.

Cockerell was as good as his word. To the printers of the
community he brought volumes of the Kelmscott and Doves
Presses for study, and Emery Walker and St. John Hornby in
person to criticize and advise. Katie Adams was engaged to give
instruction in book-binding, and Perrins and other of Cockerell's friends were easily persuaded to lend manuscripts from
their collections. Thus was taste added to the enthusiasm
which had never been lacking at Stanbrook.

*   *   *

From the very start of his friendship Cockerell had made clear his position with regard to religion. The French painter Renoir once said that he found it hard to believe that two hundred and fifty million Hindus had been mistaken for four thousand years; this, in a nutshell, was Cockerell's attitude:

> I am [he wrote to Dame Laurentia] a man without any set creed—too much in sympathy with all great religions to adhere exclusively to one, too much aware of the great mysteries to accept any solution of them. I have been to Assisi, as I told you, for love of St. Francis and of the things he loved—and have looked at Damascus with more reverence for the sake of St. Paul and his 13th chapter of 1st Corinthians. But I should look with similar feelings on places associated with Buddha and Confucius —and having seen a little of Mohammedans and known the late Grand Mufti of Egypt, who was one of the wisest, gentlest and most venerable of men, I am opposed to their being converted into Christians or into anything else but more enlightened Mohammedans. I tell you all this that you may realize what manner of infidel you are dealing with. . . .

Dame Laurentia replied:

> It is very nice of you to tell me your religious views so frankly. You won't mind my saying that I think a man without set creed is very much to be pitied. While acknowledging all the good there is in the different ways men have of expressing their religion, one cannot see how all can be equally right—especially if we grant (as you perhaps do not grant) that God has made a definite revelation to men. I am not going to believe that you are a plain infidel, but I do not see where God and Christianity come into your system. . . . Of course we do not believe in indiscriminate proselytising. . . .

Nor did Cockerell conceal his opinion that Dame Laurentia, by joining an enclosed order, had needlessly deprived herself of so many of the interesting things and innocent pleasures that life had to offer. That April he wrote to her, 'When I saw Stonehenge yesterday, and the hares playing on the downs (nine at one time!) or the plovers and the larks overhead, I was sorry that you were cut off from the thrill it all gave me — but no doubt you have other thrills that I am a stranger to, so perhaps I ought not to be sorry.' Dame Laurentia replied:

> I could not help smiling at your regrets on Stonehenge. You do not think of us, I hope, as caged birds (or lions); we do not answer a bit to that description. The only place where there is any impression of cutting off is in the parlour, and we look on the grate as a barrier not to keep us in but to keep you out. We are not debarred either from enjoying nature, though we have not the variety that you so-called free people can procure. . . . You won't be sorry for me again, will you?

But Cockerell would not budge from the position he had adopted:

> I believe all you tell me about the joys and compensations of the life you have chosen. None the less I *do* regard you as caged birds. You may tell me that we are all caged in one way, by fashion, by prejudices, by duties, by principles, by lack of health, strength, understanding, means, etc., etc. and that you are free from some of the bars that enclose other women — of course I admit it. And as to keeping *me* out I accept the situation cheerily, and if you like you may say that it is I that am imprisoned on the wide earth. But why should you want to keep out Miss Adams, any more than the doctor? Until I know you better I shall still be sorry that you cannot see Stonehenge and the barrows of the ancient chieftains of that countryside — that you cannot see the British Museum, the National Gallery and Chartres Cathedral and that you cannot see the faces of those persons, men and women, who form so large a part of my world. . . .

Dame Laurentia replied:

> If you persist in being sorry for me I suppose I can only
> hope that time will bring you to a better way of thinking.
> But in the mean time please take Chartres off the list of
> things to be sorry about, for I am happy enough to have
> seen that most wonderful and glorious Cathedral, one of
> the most delightful experiences of my life. . . .

So they could only agree to differ — to differ upon matters
which were to Dame Laurentia fundamental — though she
never entirely abandoned the hope of one day converting him.
He for his part continued to act as her link with the outside
world. He was always ready to examine a manuscript for her
and to report on it, and many of their letters deal with problems of attribution and dating, or with liturgical matters. He
plied her with books, sometimes warning her of their contents
so that she might refuse them if she so wished. There were 'the
works of the blessed Borrow. . . . He was a militant Protestant
and unless you are prepared to bob your head when he tilts at
you and come up smiling (which for aught I know may be
against the rules) you must live and die without reading him.'
But of Borrow Dame Laurentia had no fear.

Strangely enough, secular music of the most innocent kind
proved a greater obstacle. After a musical evening in Paris
Cockerell wrote enthusiastically:

> I wonder whether you know the blessed songs — my
> favourite ones — that were exquisitely sung to me last
> night. Caccini's *Amarilli* (the best of all) and *Voi che
> sapete* and *Vedrai carino*, and *Ombra mai fu* and such
> lovely things of Gluck that a French friend exclaimed
> (and I agreed with him), 'C'est la musique du Paradis!'
> If the words are not allowed in convents have not the
> heavenly airs been left you?

But not even the works of Gluck, who had been given the
order of knighthood by the reigning pope, were acceptable. 'I

do not know your songs,' Dame Laurentia replied, 'but I have
no doubt they are lovely. There is room in my mind for all
truly beautiful music, but there are songs, just as there is
literature, which would not suit our atmosphere, and to tell
the truth would not interest me.'

On several occasions during her seventy years at Stanbrook
Dame Laurentia was accorded permission by the Holy See to
visit other Benedictine nunneries. In June 1923 she received
a dispensation to spend a fortnight at East Bergholt, in Suffolk,
to train the monastic choir. She immediately informed the
delighted Cockerell.

The layman might be excused for imagining that the
journey across England of an enclosed nun would have to be
made in a kind of Black Maria, or at all events that she would
not be allowed to stray a single step from the directest path.
When Cockerell wrote to point out that the British Museum
stood midway between Paddington and Liverpool Street, and
that Cambridge and Oxford lay on an alternative and reasonably direct return route to Stanbrook, he probably had very
little hope that the plot that he was hatching would succeed.
But no obstacle was put in the way of a day's sightseeing in
London, where Dame Laurentia had not been for nearly forty
years, and a swift visit to the two university cities.

Of course Cockerell planned, to a split second, every detail
of these memorable days. By rising at 4.30 a.m. — no hardship
for a nun — Dame Laurentia and her companion, Dame
Francis Kenyon, were able to reach London by ten o'clock.
Here they were met and conducted to Westminster Cathedral,
where Cockerell awaited them. After hearing mass, the party
divided, Cockerell taking Dame Laurentia and her friends and
relations to Westminster Abbey, which she had never seen,
and thence to lunch with friends in South Kensington. He
wrote in his diary:

Then, at 1.50, we started for the British Museum, calling
on the Yates Thompsons, who were out, and visiting

Cayley Robinson's lovely wall decorations in the vestibule of the Middlesex Hospital on the way. At the British Museum Eric Millar had made preparations for us, and after politenesses from Sir Frederic Kenyon and J. A. Herbert, Dame Laurentia settled down to enjoy the Lindisfarne Gospels, Queen Mary's Psalter, the Duke of Bedford's hours, the St. Cuthbert book, several fine Psalters and the Lambeth Bible in undisturbed quietness until 4.40, when we left the B. M. (which she had never seen before) and motored to Liverpool St. station. . . .

A fortnight after this 'most successful day imaginable' came another 'never-to-be-forgotten day, to be ranked with 11th June.' Dame Laurentia reached the Cockerells at Cambridge in time for breakfast. There followed a sight of his own manuscripts, and what she described as 'a hectic tour of Colleges, Libraries, etc.' including, of course, the Fitzwilliam. Jesus College, of which Cockerell had at one time been a Fellow, was of particular interest to her, the building having originally been a Benedictine nunnery. The afternoon train carried Cockerell and the two nuns to Oxford, where the Bodleian had been prevailed upon to open its doors after hours so that Dame Laurentia could see a Worcester manuscript important to her work. Then five minutes in New College garden and a wild rush for the station. No American could have seen more of Oxford in exactly fifty minutes, from train to train, than did Dame Laurentia. 'For the rest of her life,' wrote Cockerell, 'these two days were counted as red letter days in her calendar, and were suitably commemorated.' He too remembered each year the anniversary of 'our blessed and never to be forgotten romp in London' and wrote a loving letter.

Cockerell was always as generous with his friends as with his books, and many of the former found their way to Stanbrook at his suggestion; he must, however, have realized that in sending Bernard Shaw[1] to Dame Laurentia he was taking a

[1] See *In a Great Tradition*, pp. 231–78.

considerable risk. For many years Cockerell had planned to bring these two friends of his together, but it was not until 1924, when the first performance of *Saint Joan* had aroused her curiosity and the Malvern Theatre had drawn Shaw to her neighbourhood, that the project became practicable. On 24th April of that year, the Shaws appeared at the gates of Stanbrook.

At this first meeting all went well: Dame Laurentia found her guests 'charming, and *St. Joan* was discussed, with other subjects, in a very pleasant conversation,' she told Cockerell. 'I was greatly interested to meet such a famous man, one more privilege for which I have to thank you, and my impression is that we got on very well together.' Shaw too was no less delighted; he promised to 'pop in' again soon, and in the autumn a copy of *Saint Joan*, inscribed 'To Sister Laurentia from Brother Bernard' was delivered at Stanbrook.

For seven years no serious rift occurred in their friendship, though Shaw was at times dangerously provocative. In a long and brilliant letter written to her from Damascus, he dared to assert that the author of *Revelations* was unmistakably a drug addict and his book 'a disgrace to the Bible;' but he sugared this particular pill with the gift of a pebble from Bethlehem set in an exquisite silver reliquary. It was with the publication, in 1932, of *The Adventures of the Black Girl in her Search for God* that he finally overstepped the bounds of her tolerance. Dame Laurentia was scandalized by what to her seemed nothing but a grotesque parody of all that she held most sacred; 'his book is horrible,' she told Cockerell, 'and quite unworthy of him.' To Shaw she also expressed her deep displeasure and several years were to pass before he again dared to show his face at Stanbrook.

But though Dame Laurentia could never forget, she came to forgive this blasphemy, and the old friendship was resumed. She acknowledged again what she had recognized at her first meeting with him — his 'absolute sincerity and simplicity;' and he, for his part, continued to admire the phenomenon of an enclosed nun who had not 'an enclosed mind, as so many women at large have.' Shortly before his death he wrote to her, 'the thought of Stanbrook is a delight to me. It is one of my holy places.'

Cockerell's friendship with Dame Laurentia was never to suffer so rude a shock. Though Dame Laurentia was saddened by his 'unbelief', as indeed was he by her belief, they could agree to disagree. 'We will leave our differences alone,' she wrote to him, 'and wish they did not exist.' Whenever he was within striking distance of Stanbrook, Cockerell would appear, with or without warning, at its gates. '6th July 1924. . . . Spent 3½ hours with Dame Laurentia, who was delighted to receive me so unexpectedly. . . . Passed judgment on the various monastic industries, the weaving, the embroidery, the printing, the wood engraving, and the writing.'

Year after year, too, the correspondence between them continued. But not until seventeen years after their first meeting did they discover that each had been keeping the other's letters; it was then agreed that the survivor should inherit the complete correspondence, to keep or destroy as seemed best. When, in 1951, illness made Cockerell as much a prisoner at Kew as was Dame Laurentia at Stanbrook, the telephone sometimes bridged the gap between them. But both were now growing deaf, and the written word remained the most satisfactory method of communication.

On 6th January 1953 Cockerell wrote in his diary: 'Grievous news from Dame Laurentia that she is dangerously ill with congestion of a lung. This may be the last letter that I shall receive from her. It is written in a firm hand. She says that she is holding her own. . . .' In melancholy mood he began to write her obituary for *The Times*. But Dame Laurentia rallied; when, some days later, Cockerell rang up Stanbrook for news of her, it was Dame Laurentia herself who answered. In August, however, he learned that his 'beloved Abbess' was dying, and three days later that the end had come. She was eighty-seven.

10

'MY' MUSEUM

WE return to Cambridge.

The Fitzwilliam Museum — 'one of the last great public edifices erected in the Classical style in England during the nineteenth century' — had been designed by George Basevi. Begun in 1837, the building was continued by Charles Cockerell[1] after Basevi's death and completed by Edward Barry in 1875. It was splendid, rather pompous, and extremely richly decorated internally.

The design for the extension of the Museum, which Messrs. Smith and Brewer had made before the War and which had been approved by the Senate in 1915, consisted of a long two-storeyed gallery ('the Marlay Galleries') connecting the original building with one side ('the Marlay Wing') of what it was hoped might eventually, through future benefactions, become a quadrangle. But by the time peace came, building costs had risen so much that there was no longer money enough for the Marlay Wing; it was therefore decided to build the Marlay Galleries, leading for the present to a hypothetical quadrangle, and small Coin and Manuscript Rooms (the gift of the McClean family) adjoining them.

No sooner was the decision to start building made known, than the design of the Marlay Galleries was savagely attacked by the Slade Professor, E. S. Prior. Cockerell had known and been on friendly terms with Prior in the Arts and Crafts circle in the nineties, and he had welcomed his appointment as Slade Professor. But Prior was an architect, and his hostility may conceivably have been connected with the fact that he had not

[1] No relation, so far as is known.

been invited to submit designs for the Fitzwilliam or even consulted as to a suitable architect. 'He attacked the scheme,' wrote Cockerell, 'with violent venom in the Senate House, in *The Times* and other papers and on all possible occasions. However his arguments, always wide of the mark, failed to carry conviction and I got my scheme through.'

Cockerell jotted down some of Prior's more caustic *obiter dicta* on the proposed extension: 'It would degrade and disfigure the building for all time . . . it would be a blotch . . . it would be like looking from a drawing-room into a cupboard . . . sloppy thought and ill-digested design . . . mere passages . . . corridors unfitted for the hanging of pictures . . . etc., etc.' Prior issued a fly-sheet in which he misspelt the architect's name and miscalculated most of the figures he quoted. Cockerell pounced mercilessly on his opponent's errors in another fly-sheet, and pointed out that what Prior had dismissed as 'mere passages' were, in fact, only a foot narrower than the side galleries of the original building.

There is no need to follow each blow that was struck and cunningly parried. On 18th February 1921 'the Grace in favour of the building of the connecting galleries to house the Marlay Collections was passed, after many delays. There was a large gathering in the Senate House to defend the Grace but Professor Prior, who has spoken twice in the Senate and has issued three fly-sheets against it, did not turn up with his *nonplacet*.' In fact, Prior troubled his redoubtable opponent no further. There was no reconciliation for many years to come; but on 7th March 1931 Cockerell wrote in his diary: 'Met Professor Prior, with whom I have been on distant terms for the last ten years because of his random and intemperate attacks on my building schemes. Suggested that we should bury the hatchet and got him to come and go over the Galleries with me. The episode went off very amicably.' Prior died the following year. 'He was an unsatisfactory lecturer and professor,' said Cockerell. 'His wife had to wake up undergraduates who had gone to sleep at his lectures.' And he wrote in his diary: 'In the twenty years of his tenure I am not aware that Prior ever did the Fitzwilliam a good turn or that any object came to it through his influence. But he had many good points, and in conjunction with Gardiner he produced a very useful book on English medieval sculpture.'

The Marlay Galleries were completed in September 1922, and after they had thoroughly 'dried out' the collection was hung. They were opened on Marlay's birthday, 18th June 1924. It was a great day for Cockerell. No ceremony took place at the Fitzwilliam itself, but there was a luncheon at King's, a speech in the Senate House in praise of Marlay and Cockerell, a garden party at Pembroke, and a dinner at Trinity followed by a party in the Lodge of Trinity. 'Home at about 11.30,' wrote Cockerell, 'tired but content.'

And well might he be content! For the Marlay Galleries were something without precedent in a Museum at that time. In particular, the Upper Gallery, with its cleverly designed bays, its dull-gold Japanese wall-paper, its rugs, occasional furniture and bowls of flowers (specially grown and arranged by two admiring ladies, each of whom had her own inviolable territory allotted to her) was revolutionary; even after the passage of forty years, during which the humanizing of museums has become a commonplace, the shock of its beauty and fitness has not staled. There is no question of 'looking from a drawing-room into a cupboard' as one enters the Gallery from the old building; the view is rather that from a very large and pompous cupboard into a very exquisite little drawing-room. If Cockerell (who had of course been hand-in-glove with his architect) had done nothing more than bring the Marlay Galleries into being, his name would deserve to be remembered with gratitude by all who ever set foot in a museum.

He knew that he had done well. A week after the opening he wrote to Lethaby, 'I am not sure that the Upper Gallery is not going to be an object lesson for the future. I have never seen pictures look more friendly and comfortable.'

The rising cost of labour and materials having made it impossible to build the projected 'Marlay Wing' with Marlay money,

Cockerell now began to cast his eyes around for a new victim. In his diary for 24th June 1925 he wrote:

> Called on Major J. S. Courtauld, M.P. at 7 Grosvenor Sq. and appealed to him and his family to provide the Fitz-william with a new wing. He was very sympathetic . . . but he said that the claims on him were numerous. I then went to his brother, Mr. S. L. Courtauld, of 47 Grosvenor Sq. He was most friendly and wished to have particulars as to the dates when the money, about £90,000, would be required. He arranged to come to Cambridge on Tuesday and I went away rejoicing.

The Courtaulds were a Huguenot family grown wealthy through the development of artificial silk; three brothers and a sister had been educated at Cambridge and were thus fair game for Cockerell. 'I did not know him (I may just have met him in Cambridge) when he called on me in Grosvenor Square in 1925,' wrote Sir Stephen Courtauld.[1] 'He then showed me the plans for the additions to the Fitzwilliam and explained their merits: he did not invite suggestions for improving them. I was impressed. . . .'

His visit to Cambridge confirmed this favourable impression. He was shown round the Fitzwilliam, excellently lunched by John Charrington at Trinity, treated to 'tea and books' at the Cockerells', and finally escorted to the Station to catch the 7.7 to London. That night Cockerell noted in his diary, 'Everything points to the early beginning of our next extension at the expense of S.L.C. or of his family.' He was not mistaken: a fortnight later Stephen Courtauld wrote to say that he and his sister, Renée Courtauld, would guarantee a sum of £50,000 between them. Thus, within three weeks of the opening of his campaign, Cockerell had succeeded in raising more than half of the money estimated as necessary for carrying out his project.

It might have been imagined that Cockerell would have been content to look elsewhere for the £40,000 that still

[1] In a letter to the Author, 1963.

remained to be found; he decided, however, to think in terms of a 'Courtauld Wing', and to continue his pursuit of the other members of that most generous family. Major J. S. Courtauld, the first of them to be approached, still eluded him; he had recently been elected M.P. for Chichester, and had too many other calls. Samuel Courtauld, another brother but not a Cambridge man, was visited and appeared to be interested; but he could not be pinned down. 'As I came away,' wrote Cockerell, 'I said, "May I regard the prospect as hopeful?" And he said, "Yes, certainly".' He too, however, managed to make his escape, but was later to give his fine house in Portman Square (the Courtauld Institute) and many of his pictures to London University. Yet another brother, W. J. Courtauld, was sounded, and he responded at once with the offer of £20,000. By March 1928, by means of a skilfully manipulated rivalry between brothers and sister, Cockerell had succeeded in stepping up their joint contribution from £70,000 to £100,000 — the precise sum now estimated as necessary.

Dunbar Smith, the surviving partner of Smith and Brewer, again acted as architect, and on 5th June 1931 the Courtauld Wing was opened. The arrangements for the occasion were much the same as those that had been made for the opening of the Marlay Galleries. Cockerell wrote:

A fine day (until the evening) for the opening of the Courtauld Galleries. There was no ceremony in the building, which was open to ticket holders from 10 to 7. 3648 persons attended in the course of the day, a great many coming from a distance. At 1 there was a grand Luncheon in Trinity College, after which the Chancellor (Stanley Baldwin) delivered a little address in the Senate House on the Fitzwilliam Museum before conferring Hon. Degrees on Lord Irwin, Lord Lee of Fareham, John Masefield and others. This being over I accompanied him to the Fitzw., conducted him through the crowded Galleries and then went with him to a big garden party at Pembroke. The last function was a dinner at King's to which the four senior members of my staff were invited.

The following day Cockerell added, 'The new Galleries are pronounced by all the experts to be a triumphant success.' Approval was indeed general and sustained. In 1936 the architectural correspondent of *The Times* wrote:

> Depending entirely upon the proportions of masses, the modulation of planes, and the relations between voids and solids, [the new block] is a model of how to preserve classical feeling with a single eye to the practical requirements of a museum. In comparison with the original Fitzwilliam it is a perfect illustration of the difference between the spirit and the letter of tradition.

The Queen paid a visit to Cambridge in July 1932 and was shown round the Fitzwilliam by its Director. Cockerell found her 'very affable and appreciative, though she speaks with a German accent,' and he was informed that she 'continually dwelt on the beauties of the Fitzwilliam during the drive back to London.' Cockerell said, 'I think I could have made a friend of Queen Mary if I had gone to Buckingham Palace and written my name in the book. She would have asked me to tea.'

To someone who congratulated Cockerell on his new Wing, he is said to have replied, 'Wing? No—*just a feather*!' The Courtauld Galleries did, of course, constitute little more than one side of Dunbar Smith's projected square, which to this day remains less than half completed; before his retirement in 1937 Cockerell was, however, to be able to add to it two more small feathers: the Charrington Print Room and the Henderson Galleries. He also succeeded, though not without a battle, in getting bays and a gallery built into the Central Gallery of the original structure. In his final Annual Report is shown a plan of the Museum, variously shaded. 'Intending and potential benefactors,' runs the text, 'will observe that the oblique lines indicate the portion of the building scheme that remains to be executed. A further extension is urgently needed for the housing of the additions that constantly accrue.'

Cockerell was incorrigible. Dunbar Smith's great project

might remain—will perhaps always remain—incomplete. Cockerell could, however, pride himself on the fact that, during his twenty-nine years as Director, he had more than doubled the size of the original building. He had added incomparable treasures to the Founder's original bequest. More important still: he had transformed a dead-alive, almost static little provincial gallery into one of the most vital, best displayed and choicest museums in the country.

Not surprisingly, the fame of the Marlay and Courtauld Galleries was soon spread far and wide. An American benefactress, after visiting Cambridge, offered $150,000 to the University of North Carolina for the building of an art gallery, provided that the Fitzwilliam additions were taken as a model. Deputations from several museums, both British and Continental, arrived to study the Cockerell technique of lighting and display. 'What *book* do you use for arranging your museum?' inquired the Director of an American art gallery, and flatly refused to accept Cockerell's assurance that he and his architect followed no written code of instruction.

Amongst a number of papers placed by Cockerell in an envelope inscribed 'for the use of a future historian', is a small slip upon which he has written the following:

Fitzwilliam Museum

I am most proud of the two achievements that met with the greatest opposition:

1. The opening of the Museum on Sunday afternoons.
2. The remodelling of the Central Gallery, as well as of the plywood used for the wall coverings in many of the Galleries and of the Japanese gold paper in the Upper Marlay Gallery and for backing in the ceramic cases. These were my choices, not the architect's.

S.C.C. 1937

The Syndicate who managed the affairs of the Fitzwilliam was composed of nine senior members of the University, the Vice-Chancellor being *ex officio* Chairman. Though Cockerell had, at one time or another, a few staunch supporters among his Syndics, he regarded them collectively with a mistrust that he made small attempt to conceal. Those Syndics who knew little about art were, in his opinion, fools; those who were knowledgeable, but held views that differed from his, were either fools or knaves. It is, therefore, greatly to the credit of the Syndics as a whole, that they realized Cockerell's many admirable qualities and, though often provoked, supported him in almost all his enterprises.

There was, for example, Dr. Guillemard, a distinguished traveller, naturalist and writer, who 'does not know a good drawing when he sees one.' There was Mr. A. S. F. Gow, who undoubtedly did, but who did not always find himself in agreement with the Director. As Cockerell wrote to a friend just after his retirement, 'When I was at Cambridge I got on much better when half my Committee were elsewhere;' and it was a favourite saying of his that 'a committee should consist of two people with power to reduce their numbers.'

No doubt it sometimes, perhaps not infrequently, happened that Cockerell was right and the Syndics wrong. His diary records what certainly appears to be one such occasion:

23rd April 1918. Syndicate meeting in afternoon. Only four present, and they stupidly voted for the acceptance, but not for the exhibition, of two bad watercolours of flowers offered by an artist called Mercer.

24th April 1918. On my way from the Museum met M. D. Forbes of Clare, one of the four members of the Syndicate who voted for the acceptance of the shoddy Mercer drawings. I remonstrated with him and he said that he did it as a matter of principle (he stupidly imagines that it is bad for the Museum to refuse things, as though I were not always refusing things) and that he 'seriously' considered one of the silly flower-pieces better than the 'absolutely rotten' Turner of Kirkstall Abbey which has just been presented by Mrs. Dewick. What is to be done with such a foolish young man?

27th April 1918. Met Guillemard, one of the guilty four on Tuesday, and reproached him for voting for the silly Mercer drawings. He defended himself and made the absurd remark that he regarded the Museum as a place of education, whereas I regarded it as a home for beautiful things — as though my whole aim during my ten years' Directorship had not been to increase and develop its educational value.

Cockerell liked to have personal control of every corner of his Museum; it was therefore inevitable that his second-in-command should fare badly. Nothing was delegated to him; he was a slave. On the other hand, Cockerell treated his junior staff admirably. He got to know their private affairs, their little domestic troubles, and helped them with counsel and with money; he fought to get their wages raised; he invited them to his house to see his books. 'When one visited the Fitz-william,' said his son, 'instead of bored, loud-mouthed officials in uniform one found quietly-dressed men (ex-gardeners, etc.) whom he had enthused and encouraged to make a study of some part of the collection. One or two of them (Mr. Parr, for instance) became experts, and they would do anything for him.'

In fact, Cockerell's creation of a new type of museum attendant was in its way as revolutionary as his creation of a new type of museum; unfortunately, though the civilized museum has now become a commonplace, the old type of attendant is as yet by no means extinct in this country.

Mr. A. Cousins, for many years an assistant at the Fitz-william, wrote:[1]

Sir Sydney made us feel that we were not merely em-ployees but fellow-workers with him. . . . Humbug and pretence had no chance with him; the passport to his favour was to be sincerely interested in museum tasks and to give ungrudgingly of the best that was in one, nor was he slow to praise anything well done. . . . He delighted to

[1] In a communication to the Author.

say to parties he was conducting round, 'A thousand pounds if you can find a speck of dust' — and indeed, any blemish on the spotless perfection was extremely rare.

It was characteristic of Cockerell that when Bernard Shaw came to the Museum he introduced each of his assistants in turn to the great man. Queen Mary's intention to visit the Fitzwilliam was a carefully kept secret, but the staff were told of it in confidence and informed that if their wives chanced to be 'just looking discreetly into the cases', no objection would be taken.

When Cockerell finally came to retire, he received from many of his staff letters of gratitude which came straight from the heart. One who had served under him throughout the whole of his time as Director wrote:

May I be allowed to renew with sincerity my thanks for all you did for me. I fear my words have been all too few in this respect, but my appreciation is all the greater. You have been a very real friend and consequently it made my work at the Museum a work of love. I have known my limitations and realize the errors I have made (many in my enthusiasm to please), but you have always taken a kindly view; this has endeared you alike to old and young, responsive as you have been to all varieties of character or pursuit and remote from nothing that concerns mankind.

Three years later, as he lay dying, he wrote again, 'To me you have always been my ideal, for I know no better man.'

When Cockerell came to the Fitzwilliam in 1908 there was no typewriter, no secretary, and only one telephone. He answered every letter by return, in his wonderful hand. Yet those who called on him at the Museum seldom if ever found him too busy to see them. In the Galleries he was a familiar figure in his dark blue serge suit with its high buttons and

narrow lapels. He loved to get into conversation with anyone —
friend or stranger — whom he encountered. A few chance
remarks made one day to a young man sheltering gloomily
from the rain among the ceramics, started him upon his lifelong hobby of collecting Chinese pottery — as, many years
later, he told Cockerell with deep gratitude. Cockerell was
always particularly good with the young. One who used, as a
girl, to visit the Fitzwilliam, recalls her experiences:

> It must have been around 1910 and onwards for a few
> years when I used often to be in the Museum with my
> father or my uncle. But the times I liked best were if I
> was alone and came across Cockerell. I was about 14 —
> *very* shy, very bored with ART but very interested in
> pictures. Cockerell was always welcoming and gentle and
> treated me casually and as a grown-up and always had
> time to show me something, as it were *en passant.* . . . I
> could never understand why he was always looked on as
> prickly, but I realize now how fierce he could be. I
> remember staying with the D. Y. Camerons and a letter
> arriving for D.Y. 'Another letter from that *fellow* — now
> the morning's wrecked!' Cockerell was trying to extract
> a picture. He wanted a dark one, and D.Y. was in a 'blue
> mood — or was it vice versa? I can't quite recall. Anyway,
> D.Y. sent him one and Cockerell sent it straight back say-
> ing it wasn't good enough. D.Y. was affronted. . . .

Many have spoken of the cold water that Cockerell could
pour, when he felt that circumstances warranted it, upon a
pompous or pretentious collector whose standards fell short of
his own. 'And now *I* have something to show *you,*' a visitor
to whom he had been showing a superb medieval manuscript
was overheard to say. The man drew a little book from his
pocket and handed it with great *empressement* to the Director.
Cockerell glanced at it without enthusiasm and handed it back.
   'I suppose,' he said icily, 'I *have seen worse.*'

11

SIR SYDNEY

THE greatest disappointment that Cockerell sustained during his time at Cambridge was that, after his Fellowship at Jesus had come to an end, no College came forward to offer him another. He said, 'I wanted it for the Fitzwilliam, not for myself.' This was the grievance that on at least one occasion tempted him to break away, and that for many years after his retirement kept him from returning to Cambridge.

In a Memorandum for the members of the Royal Commission on the Universities, who came to Cambridge in the summer of 1920, Cockerell wrote:

> It would be highly advantageous to the Museum that the Director should always have the right of entertaining visitors from a distance and actual or prospective benefactors in a College hall. If any Director be appointed to a Fellowship, the tenure should not lapse but should be held continuously as Professorial Fellowships are held.

It was no doubt true that, for the Museum's sake, its Director ought to hold a Fellowship. But though Cockerell had made several close friends at Jesus, he had also made enemies. Had he been *persona grata* with a substantial majority of the Fellows, opportunity would probably soon have been found to bring him back among them. In a community where gossip is an occupational disease, Cockerell's reputation for pontificating (and in a very penetrating voice) at high table was no doubt common knowledge, and those 'bellows of laughter that used to well up from the bottom of his lungs', though perhaps exhilarating, were also disturbing; other Colleges therefore made no more than very tentative bids to secure him. So for sixteen years (from 1916 to 1932) the Director of the Fitzwilliam was without status in the University.

Though Jesus had been perfectly within its rights in not offering Cockerell another Fellowship, his friends in the College thought (as did Cockerell) that he had been shabbily treated. Dr. Foakes-Jackson, Dean of Jesus from 1895 to 1916, wrote from the America to which he had just emigrated in disillusionment and despair:

4th December 1916   Dana Place
                      Englewood, N.J.
                      U.S.A.

My dear Cockerell,

Many thanks for your interesting letter received today. I can only say that I am disgusted with the way the College has treated you and it only shows me that I was right to get out of it when the chance offered. I fought these narrow prejudices for thirty years and I was steadily snubbed for all my efforts to destroy its egregious parochialism. Indeed till I came here I never thought that I was regarded as anything but a dissatisfied nuisance with no capacity for affairs. Lately I have been told that I was the one necessary man! However, I, who in 1910 opposed your election, may tell you this that not only did I form a real friendship for you as a man but I think your interest in the College and your loyalty to the society had a most important influence upon it. You made the Hall delightful by the many people of interest you brought. You maintained a better artistic and intellectual tone than we otherwise should have had; and that you are treated as I feel you have been, fills me with indignation. However it is no use brooding over grievances whether they be yours or mine. But I may tell you what my first steps in reforming the University would be. I would poison all those of the Council of the Senate who are not personal friends of my own, *all* bursars of colleges, all tutors and others who are supposed to have business ability, put the estates into business hands, let clerks male and female and typewriters do the tutorial work and entrust the education to men who are qualified by their training to undertake it.

Pardon these ravings but when I think of what is done by these solemn dullards I feel sick.

Yours always
F. J. F. Jackson

He had staunch supporters, too, among the undergraduates. H. A. W. Bladen, who had been at Jesus from 1909 to 1912, wrote to him from India in 1914:

> Your friendly comings and goings into my old room on F staircase; your pictures, your books, — your links with the immortals; your China tea, your breakfast parties; Mrs. Cockerell's rare bread and butter; your gifts of apples from the Wayside garden; the occasional glimpses of the great you brought to Cambridge; your manuscripts and your French plates; your generous interest in our life and the peeps you gave us at a larger; and above all your genuine and equal friendliness—you see I remember it all from that day I first met you on the staircase to the last day of all when you waved me goodbye from your own gate. . . .

More than one attempt was made to entice Cockerell away from Cambridge. In 1914 he told Lethaby, 'I have been — not exactly offered but asked to consider — a highly paid post in America, but I do not propose to give up Cambridge at present. Its only drawback is the relaxing climate, and that is a great one. In all other respects it is a delightful life and occupation.' But as, year by year, the Fitzwilliam grew in splendour and renown, year by year Cockerell's bitterness at being excluded from the University became more intense and the temptation to leave more difficult to resist. A letter written in

July 1925 to his friend Dr. Blackman, his staunchest ally among the Syndics, suggests that William Ivins, Keeper of the Department of Prints at the Metropolitan Museum, had tried to get him to New York, and that he had hesitated before refusing:

My dear Blackman,

I enclose a copy of my reply to Mr. Ivins. I have thought the thing over, in the light of what you and Glaisher said, and I feel no sort of doubt that I have given the right answer once more.

But who knows how soon I may be tempted along this road to easy affluence? I feel myself under no sort of obligation to a University which gives the heads of two of its indigent Museums the task of begging without the assistance of a Fellowship—in Forster-Cooper's[1] case ever since his appointment, in mine for eleven out of seventeen years. When I am tired of my very agreeable but very exacting job I believe I shall depart from Cambridge with a light heart and very few regrets—though I shall always be grateful to you and others (a small but noble company) for the guidance and support that you have given me. Without this I should have gone long ago.

Yours ever

Sydney C. Cockerell

The same year (according to an addition made at a later date to his diary entry for 31st December) 'Phil Burne-Jones conveyed to me an offer of a knighthood from his cousin Stanley Baldwin, then Prime Minister, which I respectfully declined.' It may well seem remarkable that he deliberately renounced this opportunity of showing the University that he was a prophet not without honour save in his own country. Moreover the manner in which the offer was said to have been made was highly unorthodox. Asked about the circumstances, Cockerell replied, 'It was only an *inquiry*—but it was definite. The knighthood was really offered to the Museum, not to me.

[1] Director of the Natural History Museum, Cambridge.

I thought it ought therefore to go to Oxford too; and the Ashmolean was not yet ready.'

In 1927 'the Master of Trinity wrote on behalf of the Council inviting me to become a member of the high table. I went to see him in the evening, and also the Vice-Master (St. John Parry) and explained that though I valued the compliment I considered that my services to the University entitled me to a Fellowship at some College (without dividend) and that I must decline as I could not afford to pay 6/6 for a dinner, when I had one provided at home. They were both very nice about it.' The offer did not appear to be generous; very possibly, however, had it been graciously accepted it might have led in due course to a full Fellowship. It led, in fact, to something of a breach with the Vice-Master, who had formerly been his friend.

Cockerell said, 'I missed a Fellowship at John's by a single vote, I was told; they offered me one at King's, but I refused because I didn't like the Hall.' Whether by 'Hall' he meant the fabric or the company, he did not explain. Neither the records of those Colleges, nor the memories of their senior Fellows, can throw any further light on these matters. The practice at John's is to record only decisions made, not motions put but not carried. At King's, no record would exist unless a formal offer had been made, and such an offer would not have been made unless there had been an intimation that it was likely to be accepted; presumably Cockerell was only 'sounded' as to whether he would like his name to be put forward. The diaries are silent on the subject.

The time arrived, however, when Cockerell's extramural fame was being sung so loudly that the sound of it became distinctly, if distastefully, audible within the walls of the University. Cockerell's diary tells the story:

25th February 1930. The Vice-Chancellor (Ramsay of Magdalene) came to the Museum and in the very kindest terms offered me on behalf of the Council of the Senate a doctorate in June. It is intended as a great compliment but it is one that I would gladly avoid if it be possible without hurting the feelings of friends who have promoted it. I asked for time to think it over and later in the day saw Donald Robertson, who is one of these. He was very nice and sympathetic and I am to let the decision depend on the upshot of another talk with the V.C.

27th February 1930. Further reflection has shown me that I ought not to decline the *exceptional* compliment — in that it is to be paid in June in great company and not at the time of the opening of the Courtauld extension — that the Council of the Senate has offered me and that has been conveyed to me in the kindest manner in a personal visit of the Vice-Chancellor. My inclination and indeed almost my resolve to do this was due largely to old grievances (which I must now forget) concerned with my (that is the Director of the Fitzwilliam's) being without any College status, and therefore without the advantage of taking benefactors or potential benefactors to any high table, which non-residents so greatly appreciate, during the last sixteen years — and just a little to my desire to remain as I am. I saw Donald Robertson, who has no doubt been one of my chief advocates, after breakfast and made a recantation. Later I had tea with the Vice-Chancellor at Magdalene College Lodge and had a very nice talk with him, accepting the proposed honour and saying goodbye to all resentments.

5th June 1930. Went to the inauguration of Stanley Baldwin as Chancellor at midday in the Senate House. . . . Baldwin rather uncouth and undignified — a great contrast to the late Chancellor, Lord Balfour — but he made a very appropriate speech. We then adjourned to lunch at Caius where I wore my scarlet gown for the first time and met my fellow recipients, the Duke of Gloucester, General Dawes (American Ambassador), Lord Beauchamp, Lord Sumner, Lord Bridgeman, Rt. Hon. Arthur Henderson, Sir James Barrie, Galsworthy, Einstein, Planck, St. J. Rose Bradford, Lascelles Abercrombie, Sir

John Withers, Prof. Meyer Lübke, Sir James Irvine, and Prof. Grierson. After lunch we returned to the Senate House which was again packed and the degrees were conferred by the new Chancellor. . . . We followed the Chancellor in procession back to the Lodge at Trinity. Then we went to a very large garden party at Magdalene, where the scarlet gowns looked very gay in the bright sunshine. Home by 6. . . .

Cockerell's Doctorate marked the turning of the tide; two years later the long-desired Fellowship was offered him:

18th October 1932. The Master of Downing (Albert Seward) telephoned that I had been elected a Professorial Fellow of that College. He is one of my best friends in Cambridge, also one of the best men in the place, and I am glad to come into this new relationship with him. He is moreover chairman of the Fitzwilliam Museum Syndicate and the College is most convenient for the Museum. I get no dividend but I gather that I shall get free dinner and rooms.

In 1933, Sir Joseph Duveen told Cockerell that he 'had urged his co-trustees to recommend my appointment to the National Gallery in succession to Daniel, to which I replied that my age put it out of the question.' He was, in fact, only three years older than Daniel had been at the time of his appointment.

In December of the same year he again received the offer of a knighthood. 'It has perplexed me greatly,' he wrote in his diary. He consulted Hornby, who thought he should take it 'on public grounds,' and Kate agreed. He therefore decided — 'reluctant though I am' — to accept. It was announced in the 1934 New Year's Honours List.

Cockerell answered, in his exquisite hand, the 438 letters, telegrams and cables he received, and listed the names of the senders in alphabetical order in his diary. 'Among those who wrote to me,' said Cockerell, 'was Kipling.' I replied, "Why do *you* congratulate me? *You* refused everything." But Kipling answered, "It's not *you* who is being honoured; it's the Museum."'

Seven publishers and two literary agents now approached Cockerell about a possible autobiography; he replied to them all that he was too busy for the present and that he was not prepared to commit himself for the future. As the time for his retirement approached, their attacks were renewed; but he refused to be tied down. 'As likely as not my memoirs will never be written,' he informed one of the most importunate of his wooers. 'I am not prepared to commit myself to the smallest degree.' Later, and with the help of Viola Meynell, he was, however, to produce the two volumes of letters addressed to him by his friends: *Friends of a Lifetime* and *The Best of Friends*. His brilliant editing of his Ruskin correspondence in the former of these gave the lie to the excuse with which he had repulsed several of his would-be publishers: 'I have no literary skill.'

12

TRAVEL AND ART

ONE of Cockerell's greatest pleasures during the inter-war years was foreign travel.

In 1920 he visited America as the guest of the Chester Beattys — generous friends who showed him many kindnesses. Cockerell had met Mr. (now Sir Chester) Beatty some years earlier and had advised him about the formation of a collection of manuscripts:

> 5th January 1916. Lunched at 24 Kensington Palace Gardens with Mr. Chester Beatty and looked at his treasures. His MSS. (about 15) are not exciting, but he has some beautiful Chinese books. Took him to tea with the Yates Thompsons, where he saw some MSS. that raised his standard. . . .
> 6th January 1916. Went carefully through Mr. Beatty's MSS. and told him which of them (about half) I should not advise him to keep. . . .

So reads the diary; but Cockerell said, 'I condemned the whole lot. They were things that had been palmed off on him by dealers, and none of them was worthy of a serious collector. He dismissed them from his library and thanked me. Before the First War he invited me to go round the world with him, but I couldn't get away for so long. He was a very generous man, and his fascinating but very temperamental wife — she always reminded me of Cleopatra — paid for my elder daughter's education. I remember Chester Beatty saying to me at the time of the Slump, "I can stand a storm, but this is a hurricane." He had to sell a number of his manuscripts. . . .'

Cockerell, the Chester Beattys and two other members of their family sailed for New York in October 1920. The outward voyage was made memorable by the presence on board of Rabindranath Tagore, with whom Cockerell soon struck up an acquaintance. Memorable on shore was Mrs. Beatty's 'wonderful creation of black unborn lambs which, with the hat and its bird of paradise feathers and a cloak to match the dress, had cost £1,500! A wicked thing, but I don't know how to be angry with this creature of extravagant impulses. Strangely enough she is not ashamed to be seen with me in my commonplace attire.'

First came a busy week in New York, which Cockerell describes in a letter to Lethaby:

> I should like to have a talk about America. You talk about their production. Except this remarkable millionaire's architecture I doubt if they *are* producing very much. The native pictures that I saw at the Metropolitan and elsewhere do not approach the European pictures exhibited near them. Of course there are Sargent and Whistler, but they were practically European. Out of all that great Continent has come little or no first class literature. Among the enlightened few there is the eager interest in the great art of the past that we give to anything that is rather exotic—say folk music and dancing. It is pathetic to see what hungry and admiring eyes these men cast on the ancient old world sanctities, and how they envy our proximity to them and suppose us to possess a culture far more profound and widespread than their own. It is immensely interesting to visit these eastern cities of America, but I can imagine no bribe large enough to induce one to settle in them. New York is by far the most wonderful, but it is cosmopolitan and very largely Jewish. . . . The Metropolitan itself is a most unsatisfactory building. I told them that it would have to

be scrapped! . . . The pictures are wretchedly shown. I
lunched twice with the staff. They are very nice men,
but not to be compared in calibre with those at the
British Museum — except Lythgoe.

From New York they went to Philadelphia, Washington and
Boston for the museums and libraries, and there was also a
week-end with friends of the Beattys at Wyncote. The Boston
Museum and its staff delighted Cockerell—'a really splendid
Museum and most beautifully arranged. . . . I lunched with
the Boston staff also, and thought them stronger than the
Metropolitan staff. Several of them Englishmen. . . .' But he
did not visit at Boston the Gardner Museum, which in one or
two respects perhaps anticipated the innovations he was about
to make in the Marlay Galleries of the Fitzwilliam.

From Boston Cockerell wrote to a friend in England, 'I continue to be treated as though I were the Emperor of Manu-
scripta, and I only hope I shan't be found out before I leave.'
'I was received everywhere,' he told Blunt, 'with generous
hospitality and with the sort of deference that belongs to an
unknown quantity hailing from an ancient University.' In
fact, in spite of his many criticisms, his first (and what was to
prove his only) visit to the States was a very great success.

Besides a number of holidays and one or two business trips on
the Continent, including a couple of motor tours with friends
in France, Cockerell went, between 1926 and 1936 on eleven
Mediterranean cruises. On these he was sometimes accompanied by one of his children, but more often he travelled
with friends. It would seem that he much feared travelling
alone, for the many letters of regretful refusal from those who
could not join him reveal how urgently he pursued the quest
for a companion — a quest in which he only once failed.

For Cockerell the cruise proved the perfect form of holiday —
three weeks' happiness for £50 or less, all told — and an inspection of the passenger list always disclosed the presence on
board of some whom he already knew and some whom he

wished to know. Besides an almost unlimited opportunity for conversation, a cruise provided time to read and good food to eat, brisk sea air and warming sun, energetic sight-seeing agreeably alternating with 'drowsy laziness.' He watched for dolphins for hours at a time, but always missed the whale that everyone else had seen. He examined, but failed to comprehend, 'the mighty contrivances which sped us along;' he admired the fancy dresses at the gala supper, but declined to don one himself. He made friends on every hand, and in a trice extracted from them the story of their lives; one young man reported that Cockerell's kindly guidance during land expeditions had made the whole difference to his holiday. When, at last, the ship entered the English Channel, it was of course Cockerell who composed and wrote the exquisitely phrased calligraphic letter of gratitude that was signed by the more distinguished passengers and presented to the captain.

Cockerell was over fifty when peace was declared in 1918; he was seventy when, in 1937, he retired from the Fitzwilliam.

For most men, the transition from middle age to old age is marked by a steady decline in energy, a dulling of enthusiasm, a deterioration of memory. Cockerell, though he had to record an inability to work for such long periods at a stretch, and though his eyesight ('it was permanently damaged by a bungling young surgeon out for blood') grew gradually worse, remained astonishingly active, eager, and mentally alert. As a young man he had been in some ways old for his years. Lady Burne-Jones had written to him in 1907, 'You seem to me, in your devotion of time and strength to those so much older than yourself, to miss something of the happy comradeship with youth which generally engrosses men of your age.' But the older he grew in years, the younger he grew in heart. So he came to treat the young as though they were his contemporaries; and they, for their part, never found him 'stuffy' or patronizing. It was unfortunate that his interest in youth had not been aroused in the days when his own children were still young.

On 16th June 1933 Cockerell wrote in his diary:

> My 66th birthday. I am now nearer to 70 than to 60 and
> have been so for a year, but though I am conscious of the
> uncertainty of life and of the necessity to get things done
> while my strength lasts, also of abating stamina, I still
> feel quite young in many ways. If health lasts I have
> four more years at the Fitzwilliam, during which I expect
> to bring it nearer to perfection.

Certainly his energy continued to be amazing. During
his frequent visits to London in the thirties — where, incidentally, he rarely took a taxi — he always managed to fit in a
surprising number of engagements in a very short space of
time. In his sixty-fifth year he could take in his stride a day
such as the following:

> 16th February 1932. Very fine. To London by the 9.25.
> Travelled part of the way with Prof. Ernest Barker and
> part with W. A. Appleton. Went first to the Public
> Trustees' office to see Mr. A. G. Ellison about the Hender-
> son bequest. . . . Next to 36 Lincolns Inn Fields to see
> Mr. C. D. Medley about the Ricketts-Shannon collec-
> tions, some of which are to come on loan to the Fitz-
> william very soon. . . . Next to the British Museum to see
> Eric Millar. On my way ran into Charlot Geoffroy-
> Dechaume. . . . Then to lunch in Belgrave Place with
> F. A. White, who will be 91 on Saturday. . . . Then to
> the National Portrait Gallery. . . . Then to Spinks. Then
> met D[orothy] H[awksley] and went with her to take
> Margaret out to tea at Buzzard's. Went to D.H.'s studio
> to see a picture over which she is in difficulties. At 6.45
> dinner with Dr. Rose Graham at the Women's Univ.
> Club, 2 Audley Sq. and went on with her to the Soc. of
> Antiquaries where she read an admirable paper on the
> Valletta MS Life of St Anthony. . . . Met various friends
> and went with Hornby afterwards to the Athenaeum
> Club to fill up time before my train, the 11.40 from

King's Cross. Travelled with the Master of Clare, fresh
from the Unemployment Debate in the House of Commons. We talked together all the time and the journey
passed quickly.

Cockerell kept in close touch with London exhibitions. Though
he mostly remained a laggard where modern art was concerned, he had praised some of Whistler's work while it was
still suspect, and as early as 1892 had found the French
Impressionists 'amazingly clever.' Kate went even further
and became an ardent admirer of the Impressionists, but
unfortunately she could not share her husband's enthusiasm
for Morris and the Pre-Raphaelites. Of the first Post-Im-
pressionist exhibition in 1910, however, Cockerell used
in his diary an epithet so derogatory that he subsequently
erased it with a pen-knife, and at the second, held two years
later, he found Morris's phrase 'sickly affectation of insanity'
constantly drumming in his ears. He heartily agreed with
Lethaby, who wrote, 'It is *alienist* art. It is how the plague of
rats would paint.' And he agreed no less with an American
friend who said that she 'almost felt it her dooty to undress
right there on the floor to show that though the Creator may
have been a little careless about some women he can make
them nearly perfect when he tries.' Fifty years later, however,
he admitted, 'I think I was mistaken about the Post-Impres-
sionists; I came to have enormous admiration and respect for
them.'

In the First World War there were 'Muirhead Bone and
Raemaekers—two mighty masters,' and 'Ernest Cole, the
wonderful young Michael Angelesque sculptor-draughts-
man.' At first he mistrusted Meštrović's 'morbid distortions;'
but when Kate returned full of enthusiasm from his London
exhibition (1915) Cockerell—very surprisingly—changed his
tune. Indeed, he turned on Lethaby, who had ventured to
criticize Meštrović, and wrote to him, 'He is a giant and a
genius, and I am sure that you are wrong in your summing
up of him. Do go with an open mind and revise your views.'

Of an exhibition of works by Epstein Cockerell wrote, 'I bestowed my thoughts on the friends present rather than on the exhibits.' Later, however, he came to approve of the portrait bronzes, but never (though Rima 'might be worse') really to accept the stone 'monstrosities'. In 1922 he visited a 'repulsive' exhibition of sculpture by Frank Dobson, which seemed to him to have 'no more than a pathological interest.' In 1937 he felt himself 'a hopeless fossil' in front of some Modiglianis, and experienced merely 'a feeling of nausea.' He found the Picasso-Matisse exhibition held at the Victoria and Albert Museum in 1945 'perfectly outrageous . . . unbelievably ugly and degraded,' though later he conceded that Picasso 'now and again hit the bull's-eye wonderfully.' He was 'utterly unable to discover the merit' of the work of Paul Klee, greatly preferring Eric Kennington's 'wholesome' drawings, and the paintings of Sargent, John, and William Nicholson ('one of the few real artists'), and of a number of lesser men who today are wholly forgotten. 'Wholesome' was an adjective that he also applied to the works of Puvis de Chavannes.

Where the Old Masters were concerned, or the writers of the past, Cockerell's taste was orthodox and authoritarian, academic rather than aesthetic: he admired all those whose work was universally accepted as great. He was never heard to confess that he himself was not able to enjoy, say, Raphael or Milton. (The three greatest men the world had produced were, he informed Miss Hawksley, 'Jesus, Michelangelo and Alexander the Great—*in that order.*')

But among painters he naturally had his favourites. In conversation he said: 'Give me a Botticelli, a *good* Gainsborough or a *good* Degas; Gainsborough is one of my *great* heroes. Rossetti? Imperfect, but great. By Jove, how *well* he drew! He had a great mind. You know he was only fifty-four when he died? Burne-Jones? *Much* less good; but in the days of my youthful enthusiasm I wasn't conscious of his weakness. Millais? Oh, a *great* man—till he fell. A *very* great man. Oh, so good! I never spoke to him. I walked behind him once in Hyde Park, but couldn't pluck up the courage to speak to him.

Watts? Not so great as I once thought. Leighton? Oh dear no! He was a fine gentleman, and that's what he looked like, but he was *not* at the top. He made a perfect P.R.A.: he knew how to behave.'

It has, in fact, not infrequently been asserted that though Cockerell possessed considerable knowledge, his taste was limited. One eminent authority went so far as to maintain that, outside manuscripts, he had 'no taste whatever; you had only to look at his house;' it was, incidentally, exactly what Cockerell had said of his predecessor at the Fitzwilliam! Yet if Cockerell had no taste, how could he possibly have achieved the miracle of the Fitzwilliam, for which he was as much responsible as his architect? Admittedly, some of his rasher purchases have rightly now been removed from the walls. Admittedly the 'geniuses' whom from time to time he discovered and patronized—for example, an animal artist whom he proclaimed to be 'the equal to Delacroix'—did not always fulfil his high hopes. But would many museum directors dare to claim that they had never blundered? At least he never purchased the equivalent of a van Meegeren. As a leader writer in *The Times* (13th July 1937) said:

> When Bode bought the wax bust of Flora, 'from the *atelier* of Leonardo' (or of Richard Cockle Lucas), the late Robert Ross remarked that every museum director had a wax bust waiting for him at the end of the passage. Sir Sydney Cockerell's wax bust is waiting still.[1]

[1] Opinion is still divided as to the authenticity of the Cretan statuette purchased for the Fitzwilliam for a considerable sum in 1926.

13

QUARRELLING AND
PEACEMAKING

MR. Christopher Cockerell[1] has defended his father against some of the charges that were not infrequently made against him:

Father has been called a prig, a tyrant, self-opinionated, rude and intolerant. . . .

A prig? I would have thought this was a mis-reading. I would judge that he had a certain Calvinistic streak somewhere, which, together with his long and penniless early struggles, left its mark. He was obviously a too-serious young man. . . .

A tyrant? Yes, certainly, to all those who got in the way and were so stupid and who tried to prevent the whatever-it-was being done. Then he would lash out without mercy, and without any respect for their feelings. (Being a Cockerell, I feel just the same: it's those fools in high places who are so prone to go to seed). But to those under him, if he was a tyrant he was a very benevolent one. He certainly received their affection.

Self-opinionated? Yes, certainly. Cockerells know their own minds, and know that they are right (and usually are, in the sea of muddle and indecision; but I think because to know and to act often wins the day, when the only alternative is not to know and to do nothing. Again an awkward attitude to live with).

[1] In a communication to the Author.

Rude and intolerant? Father was rude and intolerant, but I think mostly when someone could be doing better, or was unworthy of himself, or was blind to all the various beauties which he held dear.

Something has already been said of Cockerell's rudeness and capacity for quarrelling. Since he was always right, it followed that those who disagreed with him were always wrong. If a quarrel arose, it was *they* who started it — and he could never understand why. Of Dr. William Bateson, he wrote, 'We have been estranged for some unaccountable reason;' and he was amazed when his former friend Mrs. Tozer attributed his long breach with the Tozers to his rudeness to her husband: he had no idea that he had been rude. He could, on occasions, be incredibly tactless and insensitive. To a woman of over fifty whose beloved father, with whom she had been living, had just died, he said, 'You must feel quite grown up now, on your own.'

Yet he was not unaware of his reputation for brusqueness. It was probably, however, half in jest that he wrote to a friend recalling their first meeting: 'That bad impression I made on you when you first came here is, I believe, the one I invariably make on new visitors, who are often thankful to get out of my presence alive. I am told that I am famous for my bad manners, that I am very alarming, very cold, very priggish, and I know not what else. . . .' Those who came to know Cockerell only in his relatively mellow old age may not fully appreciate how much truth there was in this confession.

Another old friend, William Rothenstein, had come to believe that Cockerell was preventing him from getting work in Cambridge, and (what was improbable) that it was his lack of personal charm that had turned Cockerell against him. He wrote to Cockerell (16th February 1916): 'Hardy said very truly when I was drawing him last week that people whose personalities are attractive have their work praised more than those who are uglier and less agreeable. . . .' A few months later he replied to a letter from Cockerell: 'My friends wrote

me that *while you were at Cambridge it was useless to propose
me for any work there*. It was to this quite definite opposition
I referred, and the tone of your reply makes the word friendship on your lips, something very like hypocrisy. I may not
recommend a friend for work I think others may do better, but
I would not expect myself to be regarded as a friend, if I tried
to prevent his getting any work at all.'

Cockerell said of this, 'We quarrelled—or rather, *he*
quarrelled—over portraits in Cambridge. I said, "You are
quite a good portrait painter, but I don't put you in the first
six. We have two Orpens, two Sargents and one Rothenstein—
so you mustn't complain." But he took offence.'

This rudeness—for it is not possible to use any other word—
sometimes stemmed from his intellectual honesty: he always
said exactly what he thought. When the Dean of Hereford
proudly showed him the new Gothic west front of his cathedral, Cockerell 'slanged it very frankly;' when a waitress
brought some butter that he did not like the look of, he
recalled her and demanded some *cleaner* butter. If Cockerell
disliked a picture, he told the artist so—preferably to his face.
He went further—he told him it was a *bad* picture; had it been
a good picture he would have liked it. When a rather shy
young woman was introduced to him as 'a well-known
artist,' he saw nothing amiss in saying, 'You *may* be well
known, but *I*'ve never heard of you.' Nor did he hesitate to
reply to another woman who wrote to him to recall an
'unforgettable' evening spent at his house, 'I have no recollection whatever of the evening you mention.'

As a conscientious museum director he was rightly very
particular about the treatment of works of art; but it was the
schoolmaster in him that sometimes made him treat like
naughty children those who came to see his treasures. For
example, responsible adults were usually, and the young
invariably, required to examine the state of their fingers
before being permitted to handle his manuscripts. They were
made to hold cards in front of their mouths to prevent their
breath from reaching the gold leaf, and any who turned a page
by unorthodox methods were severely reprimanded. Some

people were merely amused at being ordered about in this way; others took offence and ceased to visit him.

It may seem curious that one who drew his sword so readily, and who was often so insensitive to the impression that he was making, should have been successful as a peacemaker. Yet it was so. Probably it was admiration of his moral courage that persuaded Ruskin to heal the breach with Octavia Hill. As for the Blunts, nobody could have done more than Cockerell towards the reduction of family tension to a minimum; complete pacification was an impossibility. To Phil Burne-Jones and May Morris, who were squabbling, he cried out so vehemently, 'What — the *son of Burne-Jones* and the *daughter of William Morris*!!' that they were immediately reconciled.

Here must be mentioned another occasion on which Cockerell risked a friendship in the cause of peace. One of his friends had submitted to him the typescript of a travel book in which she had vigorously attacked her travelling companion. Cockerell, his opinion having been invited, felt it his duty to speak his mind; he did so in an admirable letter:

To put it frankly [he wrote], your references to her are undignified, ill-natured, and in questionable taste — quite unworthy of anyone so perfect in most respects as yourself, and calculated therefore to tarnish your reputation. It might easily have been foreseen, and it was foreseen by me, that two admirable women so differently constructed as X and yourself would be oil and water in cramped and uncomfortable quarters under the strain of heat, glare, dirt, smells, noise, illness, and mosquitoes. I am told that Arctic explorers similarly get on each other's nerves. . . .

She has never breathed to me a syllable against you, knowing you to be my friend. But I can well imagine that if she were writing a book, and chose to bring you into it, she could find some traits and peculiarities to dwell upon that irritated and even exasperated her. Such little things suffice. Does not Dickens remark somewhere that the Romans must have annoyed other people very much with their noses? I remember a friend's wife once telling me that she was almost driven crazy by the way in which her husband always toyed with his napkin-ring at meals!

He lists X's many virtues and continues:

Who would guess any of this from your disparaging portrait of her, in which she appears to be a bundle of arrogance, incivility, and other defects?

Sargent is said to have had a screen in his studio, behind which he retired at intervals to put out his tongue at his opulent sitters and shake his fist at them. Having relieved his feelings in that way he emerged smiling and no one was a penny the worse. You have relieved your feelings by repeated tongue-protrusions. Now is the time for the screen!

There now, that is how I feel about it and how a great many other people are bound to feel. I expect you will condemn me in your mind (if not on paper) as an obstinate and fussy old prig, quite unsuitable for secretarial duties. But then you knew quite well the sort of thing I should say, so why send me the stuff and ask my opinion if you don't want to listen? I give you permission when you write chapter on secretaries to introduce all the venom you please!

It was nearly a fortnight before his friend's reply reached him. She forgave his outspokenness, and he wrote to her at once:

I will confess that your silence made me uneasy and that I was relieved to find in [your letter] warm and unabated friendship, instead of reproaches, fulminations, and dismissal from your service. Several times in my life I have felt it my very disagreeable duty to risk a breach with a much loved friend by urging an unpalatable course of action or the abandonment of what seemed to me a false position. It so happens that each of these friends (Ruskin was one of them) was as magnanimous as yourself. My interference was not resented and my appeal was effectual. It was touch and go in each case, but oh how thankful I was afterwards that I had had the courage to speak my mind without any thought of the consequences to myself. Moral courage is the only sort of courage I possess. In all other respects I am a miserable coward.

Moral courage he never lacked. When he chanced upon injustice or incompetence he attacked it fearlessly, both by direct assault and by letters to the Press. The 'systematic dragooning' of hospital nurses, the strain of their long hours and exhausting duties, had been brought home to him when his elder daughter was badly overworked while nursing at the Middlesex Hospital; when he found his younger daughter suffering the same fate at a mothercraft training home, he took up arms:

13th April 1934. Left Cambridge by the 8.25 in order to attend a Committee of the Mothercraft Training Home and deliver a protest against the shameful exploitation of the students, who pay £100 for a year's training and never get a Sunday off or the equivalent of a Sunday. In six months there was only one day on which Katharine did not wear uniform at all and she has been tired all the time. It was a large Committee of ladies and they heard me patiently. It remains to be seen what comes of it.

Something did come of it: an arrangement was made by which the students were given a week-end off every two months.

Several years later, two medical men joined battle on behalf of the nursing profession with letters to *The Times*. Cockerell immediately entered the fray with a long and excellent letter, and a considerable correspondence followed which led to improved conditions. Even so late as 1950, Cockerell, home from a long spell in a hospital where the nurses were forbidden ever to sit while on duty, appealed through *The Times* for 'such modest alleviations as the old monks had in our cathedrals and abbeys under the name of misericords and as we are all at times glad to alight on at the ends of the Tube carriages — mere flaps that would cost next to nothing.'

After Cockerell had retired to Kew he raised with the Director of Kew Gardens 'the question of the long hours of the workers in the Gardens, and I intend to raise it again.' Through the Director he attacked the 'lamentable arrangement' of the exhibits in the Museums, which were in the charge of Dr. John Hutchinson. 'I criticized very frankly and severely,' he wrote after one of a number of talks with Dr. Hutchinson; 'but I am not sure that much sank in.' Certainly very little was done, and the Museums remain to this day an object-lesson in how material should *not* be displayed.

After paying a chance visit to the Keats Museum in Hampstead, where he was 'dismayed to find most of the precious autographs seriously impaired by exposure to the light', Cockerell summoned the Mayor of Hampstead and other relevant officials to meet him there. 'I made a vigorous attack on the want of taste shown in the furnishing and arrangement of the rooms . . . I was very outspoken, but no offence was taken, and indeed I was thanked for my frank declarations.'

Cockerell usually made sure of his ground before he attacked; but occasionally an unconsidered judgment exposed him to a snub from anyone brave enough to deliver it. For example:

13th September 1938. Had a sudden impulse to visit St. Paul's School, into which I have only penetrated once (if at all) since my one term in the then quite new building, at the end of which in December 1884 Benjamin Jowett handed me a prize. His bust now presides over the great Hall, where should be the bust of the founder Colet. I walked along the passages, upstairs and downstairs, and found other busts on the tops of the lockers, classical and renaissance and later busts mixed up anyhow. Linnaeus next to Sophocles and an Elizabethan worthy labelled Psyche! Also the tablets from the end of the Hall of the old school in St. Paul's Churchyard are not chronologically arranged, nor are the engraved portraits in the Hall, which is disfigured with hideous mosaics. . . .

Having 'routed out' the Surmaster and protested verbally, he returned home and addressed a written protest to the Governors. The Chairman was not standing for any interference. He replied icily:

> As Chairman of the Governors of St. Paul's School and also as an Old Pauline, I am amazed that after having refrained, as you yourself admit, from visiting your old school for 54 years, you should have thought it necessary and wise to criticise the position of effigies in the school buildings. I think in the circumstances you should have trusted those who are responsible for the school to settle matters of this kind. I do not know whether you are a member of the Old Pauline Association but if you are I should have thought you would have been aware that the organ over which the bust of Jowett is, was subscribed for by the parents and friends of the school in memory of Jowett, and that is the reason for the bust being in the position it is.

Conscious that he had been defeated, Cockerell left the letter unanswered. And, more surprisingly, undestroyed — for it is known that he usually tore up letters which showed him in an unfavourable light.[1]

'I think your names must really be Sydney Coincidence Cockerell,' one of Cockerell's friends wrote to him.

---

[1] It may be said in Cockerell's defence that the bronze bust of Jowett looks (in so far as it is visible at all) rather absurd under a dark oak canopy. Moreover Colet certainly had some claim *historically* to occupy this position.

Like so many of those who are ignorant of the mathematical theory of probability, Cockerell was almost childishly obsessed by coincidences. His diaries and letters, and a large batch of carefully preserved newspaper cuttings, reveal his perpetual wonderment that, for example, two persons named Low should figure consecutively in the obituary column of *The Times*, or that Clara *Butt*'s and Carrie *Tubb*'s concerts should be advertised adjacently. Of a casualty list in *The Times* he wrote to Lethaby, 'eleven names, of which the first six begin with a B!' and of the three applicants for a vacant house at Cambridge, that they were named respectively '*Coulton, Coulson,* and *Cockerell*. This was due to the Great Law of *Coincidence*.'

'This is the ninth letter I have written today,' he tells Fairfax Murray, 'and out of the nine, three are addressed to people named Murray.[1] Is it fair to conclude that this name is borne by a third of the English race? My hosts on three successive nights—Blunt, Lady Burne-Jones and Hardy—were born in the summer of 1840 and I have a letter today from J. R. Holliday, also born in that year! The inference is that nearly everyone chose 1840 for his or her birth year. And yet I am not sure whether this is the fact!' Certainly Cockerell's life, from the day of his coming unexpectedly upon Ruskin in the same hotel as himself at Abbeville, was abnormally rich in chance encounters, all of course duly listed in his diary.

Odd little facts amused him. Few people would have thought of making the calculation necessary to write the following: '17th June 1934. Gloriously fine. I have lived exactly the same time, 33 years and 168 days, in the 19th and 20th centuries!' There was indeed an engagingly simple side to him.

'I have no musical knowledge whatever,' said Cockerell in one of his more modest moments. But he enjoyed music, and

---

[1] He would have been fascinated to learn that no less than three complimentary copies of this biography are to be sent to (quite unrelated) persons named Moore.

would often, in early days, pay his half-crown for a gallery seat at Covent Garden when Mozart was being given. ('You could hear excellently, and the singers looked at that distance like puppets—which was generally an advantage.') Wagner he liked less, though he enjoyed *Lohengrin* and *Tannhäuser*. 'The Ring made me *uncomfortable*. I came out feeling *broken*, and I thought, "This is not the way music ought to treat me." I came away *exultant* from Mozart.' His chief pleasure was in informal music-making in the home, and among his friends were several singers and instrumentalists who were always ready to perform for him. He liked 'Where'er you walk' and 'Amarilli' and the old favourites.

'I am not,' said Cockerell, 'a well-read man, though I can hold my own in a literary conversation. As a young man I read every word that Ruskin had written, so I had little time for anyone else. When I first met Hardy I knew none of his novels, though I read them all later.' Yet Cockerell's diaries show that he usually had a good book 'on hand', and again and again, especially in moments of stress, he returned to Shakespeare for comfort.

Moreover Cockerell's literary talent was not inconsiderable, though its field was limited. No one could write a better obituary for *The Times* than he. In his description of manuscripts he said exactly what he wished to say, and with the utmost economy. ('I think my analysis of the Gorleston Psalter is an absolutely first-rate bit of work, don't you?' he said with more truth than modesty.) The accounts, in *Friends of a Lifetime*, of his meetings with Ruskin and with Tolstoy could not, as has already been said, be bettered.

As a letter-writer Cockerell was unflagging. He was also demanding: 'It takes *two* to make a correspondence,' he told a friend who would not play ball with him. T. H. White, whom he reproved for writing too infrequently, had the courage to answer back, 'After all, we are not Héloise and Abélard, and a gentlemanly correspondence at about fortnightly intervals ought to keep up the right level of decent affection.'

Though the style of letter-writers was formerly more stilted than it is today, Cockerell was, by any standard, pompous. He never learnt that a letter to a friend and an official report to his Syndics needed different handling. To inform a friend of more than twenty years' standing that he cannot come to stay because he may have whooping-cough, he feels obliged to write, 'I have myself what the doctor thinks is a mild attack of the children's ailment and I cannot travel until it abates.' 'In the midst of all your urgent preoccupations' is preferred to 'while you are so busy;' and to Edward Johnston, who has mislaid a favourite pen, he suggests, 'Is it not perhaps lurking in the pocket of some garment hastily put on and off?' To Lady Burne-Jones, who had been ill, he could write (15th April 1903):

> It was a great pleasure to me to see you yesterday and to feel that you are on the way to getting back all your strength. You looked indeed better than I expected to find you — and I hope that the birds and flowers óf Surrey will enable you to regain whatever remains of lost ground, now that you are well enough to enjoy them. To many of us you are dear not only for your own sake but as the friend and interpreter of others who are no longer here to guide us. We could not therefore think of you lying ill without our hearts going out to you in anxious sympathy. I wish to be allowed to give each of your children, through you, a little token to remind them of your recovery, and I have chosen three coins which I enclose for their acceptance.

Praise is not stinted here; but sometimes it is spread so lavishly that the casual reader blushes. To Lord Wavell, most modest of great men, Cockerell wrote (31st March 1943) what reads like the dedicatory epistle to an eighteenth-century patron:

> I have regarded you ever since we first met at Northwick as having only one peer among the British officers that it

has been my privilege to talk at any length with, the other being Smuts. You two, besides knowing your job perfectly, besides being great soldiers, dauntless leaders, and in the front rank of strategists and tacticians, seem to me to be unique in your philosophical outlook and in your appreciation of fine literature, fine character, and of the things tangible and intangible that really matter. It is a marvellous piece of good fortune that you and Smuts and Churchill are now all in the world together, steering this dear country and its dependencies through so many stormy seas. It would cheer and encourage you in moments of perplexity to know what deep confidence is placed in you by all those who, like myself, have watched your career, and by many more who had scarcely heard of you before this war. Great is their perpetual applause.

It must be understood that letters such as these were *not* intended as flattery: they expressed exactly what Cockerell felt at the moment. Perhaps the recipients appreciated this, because there is no evidence of friendships being interrupted through excessive praise. Or possibly praise rarely falls on unwilling ears: 'I *purr* over what you write,' wrote old Lady Lytton after receiving his '*too* flattering' letter, and begged for more.

Cockerell had always been an enthusiastic writer of letters to the Press.[1] Before he was twenty he had entered the arena with one signed 'Susannah FitzPortley' on the subject of the inefficiency of the railways, and the habit grew (as it often does) with the passing of the years. He would write about Byron, Dickens, Shaw, Hardy and Kipling; about Oxford and about Cambridge; about literature and architecture, Everest, Yellow Duck Clubs,[2] split infinitives, birds, beasts, noses, ink — anything that aroused his curiosity, enthusiasm or indignation.

---

[1] A list of these will be found in the *Journal* of the William Morris Society, Winter 1962.

[2] See *The Times*, 19th December 1944, and *The Best of Friends*, p. 133.

He wrote to express his gratitude for Kew Gardens, that 'feast of beauty' still, in spite of rising prices, to be enjoyed for a penny — and the charge was immediately raised to three-pence. But his major preoccupation gradually became that of guarding the reputations of Ruskin, Rossetti, Octavia Hill, Morris, Hardy, Blunt and Shaw. Indeed, the time came when it was literary suicide for a writer to publish anything about Ruskin or Morris without first propitiating Cockerell. It was difficult to confute a man who could reply, 'I well remember Morris telling me. . . .'

Nine times out of ten Cockerell was of course right. But it 'pained' him, as he wrote, 'to have aspersions cast on my heroes and heroines,' and occasionally he would refuse to admit disagreeable facts that had been well substantiated. The love of Rossetti (whom Cockerell never met) for Jane Morris, established beyond reasonable doubt by Professor Doughty in his *A Victorian Romantic* and confirmed by several other writers, was disputed by Cockerell principally because he did not care to believe it; and in an exchange of letters on the subject in *The Times Literary Supplement* it was Cockerell who was worsted.[1] A letter to *The Times* (7th March 1962) denying that Ruskin ever mutilated medieval manuscripts was refuted by quotation of Ruskin's own admission of this vandalism — but Cockerell deserves on this occasion to be excused on the grounds of advanced age.

Cockerell took enormous pains over everything he wrote, and he was usually very well satisfied with the results of his labours. Entries such as, 'I have just reread my Report; I think it an excellent one,' 'Read through a large part of this Diary and found it very interesting,' and 'Reread a large part of Freya Stark's *Letters from Syria* which I edited five years ago . . . I think I made an excellent job of it,' are frequent in his diaries. Modesty, indeed, never appeared to be his forte, but much that looked like immodesty was in reality no more

[1] A number of letters from Rossetti to Jane Morris, now in the British Museum, were first made available to the public on 26th January 1964, the fiftieth anniversary of her death. They record Rossetti's deep affection for Mrs. Morris but afford no actual proof that he was her lover.

than a plain statement of the truth as he saw it. Of Mr. Jerrold Moore he wrote that he had 'apart from myself, an unrivalled knowledge of the Pre-Raphaelites and Morris.' At an exhibition of Edward Johnston's work that was being arranged at the Victoria and Albert Museum, he arrived at the last moment and 'disturbed' the cases that had been set up by the staff, in order to make 'readjustments that were certainly improvements.' He informed a Mr. Haslop, 'a very nice young man,' that he intended him to make his mark 'under my guidance' as a carver of inscriptions; and while at Cambridge he called upon Quiller-Couch in order to tell him which of Shakespeare's plays he was to single out for particular praise in his next lecture.

The intelligence and taste of his visitors Cockerell judged by the extent of the interest that they showed in his books and manuscripts. Professor David Knowles was 'no doubt an excellent fellow . . . but I was rather unfavourably impressed by his way of looking at the books I showed him, which did not seem to indicate any appropriate enthusiasm.' Mr. M. C. Oliver, a distinguished scribe, he found 'a very competent executant, but I doubt if he has much instinctive taste . . . he was not visibly excited or enthused by what I showed him;' and a Mrs. Webb, who came to talk to him about Octavia Hill, was condemned because she 'did not pay much attention to the material I put before her.' But those who did not praise his wife's illuminations—exquisite work, but of a kind that made small appeal to the younger generation—scored the blackest marks of all.

Yet for all his self-satisfaction there were moments—and most especially towards the end of his life—when Cockerell showed an unexpected humility. To Viola Meynell he wrote (7th April 1930): 'However successful I may have been as a Museum official, I am in most other respects a quite insignificant person. Strip off the veneer of distinguished men and women from whose friendship or acquaintance I have gained an unfair lustre, and what remains?' This was of course addressed to a worshipper who could be counted upon not to believe it. But speaking of his work on medieval manuscripts

he said—half-jokingly, perhaps—'I once thought I was a
rather smart young man; I now realize I was only a plodder. I
had only a veneer of knowledge;' and on another occasion,
'Don't put me down as a person who knew anything. I'm a
considerable humbug. I was second-rate.'

14

MELBOURNE

IN October 1936 Cockerell was appointed European Adviser to the Felton Trustees of the National Gallery of Victoria, Melbourne. With retirement from the Fitzwilliam almost upon him, he welcomed not only a new interest but also the handsome addition of £1,000 a year to his Cambridge pension. The Syndics of the Fitzwilliam approved the appointment and gave him four months leave of absence to visit Melbourne at once. There was of course no question of Kate going with him; accompanied therefore by his daughter Katharine, and by two old friends—Carolin Nias and her sister, Cockerell sailed on 7th November in the *Orford*.

The Bay of Biscay provided him with his first serious storm at sea, Ceylon with his first taste of tropical vegetation. On reaching the Cocos Islands they 'did not land but cast overboard a barrel full of provisions for the English inhabitants, and passed close to the exquisite lagoon.' As they crossed the Equator Mrs. Simpson's name was on every lip and there was talk of abdication. 'The Australians on the *Orford* are greatly upset,' he wrote; and they remained so until all thought of Mrs. Simpson was banished by still graver news from Brisbane: Australia was all out for 58.

Melbourne gave Cockerell and his daughter a royal welcome. He was made an honorary member of the city's best clubs; he was interviewed and photographed incessantly; a local paper ran a column captioned 'Sydney day by day.' Public banquets and private dinner-parties were organized in his honour, and the Victorian Old Paulines assembled to toast him. With Katharine he was taken everywhere, shown

everything from cricket (Bradman making 270) to koala bears;
and for Katharine there was also (he wrote to Katie) 'Russian
ballet, cinemas, a dance, surf-bathing, fish-spearing, etc. . . .
We like Australia and the Australians exceedingly, and are so
spoilt and puffed up that you wouldn't know us!' Over the
Christmas holidays they were the guests of Lord and Lady
Huntingfield at Government House, and in the New Year
there were expeditions to Sydney and Hobart to see the
galleries.

Overwhelmed by all this kindness and hospitality, Cockerell
must have regretted that there was so much to find fault with
in the Melbourne National Gallery and the way in which it
was run. 'It was a shocking place,' he said. 'Quite half the
Committee (which was far too large) were totally ignorant —
just people who were rich or important. The Director was a
slave, and never consulted about anything. I protested: the
Director must *direct*. I was disagreeable and outspoken.' But
it would need the strength of a Hitler, he told a friend, to get
anything done. He wrote in his diary: 'My Report on the
Gallery was very favourably received, as were my very outspoken observations;' and certainly the farewell banquet with
its flattering speeches, and the two cabins filled with bouquets
and histories of Australia, gave no hint that his visit had been
other than a great success.

The gist of Cockerell's speech at the banquet was printed as
a broadside by the Hawthorn Press, Melbourne. It was
friendly and laudatory, but patronizing:

THOUGHTS ON MELBOURNE BY A FAMED PRINT-
ING CRAFTSMAN, SIR SYDNEY COCKERELL, KT.,
M.A., Litt.D., FRIEND OF WILLIAM MORRIS
& SIR EMERY WALKER, AND LONDON ADVISER
TO THE FELTON BEQUEST

You do not realize what important people you are. You
are making history in a very wonderful way, but it seems
to me that people here are inclined to lack pride in their
achievements. They tell me that Melbourne is so young.

But it is a hundred years old! In that century it has striven for material things and has secured them in abundance. You are now grown up and are ripe for cultural developments, of which I discern many indications. I do wish you would magnify your country and stop people from saying you are less good than you are. You Australians are capable of anything, and if you believe it enough you will do whatever you want. You have plenty of self-reliance and self-confidence in cricket, and I only hope you will apply those qualities to everything else you take up. All my life I have been looking for beauty, and my opinion, for what it is worth, is that Melbourne is going ahead very well. Its best architecture is as good as any, but a great deal of it is unworthy of the city, and should be swept away or controlled. You have a National Gallery the contents of which are very good on the whole, and will go on improving each year. When I see your spacious streets, your stately buildings, your all but unique wealth of public gardens, your arterial exits so beautifully planted with trees, your miles of beaches swarming with wholesome life, and, most of all, when I scan the faces of the strong and stalwart men and the beautiful athletic women, I exclaim to myself that nothing is impossible for such a city if only it will make up its mind to excel. The great cathedrals and castles of England were created when the total population was not more than four millions. Any country might be proud of the galaxy of talent which is found among Australian artists and sculptors. What city of your size can boast of finer commercial buildings? What city of any size whatever can point to a war memorial surpassing the Shrine of Remembrance in beauty, dignity, solemnity, and appropriateness?

But within a few months of Cockerell's return to England there was trouble. This was due in part to a misunderstanding: Cockerell thought that he was allowed — indeed expected — to spend, at once if he so wished, a fairly considerable reserve fund that had accumulated; the Trustees intended this to be held for the purchase, if occasion arose, of an outstanding masterpiece, and did not mean it to be frittered away on 'numberless things, some very slightly recommended.' There was also 'a disastrous blunder'[1] in connection with the purchase of a Van Dyck. In October, finding it 'impossible to work with the Committee,' Cockerell sent in his resignation. Misunderstandings were, however, cleared up, and under pressure he agreed to remain in office. But he was not happy. In May, 1938, he had 'a long talk with D.L., who is disgusted with his countrymen in the Melbourne art world . . . and the jealousies and intrigues that make things so difficult in Australia.' There were, of course, 'one or two excellent men' among the Trustees—that is to say, men 'anxious to put into practice my ideas;' but when Cockerell's three year term was drawing to its close he did not seek reappointment. 'My heart was not sufficiently in this very difficult job,' he wrote, 'to justify an extension.'

The Chairman of the Trustees was not surprised at his decision. He had long felt, he wrote, that the job had not proved to be what Cockerell had expected. 'There are more restrictions and red tape about it than you have been accustomed to. However, there it is; and we can only be grateful for the many good things you have acquired for us.' Cockerell replied:

When I left Melbourne, where everyone I met was so very nice and so very kind, I dared to hope that, because of my thirty years' experience in an expanding museum, I should be able to make a good job of it. Now I must sorrowfully confess that I have done no better than my three predecessors, all of whom lost heart, as I have lost it.

[1] A complicated story. Cockerell was negotiating the purchase, through a dealer, of a privately owned painting by Van Dyck. The figure asked was £12,000, but Cockerell had good reason to believe that the owner was prepared to accept £10,000. Meanwhile a representative of the Felton Trust, acting without consulting Cockerell, agreed to the price originally quoted. Thanks to the generosity of the dealer, who offered to forgo his commission, Melbourne eventually acquired the picture for £10,000.

The one piece of work of which he was really proud was, he said, the formation, with the help of Mr. Bernard Rackham, of a representative collection of European pottery and porcelain; what the Gallery now needed was a similar collection of Near Eastern ceramics. He concluded:

> [Mr. Sargant and I] shall no doubt talk things over, but whether we shall arrive at any very helpful conclusions I don't feel certain. The obstacles are too great and so much of the machinery needs scrapping. . . . Perhaps some plan may ultimately be worked out that will give my successors a better chance of serving Melbourne adequately than I and my predecessors have had.

In 1944, Cockerell met Sir Keith Murdoch, 'the most active member of the Melbourne National Gallery Committee,' who was on a visit to London:

> I had not seen him since I left Australia seven years ago and I was most anxious to hear about subsequent developments. While I was there I drew up (spontaneously, as no part of my duty as Felton Adviser) a very careful Report on the better arrangement of the collections, the introduction of bays into the Galleries, the condition of the Print room, and the real need for entirely new Galleries on a cleaner and better site. This report was very well received, but, knowing the indolence and ineffectiveness of the Director, Macdonald, and the difficulty of getting decisions from an unwieldy Committee, I feared that it had been shelved and forgotten. But now I learnt to my great relief and satisfaction that my fears were unwarranted and that many of my recommendations . . . had not only been adopted but carried out, and that Macdonald had been replaced by the deaf but excellent Daryl Lindsay, a first-rate choice. . . . I feel that my visit to Melbourne has turned out to have been far more fruitful than I had supposed . . . I came away in high

spirits. The strange thing is that nobody has written to tell me about all these developments. (I have just reread my Report and I think it an excellent one.)

In 1961, Cockerell was further heartened to read in *The Times* that Melbourne was to build a new gallery; he felt, and rightly, that his work for the Felton Trustees had not been in vain.

Cockerell returned to England in March, 1937 to complete the last four months of his Directorship. He compiled his last annual report — a job that he always particularly disliked — and discussed the affairs of the Fitzwilliam with his recently appointed successor, Louis Clarke. In May came the Coronation, to which he listened with great interest on the wireless; in June his last Syndicate Meeting — 'poorly attended and quite unemotional'. In July, at his last College Meeting at Downing, he was elected an Honorary Fellow — 'a great compliment which I appreciate highly.'

Before he had left for Melbourne, a deputation from a group of his Cambridge friends had approached him about having his portrait painted for the Fitzwilliam. 'The idea is so uncongenial,' he wrote, 'that I refused point blank — but, so as not to seem altogether uncivil, I consented to sit for a drawing by Dodd. When they asked whether I could suggest any other form of memorial that would please me I said that a fund that would be earmarked for continental travel by the staff, one at a time, would please me greatly.' It was a happy and a generous thought, and he was, over the years, to receive a number of letters of gratitude from those who were thus enabled also to enjoy what had always been one of his greatest pleasures.

For various reasons Cockerell had decided not to continue living at Cambridge after his term of office had expired. He did not believe it to be fair on his successor. He had many friends in London. He felt that he had outgrown Cambridge, and also that the University had not properly appreciated him. He had no particular place of retirement in mind; but he wanted to be within easy reach of London, and possibly he thought of the Richmond neighbourhood where he had spent many happy years in his bachelor days. Now the Marlay Curatorship had come to him in 1913 most opportunely but through the death of a friend; once again the death of a friend, this time the artist Charles Shannon, provided him, at exactly the moment he needed it, with exactly the house that he wanted. Shannon had been living at Kew, a couple of hundred yards from the Gardens, in a gabled Victorian house that was admittedly ugly but very easy to run, and there was an excellent room on the ground floor for Kate; Cockerell immediately purchased the lease, which was of course of exactly the right length to see him through (unless he lived beyond the age of ninety-nine).

'Kew,' he said, 'suited me admirably. People could not be expected to come all that way from London to see me, but they would come to see the Gardens and then look in on me afterwards.' He was being unduly modest; many were to come to see *him*, and to look in on the Gardens if there was time. 21 Kew Gardens Road did, in fact, become for the next twenty-five years the Mecca of a distinguished band of scholars and calligraphers, of Ruskin and Morris enthusiasts, and of the innumerable friends that he had made, and continued to make, in all walks of life. Thus was Cockerell transformed, by easy stages, from the great Director of the Fitzwilliam into the immortal Sage of Kew.

PART THREE

[1937–1961]

1

KEW AND DUMBLETON

'Lives of great men all remind us
As we o'er their pages turn,
That we too may leave behind us
Letters that we ought to burn.
(*Dean Inge*)

IN August 1937 Cockerell moved into his house at Kew —
yet *another* house, thought poor Kate, where one could
not bear to look at the proportions of the doors or the
shape of the windows. His seventieth birthday now lay a
month behind him. All his three children were married; he
was a grandfather, though unenthusiastic about infants whom
he never believed he could see grow up; his first false tooth
had been screwed in. He had made the discovery that sherry
parties are detestable institutions, and had long since come to
deplore 'the dismal silly exercise that is called "dancing".'
He viewed with extreme distaste advanced tendencies in art,
and looked back nostalgically to the Pre-Raphaelites and the
sound craftsmanship of men like William Nicholson. Yet his
mind had never been more alert, and he was marvellously
active in body; no one who knew him could possibly have
pictured him as intending to withdraw from the world and
vegetate — or, as T. H. White put it, 'sit in Knightly cosiness
at Kew, toasting your monogrammed slippers at the gas-fire
designed by W. Morris.'

In the two years that remained before the war, Cockerell,
as if sensing that his time was short, seized the opportunity to
make a number of trips abroad. Within a month of his arrival

285

at Kew—before, indeed, his term of office at the Fitzwilliam had officially come to an end—he set out on a 2,500 mile motor tour through France as the guest of the St. John Horn-bys. He noted in his log-book,[1] 'my 14th visit to BEAUVAIS, 8th to CHARTRES, 3rd to BOURGES and AVIGNON,' and in his diary, 'one of the great holidays of my life.' At Easter the following year he was again in France, this time with various members of the Meynell family; and in June he was at Asolo with Miss Freya Stark.

At the end of January 1939, and in spite of much talk of the possible imminence of war, he sailed to Egypt as the guest of the Chester Beattys, with whom he stayed in Cairo and at whose expense he made the Nile trip as far as Luxor. While in Cairo he went to a performance of *Hamlet* in modern dress, given by the Old Vic Company. 'The name of the actor who played Hamlet,' he wrote, 'was Alec Guinness. He did it admirably.' One day Mr. Guinness came to tea—'a charming young man of 24,' wrote Cockerell, 'very serious about Shakespeare and about his profession. His wife is on the stage, and is also a lover of literature . . . I hope to see them again.' He did; Sir Alec was, in fact, to become one of his most devoted friends and admirers.

On board ship and on the Nile steamer Cockerell, as he had invariably done on his fifteen Mediterranean cruises, made friends on all sides. Every man, woman and child on board was the object of his unbounded and benevolent curiosity. Each life-history was painlessly extracted and meticulously recorded day by day in his diary. He might well have said with Abou Ben Adhem, 'Write me as one that loves his fellow-men.'

Three weeks after his return to England in the middle of March, he was off again—this time on a motor tour through France with Lord and Lady Kennet. On the last night in France, which was spent at Abbeville, Cockerell wrote, 'I slept in the same room that was Ruskin's at the Tête de Boeuf when Detmar [Blow] and I met him there in 1888. A glorious finish

[1] A notebook, probably compiled during the Second World War, giving details, extracted from his diaries, of every day spent abroad between 1883 and 1939.

to a wonderful tour in which so many of my favourite places
have been revisited. . . . We drank Chablis in the evening.
Ruskin gave me my first taste of it in the same hotel.' No
more appropriate climax could, indeed, have been contrived to
what was to prove the last of his eighty-four journeys abroad.

In July, exactly two months before war was declared,
Cockerell wrote in his diary:

> 2nd July 1939. . . . Looking back on last week's record I
> see that it includes an afternoon at Wimbledon, a Recep-
> tion in Downing Street, the R.A. Soirée, three dinners
> away, a luncheon party ditto, three plays, and several
> picture galleries — so it does not look as though I were
> quite on the shelf! In addition I had two teeth out.

But what, meanwhile, of Kate? Virtually a prisoner in her
room, and seeing sadly little of her energetic husband, she
might well have found the days long. But courageously she had
built up a life of her own. She was always occupied. She printed
books in Braille, made clothes for the poor and knitted for the
sailors, played cards or chess with neighbours and friends who
came to see her, and read copiously. If there were moments
when her helplessness made her desperate, she hid her sorrow
from her friends and even from her children. She adored her
children, and she still worshipped her husband. More than
once she told her elder daughter, 'In spite of my illness, I
would not have changed my life with that of anyone else I've
ever met.' She was a very brave woman.

When it became clear that war was inevitable, Cockerell sent
his wife to their daughter, Katharine Laughton, at Dumbleton
(Gloucestershire), where John Laughton was Vicar. He himself accepted a kind invitation from his old friends the Siegfried
Sassoons at Heytesbury, in Wiltshire, where he found to his
surprise that his other daughter, Margaret, and her children
had been evacuated to the neighbouring village of Sutton
Veney. But hardly had Cockerell arrived at Heytesbury than

he began to tremble for the safety of his precious books and manuscripts; he therefore made several expeditions to Kew to rescue the most valuable of them, which Mr. Sassoon housed and tended throughout the War.

Heytesbury was delightful, the house spacious (though soon largely overrun by evacuees), his host and hostess kind. There were a number of friends — Lady Horner at Mells and Edith Olivier at Wilton, for example — within striking distance even in the days of petrol shortage; and there were agreeable neighbours to be cultivated. Each night after dinner Cockerell produced the 'book of the evening' from his treasure-store, and, he and Mr. Sassoon would study it and discuss literary topics. Towards the end of October Cockerell went down to Dorset for a month to stay with Emery Walker's daughter, Dorothy; then he returned to Heytesbury. But when the old year died and there was still no sign of bombing, first Cockerell, and then Kate, went back to Kew.

Cockerell's chief preoccupation at this time was the progress of *Friends of a Lifetime*, a volume of letters addressed to him by friends now dead, which Viola Meynell (Mrs. Dallyn) was compiling, with his help, for Jonathan Cape. 'If we were given fewer of a man's letters to his friends, and more of his friends' letters to him,' wrote Lord Asquith, 'we should get to know him better, because among other reasons we should be better able to realize how his personality affected and appealed to others.' *Friends of a Lifetime* demonstrated the truth of this theory.

The page proofs arrived as the Germans marched into Holland, and the book was published as the Battle of Britain drew to its close. Though its sales were, and remained, small, the reviews were uniformly good. The Ruskin correspondence, linked by Cockerell's admirable narrative, and the accounts of his visit to Tolstoy, were especially praised, and he received many laudatory letters from friends to whom he had sent copies. Some of these are included in Cockerell's second volume of letters, *The Best of Friends*. Mr. Sassoon, for example, writes: 'Your letter Book is indeed a gift. Already I have had richly interested enjoyment from it — there *can't* be a dull page in it, as far as S.S. is concerned! (I will spare your blushes in regard to the testimony it provides of your unwearying good services — but, dash it, has anyone ever done more than you in being of helpful service to people of genius?)' And Noël Rooke wrote (rather ambiguously) that 'for me, the book was the most intense pleasure I have had since the fall of France.'

In 1956, Mr. Sassoon wrote:

I am re-reading *Friends of a Lifetime,* and find it means a lot more to me than 15 years ago. That is the good thing about getting old — one's responses are deeper and steadier when emotional excitability has abated. The past is such a comfort, isn't it? . . . *You* are exceptionally wealthy in memories — and the two volumes are an outline of your history of rewarding human relationships. I think you have been unusual in your methodical loyalty to the past and your ability to preserve it 'in mint condition.' Your achievement of this appeals to me specially, because I have always (since I began to mature, after the '14 War) had a positive passion for preserving experience from becoming unremembered — and became a persistent diarist for that reason. But you are much richer than I in having known so many first-rate people and acquired so much expert knowledge in the arts. . . .

But there was a letter from Neville Lytton which did not find its way into *The Best of Friends* and which courageously makes a valid criticism. He wrote to Cockerell:

Certainly you have printed a lot [of letters] which merely say: 'If you take the 3.45 train, you will arrive in time for tea,' or, 'You are certainly the best friend in the world.' I suppose you think (possibly with some justification) that anything written by a very great man has some interest. I feel, however, that nothing should be published that is not up to the standard of greatness already set by the great man. . . .

The biographer of Cockerell, too often provided only with
rather trite information about his subject's heroes, risks expos-
ing himself to a similar charge!

There is also another, and a less agreeable, criticism that no
reviewer was in a position to make. To provide space for the
more trivial letters of the famous, those of some of his closest,
but less distinguished, friends were entirely omitted. To take
but one instance of many, there was Emily Guest, whom
Cockerell had known, and regularly corresponded with, from
1890 until her death in 1919. How highly he valued their
friendship is shown in a letter that he wrote to her on 18th
January 1914:

> You have set me pondering over the little group of
> women I have been privileged to know who have com-
> bined profound knowledge and understanding with the
> ripe wisdom of which charity is so large a part. I shall
> always count you as first or almost first of these. Octavia
> Hill and Lady Burne-Jones — both blessed women and
> women of genius — contest the place with you. But about
> the one there was a touch of sentimentality and about the
> other there is more than a touch of puritanism, of which
> you are wholly free. However it is an impertinence to
> criticize any of you. The only reasonable attitude, as
> Morris said of Chartres Cathedral, is one of gratitude and
> admiration.

Surely friends such as these, though they lacked literary talent,
deserved at least a mention among his 'Friends of a Lifetime'!
In defence of Cockerell it must, however, be remembered that
though he no doubt made suggestions, it was Viola Meynell
who edited the book.

In the golden days of that early summer that seemed to mock
the tragedy of the collapse of France, Cockerell's life at Kew
continued much as it had done before the War. He met his
friends in London or stayed with them in the country, listened

to debates in both Houses (as had been his pleasure for many years past), went to exhibitions and the theatre, or in Kew Gardens 'sat quietly looking at the beauty of the trees and flowers and thinking of the devastation now taking place in my beloved France. The gigantic battle continues. . . .'

Writing to Viola Meynell, he mentioned his 'meditations in bed' during the early anxious days of the War:

> In normal times they are usually agreeable. Now they are of course coloured by the war, but I try not to make it the subject of them by summoning before me beloved friends, alive and dead — now doubly and trebly dear — and pacing the streets of Beauvais, Chartres, and other old cities in which I have been happy — or cruising in the Mediterranean — or recalling other happy incidents of one sort or another. You are often the centre of such musings — I can never be grateful enough for the dear friendship that you have given me.

On 25th June came the first air-raid warning, and a week later the Cockerells left by car for Dumbleton, which remained their headquarters for a year. Katharine was now alone there with her daughter, her husband having been appointed a Naval Chaplain.

Though Cockerell was thankful enough that he and his wife were out of the London area while the Battle of Britain was being fought, he did not take kindly to life in a remote country village:

> Dumbleton on the face of it has great advantages [he wrote]. There is no pub. Everyone is fairly well off. Exceedingly good milk is available. The cottages are well built. Much aid comes from Lady Monsell. There is a district nurse. There is a fine cricket ground and a lawn tennis court. On the face of it it is an ideal village and its inhabitants should be exceptionally healthy and stalwart. Yet they do not seem to be so. The explanations offered were (1) too much intermarriage, (2) the average wife's

ignorance of cooking, and (3) the insistence on white bread.

He said, 'I saw what village life was like, and I found it very unattractive. There were terrible jealousies. Something was doled out — perhaps it was milk; I forget now — and if somebody got a teaspoonful more than somebody else, there was trouble at once.' But he was soon to exchange village life for Winchcombe Hospital: 'In January 1941,' he said, 'I had the probate operation.' He meant, of course, 'prostate'; his mind, at that moment, was running much on his latest will.

'I am a sad coward, terribly afraid of pain,' he wrote to a friend at the time. Twenty years ago, this operation — in his case a double one — was indeed more severe and more danger-ous than it is today. Cockerell's affairs being, naturally, in apple-pie order he passed the time, while waiting for the surgeon, in reading 'again and again some of the most en-chanting passages of *The Merchant of Venice*'. And when he was not reading, his thoughts were of course often of old friends and well-loved French towns. A week separated the two operations, both of which were successfully performed.

In his diary Cockerell describes his experiences in detail — the agony of the washing and syringing, the blessed relief of morphia, the slow improvement and the disheartening set-backs. He was never too shy to summon a nurse when he needed one, and it is almost exultantly that he writes, 'Rang up the night nurses nine times — a record.' Nor did he conceal his dissatisfaction if a nurse did not take his fancy. Of Nurse T., imported specially from Cheltenham, he wrote, 'We did not click at all. She is said to be an excellent nurse, but she is very fat and I found her clumsy and professional and not very intelligent. I was very glad when she departed for Cheltenham by the 8.30 bus.' (It is, of course, highly typical of him that he not only knows, but troubles to record, the hour at which the bus left). Next day, to his 'immense relief,' he learned that she was not coming again. Even the surgeon and doctor were sharply criticized when they came 'to do some finishing touches under an anaesthetic. After jabbing at my arms five or six times without any result, they got in the gas (which they might just as well have used from the beginning). . . .'

But at last he was convalescent and laboriously relearning to walk. Seven weeks after the operation he left the hospital for 'the kind Monsells' at Dumbleton Hall, the first of a succession of hospitable friends who smoothed his way to a complete recovery. A full year, however, was to pass before he felt entirely fit again.

2

OLD WINDSOR

IN the summer of 1941, the Cockerells, feeling perhaps that they were being something of a burden to their daughter, left Dumbleton Vicarage to become the paying guests of Captain Peters at Ouseley Lodge, Old Windsor. This arrangement was brought about by their mutual friend, Miss Dorothy Hawksley, whom Captain Peters had already invited to stay for the duration of the war. The Cockerells remained at Old Windsor until the autumn of 1943, when they received notice to quit. Nine months later the house was severely damaged by a flying bomb which destroyed the nearby 'Bells of Ouseley' and caused a number of casualties.

Ouseley Lodge had been built in the eighteenth century by the Duke of Roxburghe as a dower house to Beaumont, which subsequently became a Roman Catholic Public School. It suited Cockerell admirably, for though it was more or less in the country it was within easy reach of civilization. There was an adequate ground-floor room for Kate, and a magnificent upstair study for himself. The Thames flowed delightfully near. Beaumont College was at his door, and Windsor Castle and Eton within easy reach; and within next to no time he had established good relations with all three. A cordial letter from Mr. (now Sir Owen) Morshead, the Royal Librarian, pressing him to make use of the Royal Library, introduced him to the little closed community of the Castle; Eton in turn made him welcome; and a visit to the Rector of Beaumont 'to try to persuade him to take down the stuffed heads of beasts that disfigure the walls,' opened the doors of the Jesuits to him.

(Cockerell got his way over the heads: they were removed 'for the duration' and never restored. He had always had an intense dislike of big game shooting—indeed, of shooting of any kind. Shooting went on around him when he stayed with Dyson Perrins at Ardross and doubtless he did not disguise his disapproval, though he always much enjoyed any grouse or pheasants that came his way. He said, 'In Egypt I met a young man who hoped he'd kill an elephant, kill a giraffe . . . *horrible*! I remember Hardy telling me that when he was shown a lot of stuffed heads he said, "There's one missing." "Which?" "That of the killer".')[1]

Cockerell was soon on excellent terms with the Jesuits, and he was constantly in and out of their Common Room and their Library; 'they welcomed me whenever I pleased at their tea-table,' he said, 'and never attempted to convert me to their religion.' He examined their books and manuscripts, attended the school entertainments, made a dozen friends among the more intellectual and aesthetic boys, and organized an exhibition of handwriting which proved to be the first blow struck for the revival of Italic in the Public Schools. With the Fathers he enjoyed discussing religion and education, and they seem to have taken his occasional badinage in very good part. His diaries mention some of these occasions:

> 30th August 1941. After tea I called on Father Tempest and had more than an hour's most interesting talk with him. These celibate Fathers, possessing no property and subject to the will of their superior council (or whatever it is called) which may send them at short notice to the other end of the world, seem to me to approach far nearer to the Christian ideal than do the Anglican parsons, and I respect them greatly.

[1] Much the same is related by Pietro Della Valle, in his *Viaggi* (1650–58), of a legendary Shah of Persia who had ordered a tower of skulls to be made from the trophies of a royal hunt. The architect of it rashly asked the Shah to suggest the skull of 'some great beast' to crown his design. 'Yours,' said the Shah, and drawing his sword provided for the tower 'the skull of the greatest beast he knew.'

2nd November 1941. Went up to coffee in the Common Room. Sat with the nice Rector and Father Borrett and made a new acquaintance, Father Duggan, a French master like Borrett. As it was All Souls Day I asked them how they interpreted the petition in the burial service, *Requiem eternam da eis, domine.* Was it rest in the grave? Had *requies* any other meaning but repose? Father Borrett's explanation was that it was 'rest from striving,' and I went on to *Resurrectio carnis.* I understood the Rector to say that he and his colleagues believed this in the literal sense, but when I showed surprise he qualified it somewhat. I told the story of the two children walking behind a general, one of whom said to the other, 'Tell me, where is papa's leg?' The other answered, 'Sh! Don't you know it's in heaven?' When I told this story to Burne-Jones he said, 'Yes, you can imagine it standing near the Throne,' and I repeated this remark, which led to other stories. I asked about the private possessions of Jesuits. Until their final profession, which takes place after they are 30, they can dispose of their possessions (and even their expectations) 'under advice'. After they are finally professed any property that comes to them and has not been so assigned (e.g. to needy members of their families) belongs to the Order. They have no pocket money and must apply for every penny they have occasion to spend on buses, travel or necessities.

13th December 1942. Have a lively discussion with the Jesuit staff about their attitude to theatrical performances. They are forbidden by the rules of their Order to go to any theatre, but they encourage the drama at Beaumont and recognize its advantages to the boys who take part in it. Also they realize their own loss in not being able to see Hamlet and other masterpieces. Still they must 'obey the law' although it has become a foolish one and they are well aware of this. Moreover though they obey the letter of it, they take advantage of some loopholes. Thus they can see performances that do not take place at a licensed theatre (e.g. those of the O.U.D.S. and open air performances). Moreover there is a curious anomaly of a larger kind, as the wording of the prohibition fails to embrace music halls and cinemas.

Cockerell's association with Beaumont did not come to an end when he finally went back to Kew. He returned there from time to time, and kept in touch with his 'Beaumont pets' — as he called his particular *protégés*.

Since the death of Dr. James, Cockerell had had no close friends at Eton. Soon after his arrival at Old Windsor he took a bus to the School and surveyed the bomb damage and the inhabitants. 'It entertained me,' he wrote, 'to scrutinize the features, sometimes distinguished but more often commonplace, of the Eton boys hurrying to and fro. A few had got out of their black tails and white ties into river or playing-fields kit. It is only then that they look like real boys . . . '. But it was not long before he had established contact — probably through Mr. Morshead — with Kenneth Wickham, a housemaster and an antiquarian, and so in due course became the guest at lunch or tea of many members of the staff. He renewed acquaintance with the Head Master — 'he is generally voted a success' — whom he had known at Jesus; he met the Provost (Lord Quickswood); he was invited — great honour! — to drink cocoa with the Vice Provost and his twin sister, Miss Marten, after Sunday morning chapel, and subsequently to lunch in College Hall. He visited the Drawing Schools, where his Beaumont exhibition of handwriting had been set up and was arousing a good deal of interest.

He became, indeed, a regular visitor to the Drawing Schools, where the Author, at that time Drawing Master, was fascinated to watch his easy success with the young. He would approach a boy — any boy — with his inevitable question, 'What is your *hobby*?'; and whatever the answer, he had always something stimulating to contribute. From his voluminous pockets he might pull out a coin, a manuscript, or a letter just received from Bernard Shaw. A little circle would gather round. If ever there was a schoolmaster *manqué*, it was Cockerell.

Those unfamiliar with the small and self-sufficing micro-cosms of Eton College, Eton town, Windsor Castle, Windsor town and Beaumont College may find it hard to appreciate the measure of Cockerell's triumph in establishing himself as *persona grata* in so many of these adjacent yet insulated com-munities. It was characteristic of him to wish to bring them closer together. His attempt to get a play acted by Beaumont boys in the Eton School Hall may have failed, but he did manage to entice some of the Eton staff to Beaumont to attend one of their 'speakeasies' — an admirable kind of informal 'Speeches' for small boys, which Eton might do well to imitate. Moreover he succeeded in taking the Rector of Beau-mont to St. George's Chapel, which he had never entered, and afterwards to a most successful lunch with Canon Ollard. Canon Ollard, in his turn, lunched with the Fathers in the refectory at Beaumont and 'seemed delighted, as did they all. I have been the liaison officer. . . .'

A few more catalysts like Cockerell would prove an invalu-able asset in the Windsor neighbourhood.

3

LITERARY PURSUITS

SO the anxious days passed happily enough. With his old friend Miss Hawksley he walked by the Thames or took the steamer up to Cliveden Reach. (It was on one of these river trips that he noticed that the cushions in the saloon were still covered with the 'Tulip and Rose' fabric that William Morris had designed in 1876, and managed to acquire a length of the material). He went to London fairly frequently, saw the bomb damage in the City, listened to Parliamentary debates, visited theatres and art exhibitions, lunched with friends and attended a meeting of the Roxburghe Club. He went to Hampton Court and to Holloway College. Books were a constant solace in the evenings or when in the winter he suffered, as he often did, from bronchial colds. He re-read, with much enjoyment, the fifty-five volumes of his diaries and added captions to them. And when he felt depressed by the war news or from any other cause, he 'meditated on Chartres and (now largely devastated) Beauvais, and wandered in their blessed streets, as they were, when I saw them last in 1939. I was sixteen times in Beauvais and ten times in Chartres and some of the happiest days of my life have been spent in them. . . .'

Parliamentary debates interested him particularly, and, with his habitual luck, he almost always managed to secure a seat in 'a select little recess with room only for six people' or some such coveted place. After a debate in the Commons in March 1942 he wrote to Katie:

I spent five hours there with a short interval for lunch,

and found it all very interesting. In critical times like
these I like to peep into the centre of things. Do you not
think that we have lived to witness the break-up of the
British Empire? I should feel more distressed if I could
convince myself that it deserved saving. It certainly does,
from the Japanese and the Germans. But we have
deliberately brought it on ourselves by our selfish
pleasure-seeking money-grubbing ways. I feel very
uneasy about the kind of life that my children and grandchildren will be forced to lead ten years hence. . . .

A particular literary occupation that now occupied much of
Cockerell's time and gave him great pleasure was the editing
of his friend Miss Freya Stark's Syrian letters.

It was through Miss Dorothy Hawksley that, in 1931,
Cockerell had come to meet 'a nice Miss Stark, who has
travelled alone in Persia and is going out again.' Three years
later he read 'Freya Stark's well written description of her
adventures in Persia, *The Valley of the Assassins*;' and presumably he wrote to her to express his approval, for a card or
two came to him from the Dolomites, where Miss Stark was
climbing. That autumn he met her again in London at a party
at the house of a mutual friend.

Cockerell always admired feminine charm, physical courage, and success; he had already been much impressed by the
Manchurian explorations of his Cambridge friend Dr. Ethel
John Lindgren. Miss Stark was charming, intrepid, and now
unmistakably heading for fame; and he was captivated.
Recording the party in his diary, he wrote no longer of 'a nice
Miss Stark' but of 'marvellous little Freya Stark, who is off
again in a fortnight or so for a perilous journey across Arabia
. . . one wonders whether she has sufficient stamina for such
a journey . . . Freya is very small with a strongly arched nose
and a whimsical expression. . . .' A few days later he attended
her brilliant lecture to the Royal Asiatic Society on Luristan, at
which she received the Richard Burton Medal. In November
she came to Cambridge and, soon after, armed with a coin of

Wilfrid Scawen Blunt
PHOTO: RADIO TIMES
HULTON PICTURE LIBRARY

dith Blunt
3aroness Wentworth),
om a photograph by
mery Walker, c. 1911

Thomas Hardy, 1923
PHOTO: STEARN

T. E. Lawrence
PHOTO: TATE GALLERY

Dame Laurentia McLachlan,
Abbess of Stanbrook

Sydney Carlyle Cockerell, c. 1930
PHOTO: DOROTHY HAWKSLEY

Sydney Carlyle Cockerell, in his study at Kew
PHOTO: JOAN HASSALL

Miss Freya Stark, 1943

Sydney Carlyle Cockerell, c. 1960

Charlemagne which Cockerell gave her as an amulet, left for
Asolo and thence on the adventurous journey she was subsequently to describe in *The Southern Gates of Arabia*.

Their friendship continued and prospered, for to two such
indefatigable letter-writers separation was a spur rather than
an obstacle. In the summer of 1938 he spent a fortnight with
Miss Stark and her mother at Asolo, where he was soon playing
the role of Miss Stark's literary counsellor. Then came the
War, and she was summoned to the Middle East.

Miss Stark had sent to Mr. John Murray, her publisher, a
bundle of letters that she had written to her mother from
Syria in the late twenties; they were handed to Cockerell for
his opinion, and in due course Miss Stark agreed that he should
edit them for her. 'I agree blindly to any arrangement of them
you make . . .' she wrote to him from Baghdad. 'I am most
happy to leave my book in your safe and delicate hands.'
Letters from Syria was published in November 1942, and
Cockerell was relieved when he received a letter from its
author congratulating him on the good job he had done:

> I cannot tell you how much I admire and appreciate what
> you have done for it. I feel it is your child more than
> mine and it was amusing to approach it as almost a
> stranger. It seems to me that the person who wrote it 14
> years ago was very definite, ignorant, gay and rather nice!

Cockerell had long been urging Miss Stark to write her
autobiography. She had, in fact, made a small beginning while
in Aden in 1940, but in the autumn of 1942, finding herself
obliged to rest for some weeks in Cyprus, she settled to the
task and sent the manuscript in instalments to Cockerell for
criticism. The book, which gave an account of her life up to
the time of her first visit to the East in 1927, contained much
that was of a private nature and its publication was delayed
until 1950. *Traveller's Prelude*, as it came to be called, was
dedicated to Cockerell, and in a postlude—'Letter to Sir
Sydney'—Miss Stark wrote, 'This story of my life, up to this
moment, was written for Sydney Cockerell at his request,

during a short lull that came to me in the war years, in
Cyprus. . . .' The book closes, 'But the deepest love of young
people goes, I think, to those like my father, and W. P. [Ker],
and yourself, dear Sydney, who feel tenderly about the "living
space of other human souls".'

This was written in 1942. With Cockerell now seventy-five,
with Miss Stark often ill and often exposed to danger, and with
the War still far from over, few might have dared to predict
that nearly twenty years of friendship still lay ahead of them.
Yet it was so. Many hundreds more letters were to pass
between them, and whenever Miss Stark was in England there
were (he wrote) 'rapturous encounters' in London, and later
at Kew. 'You talk of such pleasant quiet happy civilized
things,' she told him. She confided her troubles to him. He for
his part watched over her books and her literary reputation,
and more than once risked their friendship by some very
frank speaking.

Of all the women whom Cockerell came to know in the latter
part of his life, Miss Stark probably came closest to ranking
with the great heroine of his youth, Octavia Hill, and with
Dame Laurentia, his beloved Abbess of Stanbrook.

These literary pursuits were, as we have seen, only one of
Cockerell's many recreations during his exile in Old Windsor.
If local and newly-won friends did not neglect him, neither
did his family; and Kate, in particular, welcomed the visits of
their children and their grandchildren. Cockerell himself was
also often the guest of his old friends in various country houses
in the South. On five occasions while he was living at Old
Windsor he spent a fortnight with Captain George Spencer-
Churchill at Northwick Park, and probably there was no other
house in England where he met so many interesting people in
such agreeable surroundings. He stayed again with the Sassoons at Heytesbury, and with the Hornbys at Chantmarle. To
Katie Webb he wrote (2nd January 1943), 'I go on enjoying
life to a preposterous degree, thanks to the existence of so many
dear friends,' and noted in his diary (16th July):

My 76th birthday. I think I feel no older than I did a
year ago. Indeed I am remarkably fit—due no doubt
partly to my regular life, which does not tax my strength
unduly. I am never out after dark and I go to bed at or
before 10.

That same month news had been received of the bombing of
Cologne Cathedral. Cockerell immediately wrote a brave letter
to *The Times*, urging that the admittedly unavoidable damage
should be referred to with regret, rather than with indifference, in the Press and elsewhere. He was of course inundated
with letters. The large majority of writers praised his pluck
and imagination in saying what badly needed saying, though
one who had lost her home and her family during the Coventry
raid asked pathetically whether *he*, in such circumstances,
'would still express regret because we accidentally damaged
one of their cathedrals.' Then Professor Abercrombie confused
the issue by pointing out that Cologne Cathedral was virtually
a modern building; the loss of any of the small Romanesque
churches in Cologne would be a far greater calamity. However,
it gave Cockerell the opportunity to write a longer letter—
'better than the first one,' he noted—reiterating his argument.
  There was also, inevitably, anonymous and pseudonymous
abuse. 'Your letter . . . seems to point to Germany being your
"spiritual home." Why not make it your material home?
People with your namby-pamby views are not wanted in this
country. . . . You are not fit to be called an Englishman and
should be denationalized and sent to Germany where I am
quite sure if you expressed your ideas you would be promptly
shot. In some ways the Germans know better how to deal with
your type.' One who signed himself 'Newark'—a peer not
mentioned in Burke—went still further: 'I do not know you,
but assume you must be a tottering silly old fool for writing
such tripe. I advise you to seek sanctuary in the nearest mental
hospital for treatment.'
  Cockerell treated these letters with the amused contempt
that anonymous letters always deserve. He was in a thoroughly
cheerful mood. He felt extremely well; the Allies had invaded

Sicily; the Russians were holding the Germans on the Eastern front. But suddenly, on his own home front at Old Windsor, there was unexpected trouble:

> 19th July 1943. A crisis at Ouseley Lodge. Kate's attend-ant Miss Carlin is in bed and the doctor does not think she will be able to resume her work. The excellent maid Winnie is away on holiday until next week. The good Gardners [the butler and his wife] are much overdone and the coal ration has been so much reduced that there will not be nearly enough for the winter. I rang up Margaret in the evening and she will come tomorrow to help to solve some of our difficulties.

> 20th July. Margaret came for the day to see whether she could help us out of some of our difficulties by having Kate at Hampstead and hunting for a more able-bodied person to take Miss Carlin's place. She is very tired her-self and has much too much to do, but she is full of pluck and unselfishness and she was very nice indeed.

The following day Captain Peters announced that the Cockerells must go away for a month at the beginning of August, so that his overworked staff could have a holiday. When Kate said that it was impossible for her to move, Captain Peters, who had treated the Cockerells with great kindness, saw that there was no alternative but to request them to leave for good. In any case, coal was so short that he felt that he could not have kept them through the winter.

> This was a very disturbing bombshell [wrote Cockerell], on the top of Miss Carlin's illness. I rang up Margaret to tell her. She will take Kate at Hampstead as soon as her boys have gone to Cambridge. I went to bed in a very uneasy frame of mind and found it hard to get to sleep.

One trouble was that 21 Kew Gardens Road was occupied — by a Dr. Jepson. He had to be told that he must vacate the house, and he had nowhere else to go. Cockerell hastened to Kew and, as gently as possible, gave the Doctor two months' notice. 'He was of course much taken aback, but he was very nice about it and admitted that he was fortunate to have occupied it rent free for 2 years and 8 months with 2 more months to come.' Finally Dr. Jepson managed to get a requisitioned house nearby, and Cockerell and his wife, after spending the rest of the summer with various friends and relations, returned to Kew in September. Their years of pilgrimage were at an end, and peace, if not actually in sight, did now appear to be lurking around the corner.

4

THE FAUNA AND FLORA
OF KEW GARDENS

ALMOST the last thing that Cockerell had done before
returning to Kew had been once again to write to *The
Times* on the subject of war damage to a continental
cathedral. The victim now was Rouen, whose 'partial destruction' had passed almost without the shedding of a tear in
the general exultation over the Allied advance through France.

As not infrequently happened during the War, first reports
of the damage turned out to have been much exaggerated.
But Cockerell, back at Kew, had already embarked upon a
scheme for raising money in England for the restoration of the
Cathedral, and he went ahead with it. A list survives, in his
own hand, of the famous men who might, he hoped, lend
their names to his appeal: Churchill, Eisenhower, the Arch-
bishops of Canterbury and Westminster, Bernard Shaw (?),
Sir Alfred Munnings, etc. Many letters were written, but
many difficulties arose. The Foreign Secretary (Mr. Anthony
Eden) considered this to be 'not really the most appropriate
way of demonstrating sympathy with the French.' The
Treasury was extremely doubtful whether money collected
could be sent abroad. Reluctantly Cockerell abandoned what
seemed destined to be a hopeless undertaking.

Re-installed at Kew, Cockerell continued to lead much the
same existence as at Old Windsor. His energy was undimin-
ished, and when visiting Captain Spencer-Churchill at Camp-
den he found he could still walk six-and-a-half miles without

tiring. London was now more accessible and he went there more frequently, ignoring the flying bombs and an occasional tumble in the black-out:

> On my way home I tripped at a kerb and fell flat, breaking my umbrella, losing my torch, bending my spectacles and bruising my hand and chest. I was picked up by two passers by and got in a bit shaken, but very thankful to have sustained so little serious damage.

He was seventy-seven; the very next morning he was off again for another long day in London! His friends, too, found him easier to reach at Kew, and he never lacked for visitors. Above all, he now had Kew Gardens, a perennial source of pleasure to him, again at his door.

Cockerell was not a botanist, nor indeed a horticulturist; in none of his letters does he refer to any but common plants. He liked Christmas roses, but he would not have been able to tell *Helleborus niger* from *Helleborus orientalis*. He had not even a Ruskinian curiosity about flowers. He just liked them; indeed he came to love them. Yet his own garden was always neglected, and Kate powerless to help. Labour was, of course, not easy to get, but it could have been found if he had really cared and had persevered. He was singularly unlucky in such casual help as did come his way.

So the garden remained chaotic, while in the house, equally neglected, the paper began to peel from the walls behind the Rossetti and Burne-Jones and Ruskin drawings. It was indeed curious that one who loved flowers and who loved beautiful things should have remained content to live in such depressing surroundings.

Those who were familiar with Cockerell's overgrown wilderness were momentarily surprised when he wrote of a delightful hour's walk in 'my' garden; he meant, of course, Kew Gardens.

Now Kew Gardens contained flowers, but—and this was no less important to him—it also contained people. Cockerell had always been inquisitive about his fellow men and women, and after his retirement he had the leisure to indulge his curiosity to the full. 'The secret of a happy and interesting life,' he once told a friend, 'is to talk to *everyone, everywhere.*'

In his almost daily walks in the Gardens, as also on his journeys to London or his waits at bus stops, Cockerell never missed an opportunity of striking up a conversation and of extracting the maximum amount of information in the minimum of time. Thus, for example, he might fraternize with 'a nice Indian mathematician from Bangalore,' 'an employee of a boiler insurance company now evacuated to Walton-on-Thames,' 'a girl in blue employed by the Navy as a typist,' 'three Canadian bandsmen,' 'a burly American surgeon who wanted to see a robin,' 'a cultivated German silk merchant who had lived for a long time at Watford,' 'a bright little lady chased out of her home at Frinton-on-Sea by the Government,' and a 'lady doctor who had spent most of her life in India but is now much with friends near the Lizard.' 'I enjoy these chance encounters,' he wrote, 'which most other people never take advantage of.'

It may not be difficult to understand Cockerell's curiosity; it is hard to understand what prompted him often to record his gleanings at great length. One example will suffice: it shows how much information his tenacious catechism could extract on the District Railway between Kew Gardens and Turnham Green (say five minutes, and perhaps another five minutes on the platform):

> To London by the 10.54. On the platform made the acquaintance of a bright old lady carrying a large bunch of lilac, and before she got out at Turnham Green learnt that she was Mrs. Dyer of Mortlake Road, aged 70, that her house had been badly bombed in August, that she was taking the flowers to her daughter's large flat in Kensington Park Gardens, that her daughter's husband is Hon. Surgeon to the Norwegians, who fill her flat with

flowers, that she takes flowers to her from her garden once
a week all through the year, that she was in Rangoon for
14 years from 1900 and liked Burma very much, that
her brother-in-law was General Dyer of Amritsar fame,
that if he had not fired on the crowd there would have
been a great massacre of Europeans, and that Wavell was
often at her house for tennis when he was a subaltern.

These were his chance acquaintances. But in Kew Gardens
he had his 'regulars,' among whom was Archbishop Lang,
then living in retirement on Kew Green; it is most curious
how Cockerell, so staunch an agnostic, so often gravitated
towards clergymen, monks and nuns. Cockerell walked with
Lang on twenty occasions between 1943 and the Archbishop's
death in 1945, and recorded in his diary some of the subjects
they discussed:

I asked him whether he had been satisfied with his life
and he said emphatically, 'very far from it.' No marriage
is recorded in *Who's Who*, but as Vicar of St. Mary's
Oxford, Vicar of Portsea, Canon of St. Paul's and Bishop
of Stepney, Archbishop of York for 20 years, and Archbishop of Canterbury for 15 years (not to mention Fellowships of All Souls, Magdalen, and Balliol, and chairman-
ship of the Trustees of the British Museum), most people
would say that he had led a very full, useful and satisfactory life.

I realize how unfortunate it must be to be a marked man,
known wherever he goes, if only by his gaiters (which
however he had discarded for trousers when we walked
together). He told me, when we were discussing Westminster Cathedral, that he had never dared to step inside,
as it would at once have been in all the papers. . . . From
how much he is and has been cut off by the necessity to
act as though he were always under observation!

He told me that when he decided to give up the bar and

politics he had to make up his mind as to whether to
adopt the R.C. or the Anglican form of Christianity. He
had a dream in which Cardinal Newman took him by the
hand, and he evidently wavered. He agreed with me that
the Church of England failed greatly in having a Sunday
religion and in having sacrificed all the feasts of the
saints which help to make religion both real and picturesque in France. This time the Archbishop was dressed (as
I told him) 'like a Christian', with no dog collar. We got
on capitally.

Went to Archbishop Lang to give him powder and shot
for his speech in the House of Lords next Wednesday on
the bombing of sites and objects of cultural value in Italy.
I asked the Archbishop whether he didn't think Roman
Catholicism the best religion for an intellectual like
Chesterton, and he said yes. He objects less to Catholicism
than to narrow forms of Protestantism, but maintains that
within the Anglican Church perfect satisfaction can be
found. I asked him how he envisaged God—as a being
with arms and legs? He said, 'Indeed no.' Then I asked
why he spoke of him as 'he' instead of as 'it', and he said
'it' would never do. It would take away all sense of
personal relationship. I suppose it would; all the same, I
think it is the only honest way to put it.

I asked the Archbishop whether he had composed George
V's absolutely perfect messages to his people after his
critical illness and at the time of his jubilee. He said that
after the considerable lapse of time he thought he might
claim to have done so. These two messages were unique
for their simplicity, directness of appeal, and matchless
diction. I have tried many times to find out who composed them. . . . The discovery makes me feel an
immense respect for the Archbishop.

One day, on their walk, Cockerell remarked that it was
curious that 'camellia' should be spelt with two 'l's. The

Archbishop declared that it only had one, and offered to bet on it. Thus a penny changed hands, and finally passed to a small boy at the turnstile who had been unable to enter the Gardens.

It was perhaps calligraphy, and in particular the propagation of the Italic hand, that became Cockerell's most active interest during the last twenty years of his life.

During the Second World War, while he was exiled at Old Windsor, he had arranged the small exhibition of fine writing, shown first at Beaumont College and afterwards at Eton, that had led to the great revival of Italic in schools which suddenly swept the country in the fifties. Then every author contemplating an Italic tract, every teacher of handwriting burning with a fresh zeal, was to come to Cockerell's bedside as to the fountain-head of all knowledge, to seek his guidance or obtain his *imprimatur*. And when a patron for the new movement was needed, it was Cockerell who aroused the interest of Lord Cholmondeley, who in due course became the first President of the Society for Italic Handwriting and its generous benefactor.

To the very end of his life Cockerell continued to write beautifully—and always with a 'dip' pen. (Those who wrote to him with a ball pen were rash indeed!) Nor did he ever miss an opportunity to attack bad handwriting, and the Manager of the local Westminster Bank was one day summoned, like a naughty schoolboy, to his bedside to be reprimanded for the cacography of his clerks. As his eyesight grew dimmer, Cockerell's script grew yet smaller; and then sometimes a little piece of fluff, invisible to him, would play havoc with letters that were in themselves still excellently formed. He took it in good spirit when, in his ninety-fifth year, he learned that a letter from him to *The Times* had not been published because no one at the office had been able to read it. But what was so remarkable about Cockerell's writing was the level of excellence that it maintained. Many people can put on a decent hand, as they can put on a decent suit, when occasion demands;

very few make a point of being always at their best. Only one who has had to read (though admittedly with the aid of a magnifying glass) the seventy-seven volumes of Cockerell's diaries can truly assess the value, to a biographer, of such a virtue.

Calligraphers and palaeographers who visited Cockerell were, of course, always shown one or more of his splendid collection of manuscripts. His friend Dr. Eric Millar, writing in the Autumn 1962 number of *The Book Collector*, has described the sharpness of his observation and his astuteness as a collector:

> To look through a manuscript with him was always an experience, as he never failed to draw attention to some feature or other that one would have missed by oneself. He was no doubt inclined at times to be what the late Sir George Warner used to call 'Cockerellsure'—as, for example, in his confident apportionment of the different parts of an important manuscript to a definite number of decorators and figure-draughtsmen—but he had a remarkable eye, and was more often right than wrong, while his descriptions were always stimulating. . . .
>
> He once said to me that he had no money, and that his whole fortune was on his shelves . . . I think it would perhaps be true to say that he never acquired any MS., however desirable, if he did not feel it was also a bargain, and that he always had a figure in mind for which he would be prepared to part with even his finest manuscript. But his collection was indeed a remarkable one. . . . It is to be regretted that no catalogue of [it] exists . . . but no MS. ever left his hands without having a scholarly description in his astonishingly regular and microscopic handwriting on a fly-leaf, and there can never be any doubt as to its former ownership. . . . One can say that his collection was due to his faultless taste, backed by sound knowledge and judgment, and by more than most collectors' share

of good luck, for, if some great treasure slipped through unrecognized in the sale-room or elsewhere, Sydney Cockerell always seemed to be there to secure it. . . .

As a collector in a modest way myself, I never felt that any acquisition was complete until he had seen and approved it, and I also have the deepest reason to be grateful to him; for, on hearing that I was anxious to acquire his 13th-century Flores Augustini . . . he wrote to say that the price he had put on 'that uniquely attractive manuscript' was £1000, but that he should hate to think of its falling into the hands of anyone unable to appreciate it, so that he had decided to give it me 'as a memorial to our long and close friendship', with one condition attached—that it should pass at my death into the hands of another collector worthy to possess it. I need not add that this condition will be faithfully observed.

Cockerell, who had so strenuously urged Yates Thompson not to disperse his manuscripts, was not to be in a position to keep his own collection intact. Today his beloved books are scattered. Some have passed, by gift or by purchase, into the hands of private collectors; others have found a permanent home in the great public libraries of this country and of America; none, sad to say, has joined the wonderful collection that he was so largely responsible for forming at the Fitzwilliam Museum, Cambridge.

5

CAMBRIDGE, AND A
VISITOR TO KEW

IN 1946, after pointedly absenting himself from Cambridge for nearly nine years,[1] Cockerell suddenly decided to make his peace with the University which in his opinion had treated him so ill. In fact, during the course of that year he paid Cambridge no less than five visits.

It is not clear what prompted this sudden *volte-face*. Perhaps an invitation to stay with his old friends the Trevelyans at the Master's Lodge at Trinity, where his fellow guest was to be the Duke of Devonshire, was hard to refuse. Perhaps, too, he had already decided to lend Downing a hand in the choice of a successor to Sir Herbert Richmond, whose term of office as Master was drawing to its close.

His visit to the Trevelyans was a success. Though it was January the sun shone in a cloudless sky, and Cambridge soon began to weave its old spell. After tea Cockerell walked out through the Great Gate and into the town:

> The sun had just set, and I thought I should like to walk through the darkening streets. This I did feeling like a ghost. It was thrilling to see the hurrying undergraduates and to pass Caius and King's and Corpus and Cats and Pembroke and eventually to find myself, as it got dark, opposite the Fitzwilliam. Then I made my way into Downing and up the stairs of W. L. Cuttle, who received

[1] 'Though I was once in Cambridge incognito to see Katharine when she was ill.'

me with much cordiality. We talked for a bit about his affairs and those of the College and arranged to meet again tomorrow. Then I returned to Trinity and found that my fellow guest, the Duke of Devonshire, had arrived. . . . I had not intended to revisit Cambridge, indeed I had proclaimed that I would not do so, but here am I there and extremely glad to see it again. . . .

Next day he wrote:

A very beautiful morning. When breakfast was finished I walked out along the backs (yellow crocuses already showing) with the Duke of Devonshire and had much good talk with him. He had been staying at New Delhi with Wavell when Freya Stark was there. He described Wavell's reckless riding over uneven country and Freya's fall. . . . We walked on to the Fitzwilliam and spent about an hour and a half there. Louis Clarke has rehung the old upper Galleries, including the Marlay Gallery, most beautifully. . . . He was very welcoming, as were all my old staff. . . . It was indeed a treat to see the old place again and to have another glance at the many treasures that I secured for it. . . .

For the four remaining visits that Cockerell paid that year to Cambridge, Downing was his headquarters and 'College matters' much in his thoughts. No doubt the question of a successor to the Master, Sir Herbert Richmond, was often discussed. Cockerell, as an Honorary Fellow, was not an elector; he was therefore perhaps acting rather unwisely when in due course he wrote, over the heads of Downing, to inquire of several of his distinguished friends—among them Lord Wavell, Lord Mountevans and Sir Orme Sargent—whether they would be interested in having their names put forward. Lord Wavell and Lord Mountevans decided that they did not wish to stand. Sir Orme Sargent visited Downing with Cockerell, where 'I think he made an excellent impression.' But Sir Orme thought otherwise: 'I realized clearly,' he told his promoter, 'that I was not their man.' It seems possible that some, at least, of the Fellows of Downing resented Cockerell's tactics, and that anyone who was Cockerell's candidate was *ipso facto* unlikely to win approval. In May 1947 Sir Lionel Whitby was elected Master.

In 1947 Cambridge University informed its retired officers that their pensions could, on application, be increased by £60 a year. Cockerell wrote at once to the Treasurer, broadly hinting that he considered himself to have some claim to an additional increase:

> I am very pleased to hear that the Council of the Senate recommends that the pensions of retired University Officers should be supplemented. I have always felt that, considering the following facts, I had on my retirement rather a hard deal.
>
> When in May 1908 I was elected Director of the Fitz-william Museum the stipend was no more than £300 a year. Nevertheless I found on my arrival that I was also Director of the Museum of Classical Archaeology, without additional payment. Not a word had been said about this beforehand and it was a complete surprise to me. It was also a bit of a grievance. It took me much time to induce the University to relieve me of this second responsibility.
>
> The Fitzwilliam itself was then a deplorable medley. . . .
> [Here follows the familiar account of his achievements].
>
> After occupying the post of Director for 29 years and 4 months I retired on 30th Sept 1937 with a contributory pension amounting to £683. 12. This was subject to income tax, which reduced it considerably. The situation was alleviated before the war by my appointment as European Adviser to the Felton Trustees of the National Gallery of Victoria which provided £1,000 a year (less tax) for three years. My wife has been for many years an invalid, unable to walk or stand, and requiring a nurse. My younger daughter is married to a poorly paid clergyman. They have three small children and another coming, and

I have to assist them. When the Felton appointment
ended in 1939 I was forced to convert my annuities into
capital, which I sell out in instalments twice a year. My
expenses are about £1000 a year at the present value of
money. (Wages are very high and Local Rates have risen
to £77 per annum.) My invested capital is about £4000
and this may see us out if we do not survive the next four
years and if there is no more inflation. I ought to add that
I possess a very valuable library, but I do not want to start
selling it in my lifetime, as I am greatly attached to it.

I feel, in view of all the facts set out above, that I have
some claim on the University for any supplement to my
income, from whatever source, that may be available.

The Chairman of the Committee dealing with pensions
replied courteously that his Committee was not empowered to
do more than approve the increase of £60. Cockerell could, if
he wished, appeal for assistance from the Latham Fund, but it
was highly unlikely that he would be successful. The Chairman concluded, 'Much as everyone would regret it, it does
seem that you may be forced to realize some of your savings
which have been invested in books when your capital in cash
is nearing exhaustion.'

The argument was unassailable: to put it crudely, Cockerell
was 'trying it on'—though his motive may, in part, have been
to test whether the University had yet realized how much it
owed to him. Three years earlier he had invested £1,200—a
quarter of his total capital—in an immaculate copy of the
Kelmscott Chaucer on vellum, 'being convinced that by adding
original designs and proofs I can greatly increase its value.'
He was not mistaken: his money had been more securely
invested in books than it would have been in any bank, and
when he came to sell the bulk of his library in 1956 and 1957
it realized more than £80,000. In pleading poverty to the
University he was virtually saying, 'I have, of course, a great
deal of money in the bank, but I do not want to touch it in my
lifetime.'

Cambridge seems often to have been in both his conscious

and his unconscious thoughts at this time. The Fitzwilliam now had a new Director with whose policy he was not always in agreement: he worried about it by day, and at night 'had a strange confused dream' that it had become 'terribly over-crowded.' He had 'a vivid dream of Monty James, but quite unrelated to one I had of him a few months back.' And he continued to feel that the University owed him a better pension.

In July 1947 came his eightieth birthday. 'I could repeat without alteration what I wrote in my diary on my last birthday,' he noted. 'Though my strength grows perceptibly less, I am on the whole very fit. I get about a good deal and I go on enjoying life immensely.' Yet he envied his friend Gilbert Coleridge — 'aged 89, but twice the man I am. . . . He ascribes his surprising vitality to the Muller exercises that he has taken after his bath for the last fifty years. He does them for ten minutes or longer every morning, summer and winter, attired only in a truss.'

Cockerell certainly continued to lead a full life, and was still not afraid to travel by 'omnibus'. There were lunches in London with various friends — with Mrs. Chester Beatty, for instance with whom he had recently been reconciled after several years of estrangement due to 'an absurd misunder-standing on her part. . . . She is capricious and spoilt, but to me always fascinating because of her frankness, her generosity, and her other endearing qualities.' The Royal Garden Party and the Royal Academy Banquet were functions he never missed if he could help it. At the Banquet in 1949 — called that year a 'Dinner'—

to my amazement when proposing the health of the guests, Munnings[1] started with a very complimentary

---

[1] Sir Alfred Munnings had always been a warm admirer of Cockerell's direction of the Fitzwilliam. In a letter to *The Times* (4th May 1938) on the subject of the Directorship of Tate Gallery he had written: 'It is vain for us to hope that a second Sir Sydney Cockerell may be found. Under such a management the Tate might become a spiritual home for all art lovers and artists alike.'

reference to me and the Fitzwilliam and after a reference to the Earl of Athlone, did not mention by name (at least I think not) any of the other very distinguished persons who were present. The speeches on the whole were disappointing (as they usually are) and were interfered with by a terrific downpour of rain on the roof. Munnings was rather violent in his condemnation of some modern tendencies in Art. His protest would have been more effective if it had been less vehement.

Cockerell stayed with the Duke of Wellington at Stratfield Saye, and with other friends. He gave a short talk[1] on William Morris at Morley College to 'a pleasant company of "working" men and women — about 120'. He still visited museums and exhibitions of every kind, though at the Tate Gallery's loan exhibition of Art Treasures from Vienna (1949) he was

a little disappointed as the pictures, though well hung and well spaced, had rather a tired look and those I saw (I did not see them all) provided no great thrill. Perhaps it was because I am old and rather tired myself. The Galleries were crowded, and, as so often happens in Galleries, I sat down and observed the visitors with more interest than the pictures. Some very good faces. . . .

*   *   *

Several of Cockerell's friends have described their experiences when visiting him in his house at Kew. Among these is Mr. Philip Henderson, who has kindly allowed the reprinting here of an article that he contributed to the Winter 1962 number of the *Journal* of the William Morris Society:

VISITING SIR SYDNEY

I paid a number of visits to Sir Sydney Cockerell at Kew from 1948–49 when I was collecting the letters of William

[1] He said, 'I never gave a lecture in my life. I was too shy.' But though he gave no formal lectures, on a number of occasions he addressed gatherings informally.

Morris. The first time was on a bitterly cold grey day in February 1948. I had been told that Sir Sydney was a bit crusty at times, so I approached his not very pleasing yellowish brick Victorian villa with a certain trepidation.

An elderly factotum of forbidding appearance opened the door. 'Sir Sydney expects you,' she said; 'he is in the morning room.'

She took me upstairs and there, sitting with a rug over his knees in front of a dim anthracite stove—it was still the days of fuel rationing—sat the redoubtable little old man with his white Vandyke beard and black skull cap. He barely glanced at me.

'Sit down there where I can see you,' he said abruptly, indicating a position a few feet away from him. 'Who are you? What have you done?'

I said I had written this and that, edited this and that. He was not impressed. 'What do you know about Morris?' he said.

Compared to his knowledge, I felt that what I knew would not be worth repeating and that it was his purpose to make me feel this. Nevertheless I managed to convince him, somehow, that my interest was not entirely frivolous and he said he would help me as far as he could. He warned me, however, that my task was not likely to prove a very rewarding one, as Morris was a bad correspondent: he had always begrudged the time given to writing letters, and in any case all his best letters had already been published in the life by Mackail—'the only life of Morris,' he said looking at me sternly, 'worth anything at all. Unfortunately other people are now taking upon themselves to pry into matters that do not concern them.'

I guessed what was in his mind. 'You refer, perhaps, to Mrs. Morris' relationship with Rossetti?'

His spectacles flashed. 'That will not concern you, of course.'

My afternoon promised to be as wintry as the weather.

'Unlike Rossetti, Morris was not a ladies' man,' he added, after a short pause in which I had time to reflect upon the implications of his last remark. 'He was not at all prudish, but he would not have understood the modern tendency to explain everything in terms of sex, which, by present-day standards, does not make him a very lively correspondent.'

I began to appreciate the wry humour beneath the abruptness of his manner. 'Have you been to Kelmscott?'

My embarrassed admission that I had not produced an incredulous stare, this time over the top of his gold-rimmed spectacles. 'I should take the first opportunity of going there,' he said.

After tea, which we took in the room of his invalid wife — with whom Sir Sydney appeared to preserve the same unbending sternness of manner as with me — he got out some of his treasures. Among them were the trial proofs of the Kelmscott Froissart, which was to have out-done in magnificence even the Chaucer. This, he said, was the last work projected by Morris before his death. Reverently he placed the Chaucer in my hands, saying that if I wanted to look at it I should take it to the table. He watched me as I turned the all-too sumptuous pages as a cat watches a bird.

'Be careful how you handle that book,' he barked suddenly. 'Place it on top of that piece of tapestry.'

I asked whether the massively mediaeval table I was sitting at was Morris' table.

'It was Webb's,' he said. Fixing me with a piercing regard, he added: 'Like himself it is solid through and through. Those men were giants!'

Indeed, I already felt that such a table must have been designed, if not for more than mortal use, at least for more worthy occupants than myself.

'Giants!' he repeated suddenly. 'Ruskin used to say, "Morris is beaten gold!"'

From the low reverent tone of Sir Sydney's voice and the hushed atmosphere of the study, I felt as though we were both taking part in a religious ceremony, an act of devotion to his beloved friend and master. Unluckily I

asked him if the curtains in the room where we were
sitting were from the Strawberry Thief design.

'There are no strawberries there,' he said shortly.
There *were* birds in the design and, at first sight, it looked
as though they *might* have been stealing strawberries.
But, on closer inspection, I saw to my shame that there
were indeed no strawberries there, and that, of course, the
Strawberry Thief was a chintz! Sir Sydney's suspicions of
me were evidently only too well founded.

I visited Sir Sydney many other times during the course
of my work on Morris, but the only time he unbent
towards me was when I told him that I had been to the
Folk Dance Festival at the Albert Hall. He asked me
whether it had been well attended; when I said pretty
well he replied that he was glad to see that there were a
few people left with some sense. I flattered myself that
perhaps I was now, in his estimation, among the happy
few.

His nearest approach to geniality was when he conceded—though it cost him an obvious effort to do so—that
the introduction to my edition of Morris' letters was
'adequate'. But then that is the only time on which I
have known Sir Sydney to have been wrong.

When the book appeared he gave it his blessing,
writing to me in October 1950 in his beautiful calligraphic hand: 'I think that your book of Morris letters
looks very attractive and that it is admirably edited. It
has come out at an opportune time when Morris is being
a good deal talked about. I shall be eager to see what sort
of reception it gets.' He concluded with one last correc-
tion. 'The portrait of Mrs. Morris [facing page 16, which
I had dated several years earlier] was almost certainly
done in 1865, when she was 26.'

As a frontispiece to my edition I decided to use a photograph I had noticed hanging in a passage of Sir Sydney's
house at Kew. I understood him to have said that, in his
opinion, it was the finest photograph taken of Morris, and
that was the reason why I had chosen it. 'The photograph

of Morris that you allude to,' he wrote to me in April 1949, 'was not taken at the Kelmscott Press, but at an outing (wayzgoose) of the Press at Taplow, I think in September 1895 . . . I don't think I said that it was the finest photograph taken of Morris, but that it represented Morris's features at their finest and ripest, as a result of his altruistic enthusiasms.' The sharp distinction was typical of the man.

6

KATE COCKERELL

BETWEEN 1943 and 1948 Cockerell had lost all his three brothers and his only remaining sister, Una.

Leslie had been a highly prosperous mining engineer, 'but he had a speculative turn and never managed to keep more of his money than his devoted wife insisted on his investing.' Una, the youngest of the family, was 'a very rare creature, with the finest perceptions, but fate was steadily against her.' Douglas had had a very successful career as a bookbinder, and after his death his business was carried on by his son Sydney ('Sandy').

Theo, the last to go, was a recognized authority on bees, but impetuous and rather undisciplined enthusiasm marred much of his work. He was immensely courageous. His brother Douglas once said of him, 'He was never deterred by the possession of only half a lung and corresponding resources, from going, if he heard of a fossil flea 10,000 years old calling him in Central Siberia, to collect it.' He was at Yokohama, on his way home from Siberia with an important collection of bees, when the great earthquake occurred, and it was characteristic of him that he cabled home to anxious relations, 'Bees safe. Theo'.

To these family losses there was soon to be added that of Kate Cockerell. In July 1949 Christopher Cockerell arranged for his mother to be taken in an ambulance for a three-weeks' holiday at his home at Danbury; it was the first time she had left Kew in six years. But soon after her return she had a slight stroke which affected her speech. Eight nursing agencies failed to produce a nurse and the Richmond Hospital had no bed, but three days later she was taken to a nursing home in Twickenham.

Cockerell, who visited her almost every day, noted that she looked 'remarkably handsome still, propped up in bed.' The family and her friends gathered round, and for a time there seemed hope that she might recover. But the improvement was not maintained, and she died on September 18th. Cockerell wrote:

> The sad news came as a relief after these days of suspense. I am very thankful that her life was not further prolonged after the stroke a month ago. I think it has been a happy one on the whole, in spite of her more than thirty years of disabling illness. I am also very thankful that I did not go first, as it would have made things very difficult for her. We were married on 4th November 1907, nearly 42 years ago, at Iffley near Oxford, as the modern churches in our respective parishes seemed very unattractive, and also because we didn't want any but relations and very close friends at the wedding.

In many respects Kate's life had not been lived in vain. Ten years earlier she had written to her husband, 'I think we are very lucky to have three children all happily married, and leading good and reasonable lives.' This had been her greatest consolation during long years of suffering, when again and again there came to her the gnawing pain of having failed the man she still loved. Or rather, of *imagining* that she had failed him: in reality it was *he* who had failed *her*. She could not conceal from herself that her illness had been an irritation to him as well as a sorrow. 'The worst of it is,' she wrote, 'that at last, when one begins to understand just a little about one's life, it is too late to do anything about it. But you are not so cursed by the sense of failure as I am and always have been.'

There was the further consolation that he had never lost

faith in her talent as an illuminator, though she herself would often dismiss her own work as 'mere pot-boiling.' In 1939, in a letter written from Egypt, he must have praised, once again, one of her manuscripts — no doubt her 'Hymn to Aten'[1] — for she replies:

> What you say about my book is the nicest thing that you have said to me for ages. It cannot comfort me much. I don't think that I ever forget, even for a day, that I failed. I was meant to be quite a reasonably good artist, but from lack of self-confidence, helped by lack of encouragement and generally lack of good food, I could not keep up the effort. My fault entirely, and the added difficulties of marriage finished me. . . . .

All three children had loved their mother and had understood her far better than their father had. Christopher[2] has drawn clear portraits of his parents, contrasting the carefully calculated way of life of his father with the sensitive and more empirical approach of his mother:

> I grew up having certain things drummed into me, all strongly held beliefs of Father's. 'Do any job you are engaged on just as well as you can.' 'Make friends and cultivate the friendships.' 'It is not worth spending your life chasing money.' 'Get a job you like, and then you have a chance of doing it well.' 'Be very meticulous about money.' 'Answer letters by return,' and 'Specialists are dull people. Be an expert at something, and then learn at least a little about as many other subjects as possible.'
>
> These were some of the rules by which Father lived his life; he had it all mapped out at an early age in nice neat parcels. But not Mother. She lived by the interplay and subtle shades of things, by the colour of life as it is and not the dry essence of a mathematical analysis. She felt things and just sometimes would share them; and then

[1] Probably her finest work. The calligraphy was by Graily Hewitt.
[2] In a communication to the Author.

one realized what a crude male animal one was. She was affectionate, but fearful of rebuff; and she was rebuffed. She was very fastidious and hated the crudeness of the body she wore, although that still does not express what I mean. Perhaps better, that she was an artist and sensitive to every shade; anything ugly — ugly objects and ugly thoughts too — hurt her . . .

And then her long illness with never a complaint. She sketched a little but had to give it up, and she read a lot; and we children, absorbed in our own little lives, ran in and out and later walked in and out and always to a smile. She expected one to live a decent sort of life, but accepted one if one failed. 'Wickedness I can forgive,' she said; 'but wickedness born of weakness — never!' Her illuminations are a lasting memorial to her.

Father tried to mould her into a skirted image of himself; but in many ways she was a stronger character than he, and she rejected his creeds and retreated within herself. Later, I would think, they found increasing pleasure in each other's company, touching lightly on the threads of the web of their life together. Was he capable of real affection? I can't be sure. But certainly he achieved an immense amount for one man, and always against odds, and a lot of it is there now for the eye to behold. . . .

Cockerell brought with him to the Mortlake Crematorium 'the five books that Kate wrote as well as illustrated. We looked at these in turn for half an hour and then came home. . . . I went early to bed feeling thankful that this difficult day had passed off so satisfactorily.'[1] The following day he wrote in his diary:

D[orothy] H[awksley] came to tea, supper, and chess. Kate had expressed to Christopher a strong wish that she should come to look after my declining days after her

---

[1] Cockerell kept his wife's ashes in a casket on the top of a bookcase in his bedroom, so that they might one day be mingled with his own.

death. My children are strongly in favour of this, so I asked her whether she could manage it. Her answer was a provisional yes, but she has to think out a way of life that would enable her to spend her days in her studio in Redcliffe Gardens and her nights at Kew. This may make the project impossible.

But Miss Hawksley was a busy woman and a successful artist, and her family would not hear of her jeopardizing her career. Eventually an arrangement was made whereby she and other friends of Cockerell's — Mrs. Griggs and Miss Joan Hassall in particular — came in due course to share a burden which his two daughters, with families of their own to look after, could take no hand in bearing. It fell to Miss Hawksley to run the household.

'Remarkable men,' wrote Henry James in *The Coxon Fund*, 'find remarkable conveniences.' Just as Wilfrid Blunt had found Cockerell, so Cockerell now found these 'devoted damosels' (as Miss Freya Stark called them) to minister to him. And it was no sinecure that they took on, for Cockerell was soon also to become bedridden. True he was wonderfully patient and uncomplaining; but he was also very exacting. Nor did he always remember, or choose to remember, that his 'angels' were at the same time mortals who had their own lives to lead, who might be weary or bored or preoccupied. Certainly he could claim to have 'the best of friends.'

In January Nell Worthington — 'my oldest friend and an exceedingly kind one to me and mine' — died, leaving Cockerell a substantial sum of money. 'I hope to be able to dispose of some of it usefully,' he wrote. 'For the first time in my life I feel that I have money in my pocket that I can bestow liberally on other people — a very agreeable sensation.' And this he did: many of his friends can testify to the arrival of the unexpected cheque for fifty or a hundred pounds that enabled them to realize the ambition of a lifetime and visit Greece or Italy or his beloved French cathedrals. But the money had to be spent as he ordered, and a woman who passed on to her mother half of the hundred pounds he had given her 'to have some fun' was never forgiven.

In March Cockerell 'foolishly tripped on the stair and came down on my left knee with great force,' breaking the patella. He was removed to the Orthopaedic Hospital in Great Portland Street, but told, after x-rays had been taken, that an operation would not be necessary—'whereat I burst out laughing with relief—and the house surgeon (a nice fellow named Smithy) . . . joined in, as did one or two of the nurses who were present. . . . This hospital is beautifully run, with an ample staff of nurses and assistants, all smiling and eager to be helpful and mostly quite young. On my way here I had grim forebodings of solemn harassed faces: I was quite wrong.'

Friends and relations paid him constant visits, and Miss Hawksley tended him as devotedly as a hospital would allow. After two months he was able to return to Kew, where almost his first act was to write a letter to *The Times* advocating seats for nurses.[1]

Cockerell now began to accuse himself of monopolizing the conversation—a not uncommon tendency of the aged and room-ridden—when visitors came to see him. But in his case the self-accusation was quite unjust: almost as 'enclosed' now as Dame Laurentia, he was always eager to listen to news from the outside world. His confession of this failing drew a delightful letter from Walter de la Mare:

> I heard what must be described as a *ripple* of somewhat elderly laughter follow the reading of that scrap in your letter: 'I am apt to do too much of the talking.' Well, for some little time now I have frequently found myself speculating why things have seemed to become so quiet and peaceful all of a sudden; only to discover that I had stopped talking. It was a genuine discovery, resembling that of Christopher Columbus. But for how long had

[1] See p. 266.

America been *there*? It is something of a pity that one has both to eject one's talk and to listen to it.

Restricted movement, to one who had always been so energetic, was a very real burden. Except for the months immediately following upon his operation in 1941 Cockerell had never known what inactivity meant, though he had had opportunity enough to see the effects of it on Kate. Though rarely a day went by without a visitor, he suddenly began to feel lonely. In his diary (24th July 1950) he sadly records this new and disagreeable sensation:

> I have always believed and declared that I could never be bored with my own company, but that was when I was able-bodied and could roam about. Today I had a feeling which I perceived to be loneliness, the result of my crippled condition and my comparative paucity of interests. Lucky am I at my age still to have so many loving friends. But the winter is going to be difficult for me.

By degrees, however, he regained some of his strength. Before Christmas he was well enough to be present at the cremation of his old friend Bernard Shaw.[1] On Boxing Day he wrote to another friend, 'I have quite recovered from my accident and am suffering from nothing but Old Age. I have become a limpet. It is more than nine months since I was in a train.' He went, however, in his daughter's car to the Winter Exhibition of the Royal Academy, and in the spring to their Banquet and to a meeting of the Roxburghe Club. He attended, with enormous pleasure, the Folk Dance Festival at the Albert Hall. There were delightful luncheons with the Cholmondeleys, the Huntingdons, the Duke of St. Albans and Lady Astor; streams of old friends and new, of calligraphic enthusiasts and scholars of every kind, made the pilgrimage to Kew. Miss Hawksley, Mrs. Griggs, Miss Joan Hassall and his good neighbours the Simnetts were angelic, and 'my two

[1] See p. 211.

archangels' (Lady Chomondeley and Lady Huntingdon)
archangelic. In May he managed to walk in Kew Gardens as
far as the bluebells and back—perhaps a mile. The loneliness
and the boredom had passed.

7

'THE BEST OF FRIENDS'

THERE were years in Cockerell's life that stand out as milestones: 1892, when he broke away from the uncongenial world of coal; 1907, when he married and almost immediately became a museum director; 1937, when he retired to Kew; and finally 1951, when as the result of a fall he became virtually a prisoner in his room for the rest of his life.

One morning 'when I was shaving I had a sudden attack of giddiness which recurred when I was half dressed.' It was the first of many such attacks. These finally led to 'a tiresome fall in my room. . . . I rose from my chair and my right leg had gone dead so I fell forward and for a little while was puzzled as to how to get up . . . I felt a good deal shaken.' During that winter he found it preferable to remain much in bed. His diary entry for 5th March 1952 reads:

> Three or four little attacks between 9 and 10 a.m. and heart uneasy all the morning as well as most of the afternoon. I suppose it will get steadily worse until it ceases to function. I am quite ready to depart, if only I can do it painlessly. I have had an extraordinary happy, varied, rich, fortunate, interesting, and in many ways successful life. Apart from Kate's lamentable illness, I should like to have it all over again. I think that never did a man have such a galaxy of kind and dear friends, both men and women. For their goodness to me I can never be sufficiently grateful.

In April Dr. Quitman diagnosed 'a perfect example of heart

block. This accounts for my lethargy.' Cockerell wondered whether perhaps he had strained his heart four years before, when helping to lift Kate out of bed. Migraine, with curious symptoms, recurred constantly: 'one of them is a splitting headache but another is a moving pattern all over the wall, usually white and green, very well designed. Often there is a mesh over everything, shimmering and intervening between the patient and anyone else in the room.' He turned for support and consolation to his memories, and to his friends.

Though it might seem that Cockerell already had more than his fair share of friends, death was constantly taking its toll not only of his contemporaries but also of many who were far younger than he. In 1950 Shaw and Lord Wavell had died, in 1951 Neville Lytton — 'the best of companions.' The following year, Edith Beatty and Katie Webb.[1] In 1953, Eddie Marsh (never a very close friend: 'there was something about him that caused some people to smile to themselves and not to take him quite seriously'); Dame Laurentia, with whom he had talked on the telephone a few months earlier; Margaret Mackail, Burne-Jones's daughter; Noël Rooke, whom he had known for nearly seventy years; and a more recent friend, Gilbert Coleridge, at the age of ninety-four. Queen Mary, Cockerell's exact contemporary, died in March.

The gaps were, however, constantly being filled by new friends of all ages and both sexes; but middle-aged women predominated, and of the latter he was in regular and most affectionate correspondence with at least a score at any given moment. Their letters were full of love and admiration; and as the septuagenarian graduated to the octogenarian and finally to the nonagenarian, the worship and affection

---

[1] To Katie Webb (Katie Adams), the beloved binder of so many of his finest books, he had written three years earlier: 'I send you my very special love for your 87th birthday, and congratulate you warmly, as I have done many times before, on being able to look back upon a very long life of usefulness, and kindness, and goodness, and generosity, and very notable accomplishment that has won you perpetual fame. I don't myself see how you could have bettered it, and I cry BRAVO at the top of my voice. At the same time I hug myself for having won and kept for so long your infinitely precious friendship. . . .'

crescendoed into a paean of extravagant praise: 'I am trying to model myself on you.' 'I think we must have known each other in a previous existence.' 'You have touched me more deeply than any other human being; the time has come to say these things to you. . . .' 'I write humbly as one of your "fair supply" of loves. . . . Is it proper to receive love letters of this kind in one's 90's?' 'I arrive usually pigmy-like, and go away gigantically refreshed after a banquet for both mind and body.' 'Time and reason have no meaning when I am with you.' 'I wish I could give you a large, larger, largest hug.' Phrases such as these occur again and again in their letters.

'In my eyes,' wrote Miss Joan Hassall, 'you seem to embody all the things I most value and love in this world — i.e. books and manuscripts, lettering, handwriting, herbals, engravings, Handel, folk music, Shakespeare, Milton, Elizabethan songs, drawings, notable men and women, and a generous mind. I dare say there are other items I could add to the list if I could think of them. . . . What a treasure!' 'It is strange,' wrote Dorothy Stevens, 'that you do not believe in immortality because even if I had not done so before I met you I should do so now.'

His room was 'an oasis of peace and you its dispenser,' wrote another — and they begged for 'just five minutes' of his valuable time. They dreamed of him, wrote him love letters in medieval French, asked (in exquisite calligraphy) if they might compare him to a summer's day, rushed to Rouen to see what *he* had seen, drank his health in Seville, and smothered him with flowers and chocolates. Those who rang him up to ask if they could 'look in on Thursday next' might be offered an hour on Friday week, while any who were rash enough to appear unheralded had often to wait their turn in the anteroom.

Moreover his visitors, for all the display of affection that was encouraged, and indeed almost demanded of them, were kept neatly in their places. To one who wrote asking if she might in future address him as 'Cocky', because she always thought of him as that, he must have sent a chilly reply, for her next letter begins, 'Dear Sydney.'

*   *   *

It was thus that the 'Sage of Kew' held court. How did it come about that he exerted, even in oldest age, this astonishing empire over both young and old? It was, as it had always been, because he understood that friendship needed constant love and attention (and, added a woman admirer, 'because he always noticed what one was wearing'!). Cockerell plied his friends with letters, with gifts of pictures and photographs and books and scraps of Italic handwriting. His store of knowledge of Ruskin, Morris, and his other early heroes was always at the disposal of biographers; at the age of ninety-four he could still write, to one who had in his opinion misrepresented T. E. Lawrence in a newspaper article, 'If you care to come and see me, I can dot some of your "i"s and cross some of your "t"s.'

There was his extraordinary vitality. Mr. J. M. de Navarro recalls[1] a visit he paid Cockerell in the fifties:

> The last time I saw him he was bed-ridden, but remarkably lively considering the state of his health. A man rang up who wanted some of his books for an exhibition. S.C. replied in his most matter-of-fact bellow, 'Sorry, I can't. I am expecting to die any moment now, and if I let you have them it would lead to complications;' after which he resumed what he had been saying, quite unperturbed. . . . He then began to ask me about new daffodils that I was raising. *What's your hobby?* I did not realize at the time that our friendship was ending on the same note on which it had begun, well over forty years previously. My relations with him during that not inconsiderable span of time were unclouded and to me most enriching.

There was his unflagging interest in scholarship of all kinds. An American medievalist who corresponded with him in the fifties wrote of him[2] after his death:

> Sir Sydney's avid interest in every detail of my medieval research was a constant source of inspiration to me. The

[1] In a letter to the Author. [2] In a letter to the Author.

standard of precision in scholarship which he set for himself made others aspire to them. His vast funds of knowledge in the realms of books and art, and his acquaintance
with the great figures of the nineteenth century, placed
him on a pedestal above all grubbing scholars — ordinary
mortals. A suggestion from him has provided a lifetime of
research for some people and saved much valuable time
for others. There was no one quite like him. We have
lost one of the great men of the age.

There was also his shrewd counsel — at the disposal of all
who asked it. And many did, speaking as frankly of their
matrimonial and other troubles as if they had been lying on
the psychiatrist's sofa. Did they always realize, one may
wonder, that these confessions would be neatly set down in his
diary at the end of the day? Did they realize, too, that their
private letters were being forced upon chance visitors to read,
or even being pasted (without their writers' leave) as examples
of calligraphy in an album destined for the unrestricted shelves
of the Library of the Victoria and Albert Museum? One or two
certainly did, eventually, and thereafter wrote more circum-
spectly.

On 7th January 1953 Cockerell wrote to Miss Freya Stark:
'The Angel of Death, after hobnobbing with me a year ago,
seems quite to have forgotten me;' and nine days later he
entered in his diary, as had now become his habit, his half-
birthday: 'I am today 85½ years old'. In March he told Miss
Stark, 'I am distinctly better and am beginning to feel a bit of
a fraud. . . .' On 16th July his diary reads:

My 86th birthday. I know of no other member of my
family who has lived so long. I never expected to have so
long a life, and I began last year so badly with heart block
that everyone (including myself) thought that I could not
outlive the summer. But I have been very well looked
after, and though my pulse does not improve I feel quite

as well as I did on my last birthday. I have not left my bedroom since the end of 1951, but many dear friends and other visitors have made my imprisonment a happy one.

He was very conscious of the goodness of his friends in 'deigning to cherish a poor relic like myself.' He could 'follow the course of spring by the flowers that kind visitors place at my bedside.' He blessed Miss Stark for writing to 'the ancient half-wit, when he can write nothing worth while in return.'

Shortly before Christmas an American friend, Mrs. Gilbert Troxell, wrote to Cockerell: '*What* do you think of *A Blessed Girl*[1] and Wilfrid Blunt? You told me he was "a ladies' man", but dear me! I hope you were not corrupted by him.' Perhaps the letter remained unanswered, for Mrs. Troxell wrote again: 'I dare say if I knew all your past and present I should realise that there was little to choose between you and Wilfrid Blunt — Don Juans both.' This provoked a reply which throws an interesting light on Cockerell's relations with his innumerable women friends. He wrote:

. . . And now I am going to give you a terrible shock. Virtuous women secretly admire Don Juans. Wilfrid Blunt, being one of the most beautiful Adonises of his day and also a writer of love poems, well connected, and under no necessity to earn his living, had plenty of opportunity for as many intrigues as he cared to indulge in with the many beautiful and very nice women who could not resist his extraordinary charm. . . .

My own attributes and circumstances were a complete contrast to Blunt's. I had very little personal attraction. My father died when I was ten, leaving my mother with six children (all but one younger than myself) and very little money. This turned out to be a blessing in disguise. We all had to buckle to, and we all made good in different

[1] By Lady Emily Lutyens. The book contains an account of Wilfrid Blunt's attempt to seduce her when she was a girl.

ways. I and my three brothers were strict in our behaviour. Like Bernard Shaw I did not kiss a woman until I was 28 — and then she kissed me first! Since then I have been on kissing and caressing terms with very many women, but I have only had the final intimacy with one of them, my wife, whom I married when I was forty.

You will be shocked and distressed by this confession I know, as you have formed and cherished a far different and more romantic picture of me. But I think it best that you should know the truth about me and cease to imagine me a Bluntian Don Juan.

Mrs. Troxell replied:

Dearest Sir Galahad,

I am utterly charmed by your confession. Can it really be true? I have never known so pure a heart, a life so blameless. Do you never wonder what you may have missed?

Cockerell answered:

Dearest Janet,

. . . I doubt if I deserve your astonished eulogy. I was strongly sexed and my chastity was severely tried, but I have never been able to make up my mind whether my abstention was prompted by honourable scruples or by fear of the possible consequences. You can choose whichever of the two alternatives you think the more probable.

In 1954 Cockerell engaged a permanent nurse, thus leaving his 'angels . . . free to come and go as they please.' He gave up using a cut-throat razor, and the following year he cancelled his subscription to *The Times*, which he had read regularly for seventy years. Though mentally he was as alert as ever, his physical feebleness was increasing: 'I cannot stand unsupported,' he wrote, 'or walk three yards from bed to armchair,

which has long been the limit of my movements, without
clinging to a chair.' There were days when he felt 'good for
nothing,' and 'wasted the morning' is a recurrent entry; he
could no longer read a book or a letter without using a spy-
glass. Though in general he was delighted to receive visitors,
both old friends and unknown admirers, he sometimes found
them exhausting; he speaks of the wearisomeness of 'a torrent
of learned information which I am now too old to absorb,' and
also, sad to relate, of the boredom of the conversation of
certain old friends, his near contemporaries, who had not, like
himself, kept in touch with the modern world. There was,
however, a new interest which now came his way: the assem-
blage, and in due course the publication, of a further instalment of letters addressed to him by his friends.

Cockerell (as his literary executor well knows) had all his life
been an inveterate collector and hoarder of letters: of letters
from friends, from the famous, and from the potentially
famous. Indeed, it used to be said in Cambridge that to have
one's letters preserved by Cockerell was tantamount to having
one's foot on the first rung of the ladder of success.

The letters chosen by Miss Meynell for *Friends of a Lifetime* had included none from writers then still living; she now
proposed a companion volume of letters from friends who had
died since 1940, and it was decided that living writers should
this time also be admitted. *The Best of Friends* was published
in January 1956. Both books were put together under very
difficult conditions: the former had appeared during the War,
and work on the latter was complicated by Viola Meynell's
frequent illnesses and Cockerell's total immobility. Miss
Meynell died the same autumn.

In *The Best of Friends* Viola Meynell adopted a new policy
and arranged the letters, not grouped under authors, but in
chronological order. Exception was made in the case of Dame
Laurentia, whose long correspondence with Cockerell was kept
together. It was not unexpected to find Bernard Shaw and
Miss Freya Stark among the most brilliant of the contributors,

but probably the best letters in the book are from T. H. White; these caught the eye of many reviewers, who praised them as 'vivid and spontaneous', 'rollicking' or 'sprightly' (though some which were not considered suitable for publication were sprightlier still). Those from (Sir) Alec Guinness revealed him as 'the possessor of a serious and searching mind,' and surprise was expressed that a successful actor should show himself to be both modest and intelligent.

Friends of a Lifetime had received almost unanimous praise from the Press; *The Best of Friends*, and in particular the section dealing with Dame Laurentia, found many warm admirers. The book was 'superb'; it was 'a joy'. John Connell, writing in the *Evening News*, could not find words to express his gratitude 'to Sir Sydney for giving the letters to the world and to Miss Meynell for the exquisite skill of her editing.' The *Manchester Guardian* found the book 'a captivating garland of friendship' unobtrusively bound together by Cockerell's 'silken threads.' To J. Lewis May, of the *Tablet*, the letters composed 'a volume as vivid as a romance, and no thriller was ever more absorbing or more difficult to lay down;' he was, however, surely rather ill-informed in writing, 'It may be said of [Cockerell], as was said of Joubert, "He never quarrelled with, and never lost, a friend".'

But there was criticism too. *The Times Literary Supplement* doubted (with customary anonymity) whether private letters should be published so soon after the ink on them had dried:

> It may do to print one's letters from the eminent dead before joining them; to allow one's letters from the living to be printed before leaving them seems just a shade hazardous. Old-fashioned ideas of privacy have largely crumbled under the bombardment of what is euphemistically called publicity, but there may still be lingering doubts as to how much or how soon private relationships or communications should be thrown open to the public.

John Raymond, in the *New Statesman*, discovered an excess of charm — 'oodles of it.' There was

Mr. Siegfried Sassoon smugly patting himself on the back for not being a cultural bounder ('I suppose I am the only well-known writer who hasn't seen a film since 1936'), Mr. T. H. White showing off his broguey Irishness with the air of a man trying on a paper hat—such antics, practised by artists and men of intelligence, are unamusing. There is far too much woolly, crickety fuddy-duddiness about this whole Squirearchy for my liking . . .

Though Mr. Raymond had praise for the Dame Laurentia correspondence—and indeed sympathy with Dame Laurentia for finding herself 'amid all these bouncing egos;' and though he singled out the two Wavells, father and son, for saying what they meant 'with acceptable briskness of men who have managed to be both soldiers and intellectuals,'

too often, putting the book down, I had an unfair but cumulative impression of a vast Georgian charm school, of some fifty pine-panelled drawing-rooms, each with its bright wood fire, its Paul Nash over the mantelpiece and its presentation copy of *Revolt in the Desert*. One grew slowly to dislike the parade of upper middleclass virtues— the cultural do-goodism that will eventually blossom in the New Year's Honours Lists, the ever-so-gentle snubs to the rich and worldly and the constant but equally gentle pressure applied to rich and worldly cheque-books.

The *Listener* found that, with the exception of the letters from Freya Stark and T. H. White, the correspondence only went to prove that letter-writing was a lost art. Its reviewer felt that if Cockerell himself had been responsible for the book, its publication would have suggested 'a topsy-turvy vanity— "I may not be a great man myself, but see how many of the eminent I can claim as my friends!"' He also hinted that Cockerell and his circle were dead to all that was vital in contemporary art; it was, perhaps, a little unfair to condemn a man in his ninetieth year, and with him his more elderly friends, for not being able to appreciate late Matisse.

'The only criticism I can make,' wrote Mr. David Garnett to Cockerell, 'is to say that it is almost indecent to prove how much you have been loved and what a delightful person you are.' Lady Wentworth, after reading a favourable notice of the book, wrote to her friend Miss Christabel Draper:

> . . . I am amused at his being held up as a model of accuracy considering the systematic distortions of fact with which his interferences cursed my mother's life and memory. He was positively not a Catholic being a rank atheist when I knew him and [if] he has come to believe in a more recent Deity his disbelief in Gods of any sort must have altered. Perhaps the Abbess Laurentia converted him. I haven't any idea who she was as he never mentioned any connection with convents. Tolstoy was his Reigning deity. He professed a high moral code of friendship but had no moral sex code whatever, and when he was H.F.'s emissary to blackmail me over the Horse Case I found him more than 'tiresome!!' and when he published the Finch libel I could have got heavy damages from him instead of his public apology and withdrawal of the libellous passages. . . .

But once again a far more damaging ground for criticism passed unnoticed. For where is Sara Anderson, with whom Cockerell claimed 'a close and unswerving friendship' of fifty-five years?[1] Where is Nell Worthington, 'my oldest friend', with whom more than a thousand letters had been exchanged? Where are Jane Duncan, Mary Spencer, Christabel Frampton, Loraine Painter, Miss Dorothy Hawksley, Mrs. F. L. Griggs, T. M. Rooke, and many others who were all more worthy of inclusion, if being 'the best of friends' was the criterion of admission, than many of those who bore a more illustrious name but whose letters were, in fact, often less interesting?

[1] In 1939 Sara Anderson wrote to Cockerell of 'our friendship, which has been such a blessed thing for me these fifty odd years. It gives me new life and warmth and comfort and happiness and has been one of the great things in my life.'

Technically, no doubt, the blame for this again attaches to Miss Meynell. But Miss Meynell had, wrote Cockerell, 'an extravagant pro-Sydney bias;' she adored him, and at the merest hint from him she would have taken any suggestion that he made. Morally the blame is again his—if it is fair to blame a man of nearly ninety for anything whatever.

In January 1956 Cockerell was taken to a London hospital to undergo treatment for bladder trouble—'a horrible journey in a Surrey ambulance which went far out of its way to pick up two other patients. My room is at the top of the building and I have to look at a great space of bare wall, which I dislike. . . .' His archangels, angels, friends and relations rallied to his bedside with flowers and fruit and sympathy, and a picture was rushed from Kew to fill the vacuum on the wall.

But this hospital did not please him as the Orthopaedic Hospital had done. The bed, declared at first to be 'comfortable', was soon discovered to be 'uncomfortable and slanting,' and he fell out of it. (One of his private nurses at Kew said later, 'He ought, of course, to have been "specialized"'.) After eleven days he was sent back to Kew 'in a very comfortable ambulance and I was in my bed at 3.30, feeling very tired but greatly delighted to be home. I think the hospital has done me no good.'

In his diary for 15th September 1956 Cockerell wrote: 'A wonderful letter from Tim White about his deaf and blind guest—but alas with a prohibition of my letting anyone else read it.'

With this most remarkable woman, Miss Florence Collier ('Puck'), Cockerell soon began a regular correspondence which continued until his death. Puck had been born with normal sight and hearing, but by the age of eleven she had become totally blind and totally deaf. Miraculously she had triumphed over disabilities that might have been considered insuperable. Her letters, typed by herself, show an almost incredible understanding of human nature and human relationships, vast courage, and a total absence of self-pity. 'She is so *right* about everything, such a fine perception and sense of values,' wrote Lady Cholmondeley who also became her friend and warm admirer. 'And I love her account of spring at Kew, "the colours were glorious" and the sun came "lacily through the branches".'

Puck's letters to Cockerell must run to sixty or seventy thousand words—the length of an ordinary novel. He and 'the deaf-blind valiant Puck' (as he always called her) never met, and indeed he somehow preferred to keep this delicately poised friendship one of the typewriter and the pen and the heart. Just as the grille had proved no obstacle to his friendship with Dame Laurentia, so he allowed neither deafness nor blindness nor illness nor distance to affect his relations with this middle-aged woman who had so suddenly entered his life. Both were enclosed women with unenclosed minds.

From time to time, over the years, Cockerell had sold manuscripts and printed books from his library. On occasions he had done this to tide him through a difficult period; but as a rule such sales had been merely the 'weeding out' indulged in periodically by every rational collector, or else occasioned by the necessity of raising money for a particularly desirable new manuscript. In 1956, however, he decided to sell the bulk of his collection in order to make a distribution to his children. Lady Astor, hearing that his Shaw letters were to be sold, and believing that he must therefore be 'desperately hard up', generously offered him £200—a gift which, needless to say, he did not accept.

Between May of that year and April of the following year he sold manuscripts and private press books to the value of more than £80,000; over half this sum came from three sales held at Sotheby's, and the Victoria and Albert Museum paid a thousand pounds for his fine manuscript of Cardinal Bembo's poems. 'I can now,' he told a visitor, 'afford to have an egg with my tea.'

His friend and neighbour Mr. Brian Cron, a collector of

manuscripts, who helped him in these transactions, said that when some of his greatest treasures were brought down from his studies to his bedroom before being taken away, he hardly cast a glance at them. Was it that he could not bear to look at them? Or was it that they had become a part of the life that he had now renounced? Whatever the reason, there is no doubt that the high prices fetched by some of his manuscripts gave him deep satisfaction.

For the rise in the value of medieval and Renaissance manuscripts has been spectacular. The twelfth-century St. Albans Psalter (Cron Collection) which Heber bought in the early part of the last century for half-a-crown, became Cockerell's in 1909 for £135 3s. and would probably, were it to come into the market today, fetch upwards of £2,000. 'It was fortunate in that I started collecting when most booksellers weren't educated—when they couldn't read Latin,' he said. Cockerell estimated that on an average his manuscripts brought him ten times what he had paid for them, but the appreciation in value of some of them was far greater. The Humanist *Six Dialogues of Plato*, for which he had paid £24 as late as 1920, realized £5,800 at Sotheby's in 1957; an English tenth-century *Boethius*, bought in 1909 for £75, fetched £6,600 in the same sale, the total for nineteen manuscripts being £27,315. The superb thirteenth-century Notre Dame Bible, once in the Yates Thompson collection, was purchased direct from Cockerell by Quaritch for £6,000 and was soon to change hands again at a far higher figure.

It was Cockerell's unerring eye for a manuscript which led to these shrewd investments. Within two years of his very first purchase—a thirteenth-century *Pauline Epistles*, in 1899—he had spotted an important eleventh-century Italian *Epistolae* which Sotheby's had catalogued as fourteenth-century, and bought it for £3 10s. On another occasion, having acquired an imperfect Paris *Missal* whose margins had been repaired in medieval times, he noticed similar repairs on an imperfect manuscript at Quaritch's and was thus able to complete his own.

* * *

On the occasion of his birthday in 1956, Cockerell had written
his customary bulletin on the state of his health — a subject
which was always of absorbing interest to him:

> My 89th birthday. I don't think I feel any older than I did
> a year ago. A very good day. I had given out that I did
> not feel equal to many callers and only Dorothy Hutton
> and Rachel Collins came, but I was kept busy by the
> arrival of flowers, telegrams, etc.

There followed a list, subdivided into 'gifts', 'telegrams'
and 'letters', of the names, alphabetically arranged, of the
donors and senders.

But soon there were signs that he was aging. His eyesight
grew worse and his deafness increased; the bladder trouble
had not been cured by hospital treatment. On 13th March 1957
he wrote:

> Twice last night I woke up with my mind out of control.
> My thoughts wandered aimlessly. This has happened to
> me once or twice before and is very disagreeable — per-
> haps a touch of madness.

Yet the very next day he is apparently almost his old self
again:

> Reginald [i.e., Reynolds] Stone, that very nice man and
> fine designer, came to tea and we — I — greatly enjoyed a
> talk with him for about an hour and a half. We are very
> old friends and it happens too seldom.
>
> Joseph Dunlop came in the evening to be shown a few
> Morris relics by Cron. Evidently a very nice and sym-
> pathetic Morrison (sic).

There were, in fact, the 'bad' days and the 'good' days —
days when sleepless nights left him exhausted and feckless, but
days also when he was as brisk and alert, mentally, as ever.
Though the handwriting in the diary never loses its character

or its quality, or indeed its microscopic scale, after a poor night it is shaky and sometimes illegible. No doubt 16th July was a 'bad' day, for a great occasion is recorded with the utmost brevity:

My 90th birthday.

But one letter that came to him that morning will especially have pleased and amused him. The writer was Mrs. Hubert Hartley:

My darling Sydney,
I do wish I could be one of the queue on your birthday, but I'll be in the letter queue, to send you my most dear and particular love. . . .
I am going to bring you my birthday present in two weeks time, when all the flowers have died and all the grapes have been eaten, and there are just a few feathers left out of their hats on the floor, and a faint trace of lipstick on the Codex Sinaiticus, and a lingering scent of Lanvin's Arpège on the housekeeper's dog. You see I understand these things and I send you all the love in the world.

Grizel

A fortnight later Cockerell participated, by means of a tape-recording, in the opening of an exhibition of 'The Typographical Adventure of William Morris,' organized by the William Morris Society whose first President he had become the previous March.

On September 22nd a happy event occurred:

Amy Tozer, 5 months my senior, from whom I have been estranged for over 40 years through some misunderstanding, came at 4.30 and we were completely reconciled. She was my sister Olive's greatest friend and Olive wanted me to marry her. At 90 she retains much of her old beauty and charm. Her brother (illegible) 10 years her junior, came and fetched her away. A very satisfactory incident.

On New Year's Eve he wrote:

A very nice finish to the Old Year. Wilfrid Blunt, whom I have not seen recently, came to tea and stayed for a good while afterwards, talking of many interesting things. Before leaving he sang 'Where'er you walk' and an amusing French song and Nina [Griggs] and I were in a happy mood.

8

THE NONAGENARIAN

THE nonagenarian continued to hold court at Kew. There were few days when he did not receive one or more visits — visits from friends, from neighbours, or from scholars and enthusiasts from all parts of the world who wished to draw on his unique knowledge of what had become an almost legendary past.

His children came more frequently now, bringing his grandchildren with them. Cranks came and, with slenderest introductions, the idly curious as if to catch a last view of an ancient monument about to be demolished. Journalists and writers came, of their own volition or summoned to his bedside to be reprimanded for having distorted the image of one of the heroes whose appointed or self-appointed champion he had become. Some came with gifts of fruit and flowers and game; others went away with scraps of calligraphy, a book, a little drawing, or a photograph of a page of a medieval manuscript. And he had time, and counsel, and kindness (though sometimes brusqueness) for them all.

There were many visitors from the United States. Cockerell admired the enthusiasm and vitality of Americans, and they for their part found in him qualities which their own scholars lacked. One wrote to him on his return home:

> Wherever I went in England I found confirmation of my feeling that what our world badly needs is at least a dozen more like yourself: men whose long years of study have given them so strong an awareness of tradition and experiment in all the arts of civilization. What we lack over here

349

is not museums, but men of your all-encompassing interests — interests which become also the interests of your every friend and visitor. We have plenty of museums, plenty of collectors, but no informal influence (such as yours) upon taste, perception and judgment in the arts — and notably in the so-called lesser arts. . . .

Another American admirer was Mr. Jerrold Moore, Assistant Librarian of Yale University, a young man much interested in Morris and the Pre-Raphaelites. He has described his visits to Cockerell, who seems to have given him a warmer welcome than that which he accorded to Mr. Philip Henderson a dozen years earlier;[1] Cockerell had, of course, mellowed in the interval, but he could still intimidate a visitor if he felt so inclined. Mr. Moore writes:[2]

Happening to be in London, I took my courage and wrote to ask whether Sir Sydney would honour me by allowing me to pay him a visit. By return mail there arrived a note — beautifully written by Mrs. Griggs — containing a courteous invitation, together with his own hand-written postscript: 'I expect you know that I am an old fogy of 93.'

When I arrived he was sitting up in his immaculately arranged bed — as I was always to see him — and Miss Hawksley was there. We talked about so many things, then and on my two subsequent visits. Once I brought him a copy of the Kelmscott Press *Sidonia the Sorceress* and asked him to inscribe it. He protested vigorously, saying it wasn't his book, he hadn't designed it and wasn't worthy of it, etc., etc. Finally he acquiesced, but would not sign it in the upper-right-hand corner of the first fly-leaf, as that was the customary place for authors' and makers' dedications. No, he would only put an especially tiny signature well below the middle of the page: 'Sydney Cockerell, once secretary of the Kelmscott Press.' It typified — as did his original invitation to me — his modesty and great good will.

[1] See pp. 319–23.   [2] In a letter to the Author.

The circumstance of signing the *Sidonia* occasioned his telling us an anecdote about Morris. The British Museum Trustees had requested a copy of one of the Kelmscott Press books on vellum for the Museum Library. Morris offered either *Sidonia* or *Godefroy of Boulogne*. The *Godefroy* was chosen, and Morris said that it was the intelligent choice, for *Godefroy* was the better book. He was so pleased at the choice that he gave the Museum a copy of each book. Later, as we were leaving Sir Sydney's house that day, Miss Hawksley told me that she had never heard that story before, and that it was typical of Sir Sydney to bring things of that sort up out of his memory for an occasion. He needed no developed repertoire of stories, for he apparently had the faculty of total recall.

We talked of Morris, of Marshall, Faulkner and Ellis, of Ruskin and Rossetti, of Lizzie Siddall, and finally of T. E. Lawrence. 'Oh, I didn't realize you were interested in him!' said Sir Sydney. 'What a pity—he wrote me some letters but they were sold last year. You could have had them.' I am quite certain he would have tried to give them to me on the spot if he had still had them. He did insist on my taking an envelope of 'cuttings' (as he said) about Lawrence, which were to be thrown away if they were of no interest. Visiting him the following week, I pointed out to him that when I had had the chance to examine the packet carefully, it appeared that there were valuable privately printed pamphlets, letters from Lawrence's family and friends, and other treasures among the 'cuttings'. But no: nothing would do but that I must keep them. 'I am glad,' he wrote a few days later, 'that the Lawrence envelope proved worthy of your acceptance.'

That was the extravagant, sincere note he always struck in our meetings: how fine it was to meet someone who knew and cared so much about Morris as I (!), and how nice it was of me to visit him. On the day of my second visit he presented me—having carefully made sure that the gift would be welcome—with a copy of *The Best of*

Friends, which at my request he inscribed—this time venturing the upper-right-hand corner. As I re-read the letters in that book in the light of those wonderful hours that I had spent with Sir Sydney, I felt one could understand a little his marvellous ability to make and keep friends. He was a real genius for friendship—it cannot be described in any other way—and was no lionhunter, as is proven by what I am proud to call his friendship with me. He turned his whole attention upon you, and made you feel that you were to him a new and a delightful manifestation of just the kind of person he liked best. The very insignificance of his friendship with me is, I think, a tribute to his generous and wonderful personality.

The pattern of Cockerell's life at this time is best shown in extracts from his diary. These will give the quality of his daily living; they cannot do more than hint at the fullness of it:

3rd January 1958. Sunday is the 51st anniversary of my first visit to Stanbrook Abbey. To commemorate this, Dame Felicitas [of Stanbrook] sent me an enchanting assortment of the flowers now growing out of the doors in its territory . . . snowdrops and a primrose or two, hellebores, celandine, polyanthus, ling, pansies, red berries, hazel catkins, etc. This gave me very great pleasure.

6th January. An enchanting visit from Grizel Hartley. . . . She seemed as young and lovely and affectionate as she was when I first saw her at Eton about 15 years ago. . . .

16th January. Today I have lived to be 90½ and am a very poor thing now and do not expect to live to be 91.

10th February. D[orothy] H[awksley] came to tea in order to meet our beloved old friend Freya Stark. . . .

15th February. Toye Vise, a journalist and a keen supporter of the Church of England, a decent man with whom I found myself out of sympathy, came to get my signature to an appeal for a memorial, which I reluctantly gave him.

15th April. Allan Chappelow of Trinity College, Cambridge, the very skilled photographer of distinguished human beings, called in the afternoon to add me to his gallery. He somehow won the confidence of Nurse Bartlett who forced me to obey him and went off happy with several negatives. He tried to persuade me that I was a person of importance but failed. He was here once before with photographs of G.B.S. on his 94th birthday — very good.

29th April. An unexpected visit from my old unsatisfactory nurse, Miss F., whom I mistook for Mary Thomas's nice friend Miss Gimslow and greeted too cordially.

2nd May. D[orothy] H[awksley] came at 12.30 to my delight. Mary Corrigan came at 5.30 and stayed till about 7. I was glad to see her, but I was tired. She and Dorothy discussed plays by Graham Greene with great animation and I was glad to be unable to join in, not having seen them.

25th May. Christopher's portrait in *Sunday Dispatch* together with information about him and his great invention the Hovercraft, with only a few details obtained from me. These are quite harmless, so my apprehension was not justified.

28th May. Allan Chappelow came about 3.30 with photographs of me taken on 15 April. Unfortunately I was very unwell at the time and I look it.

1st June. Happened to take up my diary for 1952, the first of the 6½ years during which I have been in bed, and perceived that I am better now than I was then.

29th June. Margaret Huntingdon [Margaret Lane] came to tea. . . . She was quite enchanting and looked to me younger and prettier than ever before. The BBC want me to do a broadcast with her, but I decided that I had not enough wits left to make it a success.

16th July. My 91st birthday and a very happy one. Messages from my 3 children and from many friends. Very few visitors . . . so I was not tired. [The usual list follows].

22nd August. Virginia Clarke [Mrs. Surtees] came to tea and was enchanting. She takes no breakfast and is much too thin. She enjoys her life in Rome. . . .[1]

22nd October. I had a very bad night of choking and coughing, the worst I have had since I took to my bed nearly seven years ago.

23rd October. For the first time in many[2] years I have a letter in *The Times* today. It is about Ruskin's book.

2nd November. Alarming symptom in afternoon. I had a sudden temperature and did not recognize people, even Dr. Quitman. . . .

9th November. A red letter day.[3] Yesterday I had visits from my two fine daughters, today I had one from Christopher and his ever faithful wife to proclaim that at last after so many years of mental toil, his great invention has been definitely taken over by a great Government office, immense funds at its disposal. . . .

15th November. A wonderful visit after lunch from my incomparable Sybil Cholmondeley, who left roses, a chicken and grapes. She cheered me up greatly.

[1] Where her husband was British Ambassador.

[2] In fact only three.

[3] The rest of this entry, and a few passages in subsequent ones, were dictated.

1st March 1959. My letter about portraits of Byron is in the *Sunday Times*.

6th June. This is the 42nd anniversary of my first meeting with my very much loved friend Dorothy Hawksley.

8th June. A great day for Christopher (and for his father). The BBC announcements at 7 and 8 a.m. opened with the news of the 3 successful trials of his Hovercraft at Cowes yesterday. . . .

5th July. *One of the happiest days of my life.* CHRISTOPHER, whose Hovercraft, which has had immense publicity in the newspapers and has apparently been successful in all its tests, came to tea. He pleased me very much by not seeming to be a bit stuck up or spoilt by his triumph. On the contrary he is very modest and dignified and immensely more grown up than when I saw him last. He said that his invention will take 20 years to perfect. I am exceedingly proud to be his father.

10th July. Douglas Cleverdon, a charming man, at one time a bookseller in Bristol, but for 20 years connected with the BBC, came at about 4 with a recording apparatus to take down a few remarks about Christopher as a supplement to an interview with Christopher already recorded. . . .

25th July. Another triumph for Christopher. His Hovercraft crossed the Channel from Calais to Dover in a little more than 2 hours. . . .

13th September. SOON AFTER 10 P.M. THE MOON WAS HIT BY A RUSSIAN MISSILE . . . A MIRACLE OF SCIENTIFIC ATTAINMENT.

8th October. ELECTION DAY. [added later: 'It was a Tory victory, to my great relief, as they have been governing the country very well'].

14th October. Siriol Hugh-Jones . . . came at 3.30 . . . to talk about Tim White, to whom she wrote a very long and fine tribute in the T. L. S. I told her about Puck, of whom she had never heard. . . . It looks as though we might become great friends. . . .

16th October. Today I have re-read [Siriol Hugh-Jones's] article in the T.L.S. and have found it even more masterly and powerful than I thought. She is a wonderful woman and, in my present half-witted condition, I doubt if I shall be able to keep pace with her or to retain her friendship and attention.

25th October. I have heard nothing more from her. . . .

26th October. Dr. Quitman came at 11.45 and stayed an hour discussing postage stamps. . . . He said that I was much better than I was three years ago.

3rd November. Today, when I had made up my mind that [Siriol Hugh-Jones] had quite dropped me, I have a very long and affectionate letter from her.

9th November. Lying awake in the small hours I thought of all the beautiful birds I had seen in my life. . . .

26th November. I have been having a correspondence with the Post Office about the illegible nature of our postage stamps for Americans and foreigners in general. . .

1st December. Arthur Wheen, head of the Library at the V & A Museum, came in the afternoon and I gave him for the Museum all my Edward Johnston material (Book of Sample Scripts, valued by John Carter of Sotheby's at £2,000, Book of Letters addressed to me, etc., etc.). These, along with the five specimens of Graily Hewitt that I have already given, make a very notable addition to the Museum's collection of modern calligraphy. I urged Wheen to extend this. . . .

18th December. Prince Philip went for a ride on Christopher's Hovercraft at Cowes and steered it himself at a rather alarming speed.

25th December. Our accustomed Christmas lunch party presided over by Dorothy Hawksley. 7 guests in the dining-room and myself in bed. Eleanor Spencer, D.H., Joan Hassall, Winifred Hooper, Mary Thomas, the two Mabels. All very nice people who got on excellently together. They all came in, one at a time, to tell me how much they had enjoyed it. . . .

31st December. . . . So ends 1959, during which the great perils that threatened a large portion of the human race have been greatly reduced by the personal contacts between the politicians of the leading countries of Western Europe, Russia and the United States.

15th January 1960. After two ghastly nights of coughing and choking when I thought I was going to die, I am rather better this morning, though very feeble.

16th January. I am 92½ today.

19th January. Had a perfectly horrible night of choking, kindly looked after by Mrs. Fletcher. I thought my end was near.

8th April. Read most of my Ruskin story in *Friends of a Lifetime* with keen appreciation and some surprise, as though it were about Ruskin and somebody not myself.

4th May. Spent most of the day reading my Diary for July–December 1940 and found it absorbingly interesting.

11th May. Christopher Sykes came at 3.30 and stayed till 5. His object was to ask me questions about Charles

Doughty, with a view to a broadcast about him in the autumn. . . .

17th May. Today I have had one of the great surprises of my life. Mrs. Janet Webb of Richmond, who contemplates writing a Life of Charlotte Shaw, Bernard Shaw's wife, whom I knew very well, or thought I did, for a great many years [came to see me]. I introduced T. E. Lawrence to the Shaws, and Charlotte took a violent fancy to him. Mrs. Webb has found in the British Museum seven letters from Charlotte to Lawrence, copies of two of which, amazingly frank and self-revealing, she left at my door this morning. When I read them I was quite astounded and I invited Mrs. Webb to come to tea. She came and we had a good talk. She will let me see copies of the other letters when she has got them.

26th May. Janet Webb came to tea. We had a long talk. I read her letters from Judy Musters and Dame Felicitas, strongly deprecating the writing of a life of Charlotte Shaw. . . .

29th May. My oldest friend, Alfred Powell, architect and pottery decorator, died aged 95. He was the only survivor among those who called me by my boyhood name Carlie — short for Carlyle. . . .

31st May. Had an extraordinary dream that Stanbrook Abbey had been secularised. No such idea has ever come into my mind. . . .

2nd June. Alec Guinness, who is taking the part of T. E. Lawrence in Rattigan's very successful play 'Ross', came at 12 and stayed nearly an hour. He was absolutely charming, as he always is. He brought a mass of beautiful roses and kissed the top of my head when he said goodbye. I gave him my old Arab cloak in which I was shipwrecked with Wilfrid Blunt in the Gulf of Suez in 1900 and which

I wore frequently at Cambridge in winter as a great protection from draughts. It had been worn by . . . G.B S and T.E.L., the second of whom he is now impersonating. A very happy occasion.

Mrs. Janet Webb came to tea. I think she has now abandoned her project to write a Life of Charlotte Shaw, as she can find no information about her between the years 20 and 40.[1]

8th July. I happened to take up Lady Burne-Jones's Memorials of E.B-J. which I had not looked at for many years. I became absorbed in its early chapters. It is a grand book, unlike any other. I was to have dined with Burne-Jones on the day of his death.

16th July. My 93rd birthday. I think I am as well as I was a year ago. Katharine and Clare came in the morning to wish me HAPPY RETURNS.

9th September. Reread my Introduction to Mackail's Life of Morris and was well satisfied with it. I could not now do it half so well.

11th October. Wrote to the Abbess of Stanbrook appealing to her to give all her nuns the equivalent of a Sunday in each week to be spent in study, contemplation, letter-writing, rest and sleep. . . .

29th October. Mabel Hartland, my excellent cook and housekeeper for 8 or 9 years, left at 3 p.m. after many expressions of devotion on both sides. Her place was taken at the same time by Mrs. M., who seems likely to be a success. . . .

30th October. When I saw Mrs. M. in the morning, she told me that her bed was very comfortable, but that she

[1] *Mrs. G.B.S.*, by Janet Dunbar (Mrs. Janet Webb) was published by Harrap in 1963.

had not slept a wink owing to heart trouble. She knows that she ought to have informed us. . . .

31st October. Mrs. M. having proved a failure I engaged a Mrs. C. as cook and housekeeper, coming in by the day — an experiment which my good nurse thinks will succeed.

25th November. At 8 p.m. took a small part in a broadcast to commemorate the 50th anniversary of Tolstoy's death, the other participants being Sir Shane Leslie and a daughter of Tolstoy living in America.[1]

26th November. I am much relieved to hear that I was audible.

30th November. My best night for ever so long. Slept from 9.15 to 5.15. . . .

5th December. Miss N.,[2] a deplorable failure as a cook-housekeeper (perhaps a mental patient somewhere or other) departed at 11.30, to the great relief of all concerned.

25th December. [Long and detailed description of the Christmas party and visitors, ending] A GREAT SUCCESS.

30th December. A splendid and emotional visit in the afternoon from Beatrice Warde, our leading authority on fine printing. . . . She was most affectionate. . . . P.S. For years I have not been able to get in or out of bed unaided, or to stand without support, or to walk a single step — but I am without pain. Only once in nine years

[1] Cockerell's contribution had been recorded in September. The talk appeared in the *Listener* on 15th December.

[2] The first mention of Miss N., who had presumably replaced the promising Mrs. C. engaged on 31st October.

have I been through my bedroom door, and that was in a wheel-chair to please a workman who had been doing something to improve the scullery.[1]

31st December. Another year gone. Past 93 and, except perhaps for a slight weakness in the chest, I feel quite as well as I did a year ago. My friends have been very kind to me. I have in Mabel Moore a perfect nurse, and though quite ready for my departure, if it can be painless, I am content to live on, rather blind, very deaf, and with failing memory and wits, until I become a greater nuisance to those about me.

On the opening page of the 1961 diary is a list of eighty-one persons to whom Cockerell has sent a photograph of himself holding a cat. The photograph had been taken by Miss Hawksley many years earlier, and the negative had suddenly turned up. Cockerell did not much care for animals (other than birds), and the cat, placed by Miss Hawksley in unwilling arms, looks ill at ease; but the portrait of Cockerell, dimpled and smiling, is excellent.

8th January 1961. A happy surprise in the morning. Mary Thomas arrived with a tiny garden of winter flowers which she had brought from Stanbrook yesterday —most beautifully arranged in a large dish by Dame Felicitas. It is giving me immense pleasure.

14th January. My deafness became acute in the night. I sent for Dr. Quitman, who removed a little wax and prescribed drops of olive oil, but did not improve my hearing.

16th January. I am 93½ today. Almost stone deaf. Sent for Dr. Quitman. . . .

---

[1] A rather charming episode. It seems that the workman was enormously proud of the improvements he had effected, but dashed that Cockerell could not see them for himself, so Cockerell allowed himself to be wheeled into the scullery.

19th January. A perfectly enchanting visit from Sir Kenneth and Jane Clark, whom I had not seen for years. They had to write down their share of the conversation with me, because of my deafness. . . .

24th January. Elsa, the lioness made famous all over the world by Joy Adamson's book *Born Free*, a best-seller that has been translated into 13 languages, died in Kenya today 'of natural causes'. A sad event.

29th January. Oliver Bevan, a young Etonian studying painting at the Royal College of Art, sent by Wilfrid Blunt, came to tea. . . . He is shy and I am stone deaf, so we didn't make much progress.

15th February. . . . Deaf as ever . . .

27th February. *The Times* announces that Melbourne has decided to build a splendid new Museum and Art Gallery. This is what I advocated when I was there in 1936–1937.[1]

9th March. My short letter in the *Listener* on Thomas Hardy's heart. . . .

18th March. C. G. L. du Cann . . . who has been writing a series of articles in the *Evening Standard* on the Love Affairs of Bernard Shaw, giving a totally false impression, came to tea by my invitation in order that I might reprimand him for what I thought was a very shabby perversion of the facts, detrimental to Shaw's reputation. I spoke very frankly, and when he asked leave to come again I declined his request.[2]

[1] Cockerell wrote to *The Times* on the subject on March 4th.
[2] *The Loves of George Bernard Shaw*, by C. G. L. du Cann, was published by Arthur Barker in 1963. In a review in the Tatler (1st January 1964) Miss Siriol Hugh-Jones described it as 'fairly vulgar, sensational and written in the style of a school essay on a night when the weight of homework was overwhelming. . . .'

3rd April. Finished reading *A Calabash of Diamonds* by Margaret Lane (Countess of Huntingdon) which she sent me about a fortnight ago. It is amazingly well written.

12th April. A tremendous triumph for Russian science and prestige. They succeeded in putting a man into outer space and in bringing him back safely. . . .

21st April. An important letter from Wilfrid Blunt, who has just returned from Portugal with a bad leg.[1]

19th May. Leonard Clark came to tea. He was eager to talk about a possible memoir of me, to be written after my death, and he evidently aspires to have a hand in it. The difficulty is that I can think of no one now living who could testify to the appalling uncivilized muddle the Fitzwilliam was in when I became Director in 1908.

24th May. Wilfrid Blunt came at 3 and stayed till 5 and agreed to be my principal executor in charge of all my letters, and to write a memoir.

[1] In reply to a letter inviting the Author to become his principal executor.

EPILOGUE

[1961—1962]

EPILOGUE

I love everything that's old; old friends, old times,
old manners, old books, old wines.
> (*Mr. Hardcastle in Goldsmith's*
> *'She Stoops to Conquer'*)

AS a regular visitor to Kew I had many opportunities to study the devotion of those who looked after Cockerell, both his wonderful 'gentle ladies' (as de la Mare called them) who came in turn to act as hostess, secretary, comforter, audience and general factotum, and the professional nurses who for some time past had also been necessary.

For the right person, nursing Cockerell or housekeeping for him was an interesting job. It was also an exacting one: he could not be brought to understand that one free afternoon a fortnight was not enough. For the wrong person it was a torment, though usually of short duration. For example:

21st November 1956. At about lunchtime, when Nina Griggs was sitting with me, Nurse F. came in and gave up her latchkey, at the same time announcing that she was leaving the house in half an hour. This abrupt conduct rather startled us, but we were also relieved when sure enough, in half an hour, a car arrived and carried her and her luggage (presumably) to her [illegible] at Chobham. She gave as her reason for her sudden departure the fact that D[orothy] H[awksley] had changed my woollen cap for a silk cap which she thought more becoming, but which Nurse expected would give me a cold. She nursed me well, but she is a very jealous and touchy woman, interested only in Football Pools, and we are glad to see the last of her.

In 'Mabel' (Miss Mabel Hartland) he found, for most of the last ten years of his life, an admirable and sympathetic cook-housekeeper who was ready to discuss serious topics ('Mabel, do you believe in the Resurrection of the Body?') and hold her own in discussion until he was driven to 'agreeing to differ.' When Cockerell denounced the absurdity of the Christian comparison of human beings to sheep—'which are silly, and all just alike,' Mabel declared that this was quite untrue: that every shepherd knew his sheep apart. 'You may be right,' said Cockerell. 'I *know* I'm right,' said Mabel. Among other services, Mabel saved his life when the newspaper that he was reading caught fire.

Cockerell needed stimulating companionship. Only a few weeks before his death he wrote, 'I had for my night nurse last night Mrs. Wilsted who is a very keen student of astronomy. I asked her how many named stars there were, each equivalent to our sun. She said, "About ten thousand." "And how many unnamed?" "Millions." This set me thinking. . . .'

In December 1958 Nurse Mabel Moore came to take temporary duty while his regular nurse was on holiday. Cockerell's first question to her had nothing to do with her professional qualifications. 'What,' he asked, 'are your hobbies?'

'Singing', said Nurse Moore.

'Could you sing "Have you seen but a white lily grow"?'

'Yes', said Nurse, 'if you give me twenty-four hours to think about it.'

'We "clicked",' said Cockerell, 'from the first.' In spite of the protestations of Nurse Moore, the permanent nurse was given notice and she was appointed in her place. Nurse Moore was extremely efficient, but her spectacular success was entirely due to the fact that she was also very intelligent, and that, like Mabel, she too refused to be trodden upon. When Cockerell attempted to stop her reading the *Daily Sketch*, offering to pay if she would take the *Telegraph* instead, she stubbornly refused. '*I* pay,' she said. 'I shall read whatever paper I like.' Cockerell was filled with admiration, then with remorse, then with fear that she might leave. He could not sleep. Next morning he said, 'I've had a terrible night. I'm afraid I've hurt your feelings.' 'Not in the least,' said Nurse. 'But I shall go on taking the *Sketch*.'

Nurse, for her part, was amazed at Cockerell's alertness of mind and fascinated by his 'funny little ways. He's a *real character*,' she said. He could tell her exactly which buses to take in London, where to change on the Underground. Yet when she suggested that he might like to sit for a while in a chair near the window, he refused. 'I've finished with the outside world,' he said. But though he no longer wished to see the passers-by, his ginkgo tree and the handful of plants that struggled for survival in his unweeded front garden, his interest in what went on outside his prison walls was as lively as ever. He gave Nurse a season ticket for Kew Gardens demanding in exchange a written report on the progress of the flowers. 'Keep these carefully,' he told her when he had read them, 'and then *have them bound*.'

One day he said, 'Nurse, I want to give you something of mine to remember me by. What would you like?' Nurse chose the little magnifying-glass that was always tied to his bed-table with a red ribbon. 'It is yours,' said Cockerell; 'but perhaps you will allow me to borrow it for the present.' Some months later, however, he suddenly announced, 'You can't have my spy-glass after all; I've given it to Lady Huntingdon. You must choose something else.' Nurse was, very naturally, annoyed. She said, 'I chose a small thing before. This time I'm going to choose a big thing. I want your wireless.' And I am very glad to say that she now has it.

What most impressed Nurse Moore was that Cockerell never complained—'Never once,' she said, 'in all the time I was with him.' This did not mean that he was not exacting. He might ring his bell incessantly for trifles that could easily have waited. He might seem curiously unappreciative of the sacrifices that his 'angels' made for him. But he never grumbled at being bedridden and helpless and dependent. He realized that, tied though he was, he still had much to live for.

'One morning,' wrote[1] Nurse Moore, 'Sir Sydney asked me, when he woke, whether later in the day I would take down at

[1] In a letter to the Author.

his dictation a list of the manuscripts that he was presenting to the Victoria and Albert Museum. Unfortunately, as he was being got back into bed, his foot slipped. To save him I lowered him to the floor. While waiting for help, there came, from the depths and in a very strong voice: "Confound it! This will *hold up the work!*"'

There were, of course — as his diary shows — the sleepless nights and the bad days. '8th July 1961. I am feeling desperately tired and done for.' '1st August. Had the worst night I have had for years and thought I was going to die. . . .' '21st August. Spent an absolutely shocking night with scarcely a wink of sleep.' '21st November. A good night, but felt weak and silly.' '2nd February 1962. Had a shocking night. . . .' '17th February. Out of bed on the floor for the second time in ten years. Mrs. [illegible] came to the rescue and I was reinstated with no damage done.' Yet to those who visited him he gave little or no sign of his troubles.

All who had known Cockerell in his Cambridge days would agree that old age had considerably mellowed him; on occasions, however, it became evident that the old fighting spirit — the frontal attacks that had won him a quarter of a million for the Fitzwilliam and a dozen enemies — was by no means extinct. There was, for example, the day when a lawyer arrived by appointment to discuss the making of a new will, the draft of which had been sent him through the post. (Cockerell was constantly changing both his will and his executors.)

'I may take it,' said Cockerell, 'that you are Mr. Z?'

'Yes, Sir Sydney.'

A pause. Then, 'I would like to tell you — straight away — that I have a strong suspicion of *all* lawyers — and that my suspicion — is based upon a lifetime of experience. They are all dilatory — inaccurate — they never admit to being wrong. They use two long words where one short one would do—' He leant a little forward, fixed the man with a cold stare, and said, 'May I hope that — YOU ARE AN EXCEPTION?'

The lawyer expressed the hope that he might be.

'Now this legacy to Mr. W,' Cockerell continued. 'I thought

I had made it quite plain—that I wished it TO BE CAN-
CELLED. And "testamentary dispositions": what *terrible*
words! Why can't you say "will"?'

The lawyer rallied a little; he promised to remove the
offending clause, but stoutly maintained that the word 'will'
was incorrect since it would not include any codicils that might
subsequently be added.

'I expect I'm wrong, always,' said Cockerell more amiably.
He liked people to stand up to him.

There is no doubt that the projected biography was a great
source of interest to Cockerell during the last year of his life,
and that he eagerly awaited my visits and catechism. He
directed my researches, told me whom I should consult, and,
though stoutly maintaining that 'unqualified eulogy' was
'intolerably cloying', attempted (unsuccessfully) to deflect me
from getting into touch with those with whom he had crossed
swords.

'I thought I might go and see X,' I would say.

'He will not tell you anything; he knows nothing about me.'

'But surely—didn't he work with you for sixteen years?'

'That is true. But he can tell you NOTHING!'

Or, 'I believe that Y is a great friend of yours.'

'He is no longer a friend of mine. We have QUAR-
RELLED.'

Or, 'When I come to write about your work on manuscripts, I imagine that I ought to consult Dr. Eric Millar.'

Pause. Then, 'The name is Mill*a*r—with an "a".'

'I know. Dr. Mill*a*r. Should I go and see him?'

Long pause. Then, rather explosively: 'My dear fellow, I
MADE MILLAR!'

I think that I was probably fortunate in being away during
the month in which his hearing suddenly grew much worse
(to one of his angels: 'You must *shriek* at me, my darling!')
till finally he became temporarily stone deaf. All communication with him had then to be written down and, very characteristically, he preserved and subsequently annotated a long

written conversation with Miss Freya Stark. But gradually a
little of his hearing returned. His deafness continued, however,
to make interrogation laborious and difficult; certain intimate
questions, that might have been harmlessly put to anyone of
normal hearing, would have sounded crude when shouted —
and no doubt several times over — at the top of one's voice.
There were one or two things that I never dared to ask him.

Cockerell always expected to be cross-examined. 'What *questions* have you prepared for me today?' he would ask. But once
he had been given the lead, he would often force the conversation into the channel of his choice. If the talk was of Hardy, he
might say suddenly, 'Did I ever tell you that Blunt never sent
a postcard in his life, never travelled in a bus, and, until his
bank manager implored him to use a cheque-book, always
wrote out his cheques on a sheet of writing-paper?' And,
Hardy forgotten, he would describe, once again, his shipwreck
with Blunt in the Gulf of Suez. 'Anthony Lytton never mentioned it in his book,' he said reproachfully.
    'About Florence Hardy. . . .' I would say.
    'The wreck,' Cockerell continued, 'was still marked on the
map when I travelled to Australia with my daughter in 1936.'
    'About Florence Hardy . . .'
    It was not always easy.

As his diaries show, Cockerell loved little innocent jokes of a
preparatory-school nature. He might say suddenly, 'Do you
know the story of the little girl and the Writing on the
Wall?'
    'No.'
    'She said it was "Mean, mean to tickle the parson".' And
the bed shook with his half-smothered mirth.
    But there is nowhere, among the millions of words of his
that I have read, in diaries and in letters, a single syllable that
could be considered even mildly coarse. He had a horror of the
dirty joke and the Stock Exchange story.

He loved having his leg gently and simply pulled. One day, seeing an enormous bunch of expensive pink roses at the foot of his bed, I said, 'Who sent you those? The Pope?'

He chuckled happily. 'No', he said. 'Guess again.'

I tried again, and again failed. They had, in fact, been sent by Sir Alec Guinness.

Yet sometimes he was unexpectedly matter-of-fact. Writing to him on one occasion, I mentioned that I was going to see an exhibition at the National Book League, and added jokingly, 'Why don't you come too?' He replied perfectly seriously, setting down his reason for having to decline my invitation: 'I have been $9\frac{1}{2}$ years in bed, because I am suffering from heart-block, a malady in which only one half of the heart operates, the other half ceasing to function. I suppose that during the night the functioning portion is apt to go to sleep.'

One day Cockerell said to me, 'Shall I tell you two things that have always been on my conscience?'

I eagerly assented.

'I used,' he said, 'to bully my brother Douglas when we were boys. He couldn't read until he was twelve, and I bullied him . . . I used to make him bowl to me and then I hit the ball ALL OVER THE PLACE. Then he became the best book-binder in England. I've left his son a thousand pounds to make amends.'

'The other thing: in 1936 I went on a cruise with a woman friend [Loraine Wyman]. She was ill — in fact it was cancer, and she died the following year. When we reached Victoria I put her in a taxi, but I didn't go with her; I was very anxious to get home. I behaved shabbily — a bit of bad manners.'

'Oh yes — there was one more thing. When I was a very small boy, and staying with my Grandmother Cockerell, I stole almonds and raisins from the store-cupboard. *Dreadful*! It preyed on my mind for a long time.

'Otherwise I don't think I've any other crime on my conscience — no murder or anything. That's why I've had such a happy life. . . . But don't try to make a great man out of me.

I'm not. You can say that I only just missed the gallows, if you like.'

And then, unfailingly at every visit, he would fumble among his papers on the bed-table, produce a photograph, and ask, 'Have I ever shown you this?'

It was a coloured photograph of Dame Felicitas of Stanbrook, his dear devoted friend. They corresponded regularly, and Dame Felicitas never failed to send him, on red-letter days and anniversaries, flowers from the gardens at Stanbrook. 'She is a very wonderful woman,' he said. 'She has a livelier sense of humour and a wider outlook than Dame Laurentia. . . .' His thoughts constantly turned to Stanbrook and, agnostic though he was, it gave him great happiness to know that the nuns were praying for him.

About a year before his death Cockerell made the acquaintance of a young man, an ardent disciple of William Morris, to whom he took a great fancy. 'I pet him,' Cockerell said. 'He reminds me of myself at the same age.'

'Meaning?' I asked.

'He loves all the best things in life. He is enthusiastic and zealous. He has impeccable taste. . . .' He paused; his eyes twinkled; he gave one of his inimitable little chuckles, and added, 'Pretty cheeky of me to say that, wasn't it?'

It was this astonishing freshness, together with his unquenchable interest in people and in beautiful things, which made him, even in his ninety-fifth year, younger in spirit than many men half his age.

On 15th March 1962, after a particularly bad night, Cockerell asked for a set of postcards of spring flowers in Kew Gardens, wrote upon each 'I think I am dying,' addressed them neatly in his own hand and sent them to his family and his particular friends. On receiving mine I rushed to the telephone, to learn that he was in excellent form, sitting up in bed and eating a hearty breakfast. He had amazing powers of recuperation.

I visited him a few days later and found him quite unchanged; it was, however, obvious — as it had been for many
months past — that death could come at any time and without
warning. He had no fear of it, nor of the extinction which he
believed to be in store for him. But he did fear pain. He never
forgot that five of his near relations had died of cancer, and
that in the thirties he had thought for many months that he
himself was suffering from it. He asked no more now than to
slip peacefully away.

As I left him I said, 'Au revoir — I'll come again soon.' He
said, 'Yes — come *soon*: I may *pop off* at any moment.'

I was to see him only once again. Then, on May Day
morning early, the final visitor came gently to his bedside:

My name is Death; the last best friend am I.[1]

---

[1] Southey, *The Dream.*

INDEX

A NOTE ON THE TYPE

The text of the book was set on the Monotype in a type face called Walbaum, cut early in the nineteenth century by J. E. Walbaum, a type founder at Goslar and Weimar, who followed Didot in the design of this modern face. His original matrices are still in existence, and are the property of the Berthold foundry, of Berlin, Germany.

Printed by Halliday Lithograph Corp.,
West Hanover, Mass. Bound by H. Wolff, New York